The Music of

JOSEPH HAYDN

The Symphonies

THE MUSIC OF JOSEPH
HAYDN
THE SYMPHONIES
ANTONY
HODGSON

The Tantivy Press/London
Fairleigh Dickinson University Press
Rutherford · Madison · Teaneck

The Tantivy Press
Magdalen House
136–148 Tooley Street
London SE1 2TT, England

Associated University Presses, Inc.
Cranbury, New Jersey 08512

Hodgson, Anthony.
    The Music of Joseph Haydn.

    Bibliography: p.
    Discography: p.
    Includes indexes.
    1.   Haydn, Joseph, 1732-1809.   Symphonies.
ML410.H4H56   785.1'1'0924   75-21259
ISBN 0–8386–1684–4 (U.S.A.)
SBN 0–904208–21–4 (U.K.)

Cover design by Mike Carney,
based on an engraving by Francesco Bartolozzi,
after a lost miniature (1791) by A. M. Ott (see plate 8)

Set in 11pt Pilgrim by Five Arches Press (Wales)
and printed in the United States of America

To
CHARLES CUDWORTH
whose writings bring the music of the
Eighteenth century vividly to life.

Contents

Acknowledgements

The Author wishes to thank:

Robert Dearling for preparing the discographical information used in the list of recommended recordings and for providing valuable information on the history of discs issued early in the long-playing era.

Mr. E. A. K. Ridley of the Horniman Museum for his thoroughness in assembling a group of instruments of Haydn's time for the coloured illustrations (plates 20–21).

Dr. Edward Croft-Murray for permitting the use of the hitherto unpublished drawing of three musicians (plate 12).

My wife, who typed everything.

Editorial Preface

This series is specifically designed to explore the sound of each composer as his most distinctive feature, and, to this end, recognises the equally important role that recordings now play in musical life. Footnotes throughout the main text contain critical references to such recordings when it is felt that they clarify or highlight the composer's intentions. In the Appendix, these and other recommended recordings are re-grouped in a purely factual listing of catalogue numbers, performance details and any divergencies from the composer's expressed wishes.

Since the aim of the series is to clarify each composer's sound, particularly for the non-specialist, this approach should prove doubly rewarding: treating concert music as a living rather than an academic entity and showing the virtues and faults of its reflection through Twentieth-century ears.

Introduction

Joseph Haydn was a brilliantly original composer and one whose style, though representative of a period, was so individual as to be a voice apart. In this way orchestral works by Haydn had an aural "hand-writing" that was on the one hand instantly recognisable yet on the other impossible to imitate. Typical of Haydn in terms of musical form is the Symphony. Into this form he poured most of his inspiration, and from it blazed the light of his greatness more brightly than from any other type of music. Under Haydn's guidance the Symphony developed into the highest of the art forms with a speed and assurance that seems scarcely credible. The tag so readily attached to this composer—"the father of the symphony"—is for this reason justifiable, but it is dangerous to use such a term if we confuse its meaning by letting it indicate that Haydn was the *inventor* of the symphony. This was not the case. As the alchemist needs base material before he can transmute it to something more precious, so Haydn needed the primitive but sturdy form of the mid-Eighteenth century symphony to quicken the response of his latent genius.

Today it is possible via the gramophone and the radio to discover

Haydn symphonies that in past years there was no chance of hearing. This is the welcome fruit of a busy musicological scene which, as will be explained later, is of very recent vintage historically: the leaders among our great Haydn scholars are still very much alive—Geiringer, Hoboken, Larsen, Landon. As a result of the communicative methods used by certain of today's Haydn scholars, the average listener has become interested in musicology as never before, and there is every evidence that many laymen comprehend its importance in a thorough way. It is no use today's writers producing the howlers that H. E. Jacob apparently meant in all seriousness in his "Joseph Haydn" of 1950: "The second movement of a Haydn Symphony is always slow" or "His popularity in England was due largely to the sudden unexpected drum-beat in the Andante of the Surprise Symphony." Mr. Jacob regales us also with how Haydn composed (Leopold Mozart's) "Toy" Symphony. The layman should, however, remember that the assimilated knowledge of the conclusions of a single musicologist should not always be equated to the discovery of absolute truth.

I have great respect for all the musicologists mentioned in these pages yet they would give me no thanks for unthinking endorsement of their every conclusion. Below I pay tribute to the work of H. C. Robbins Landon. Yet when he writes: "This is the era when Haydn myths are fast disappearing: the "Toy" Symphony is by Leopold Mozart, the *Serenade* is by Roman Hofstetter, the Brahms *Variations* are on a theme not by Haydn" and goes on to give evidence against the "Maria Theresia" Symphony meriting its title, I have to confess that of these four theories, I find only the first convincingly proven.

*

Symphonies differ from keyboard sonatas or string quartets in a very simple way—they have more instruments—and because of this the colouration available to him made Haydn mould his melody and his architecture to the sonic potential of the clothing provided. For this reason the reader will find no lengthy lists of key-sequences to explain the music; rather, there will be frequent reminders that the symphony is represented by the sound it makes—which is only another way of conveying the dictionary definition.

In modern performance the exaggeration of certain of Haydn's orchestral effects is always a forgivable fault. The unforgivable is that which mutes the brilliant colours of his orchestra. The accuracy of modern Haydn performance is important because frequently many members of the audience will be hearing the music for the first time, yet I have not uttered many "dreadful warnings." These are implicit in the non-inclusion of certain well-known recordings in the list of recommendations.

The evidence of the most authentic manuscripts of Haydn's symphonies is sufficient to give a fair idea of where modern perform- ances fall short. Nor is it too difficult to see which of today's recordings represent genuine attempts to obtain the true Haydn sound. One cannot forget the two hundred years that have passed since the concert room at Eszterháza resounded with the first performances of this music but one may at least try to avoid the worst of the pitfalls which they have brought in their wake. In Haydn's orchestra, for example, a number greater than twenty-seven players was virtually unheard of except in London at the end of his symphonic career. Modern strings have a stronger, more biting sound, fortified by a generous vibrato which would certainly have taken Haydn aback. Our trumpets are more shrill and our horns obtain their notes in a different way. Woodwinds now play more suavely and our timpani are relatively heavy and indistinct by Eighteenth-century standards. Even without a single period instrument, however, we can still make a reasonable approximation of the proper sound. We need basses which go down to a low C, woodwind players prepared to use a rustic style, timpanists with hard sticks avoiding low drum resonances, and brass players willing to match their tones by making the horns more brazen, the trumpets less so. Such approxima- tions give a very good basis. The use of keyboard continuo is frequently essential and although it is sometimes scarcely necessary and may be dispensed with, its use is never incorrect if the instrument is suitable.

*

When a musician refers today to a Haydn symphonic score as being in a "bad old edition" his use of the description "old" is strictly relative. Logically, this term would seem to refer to one which dates from the time of Haydn's own influence, and by definition any such score should be essentially authentic.

Haydn, being a popular composer throughout Europe, saw many of his symphonies published, but piratical conditions in the pre- copyright Eighteenth century were such that there were doubtless further editions of his symphonies which he did not even know about. These contemporary editions were in many instances reliable, although it is true to say that, as a rough guide, the further away geographically from Haydn's sphere of activity the less reliable they became. This is not to imply a conscious wanton destruction of Haydn's intentions. Conditions in those days meant that the term "orchestra," as applied to a group of musicians, might mean one thing in one place but something entirely different a few miles away. One princely court might have, for example, excellent flute players noted for their expressive phrasing, but no trumpeters at all, so a Haydn symphony would be modified accordingly to suit local conditions. Local taste also came into it: the rusticity of the last two movements of Symphony No. 28 might suit some regions but prove to be anathema elsewhere. A Leipzig edition of the work removed the Trio section of the third movement and the whole of the Finale, and a manuscript copy to be found at Kroměříč Castle also omits one of the movements.

Further drastic modifications were made in Haydn's often difficult brass parts. Some of the symphonies boast sections for two or four horns which are in the virtuoso class and, understandably, not every court could produce players to tackle them. Resident musicians would then rewrite the parts along simpler lines, and another suspect source would come into existence.

Even so, these are not the sources referred to by the term "bad old editions." These came much later, and it is perhaps instructive to glance briefly at the fashions which influenced Haydn performances after the composer's death.

The early years of the Nineteenth century saw a revolution in music. Beethoven led the way, and if Haydn had retained his incredible mental stamina in composing he would doubtless also have been in the forefront of the new styles. Although his music retained its appeal throughout Europe, in the fast-changing cultural climate of the post-Napoleonic world it was beginning to sound out of date. The phrasing of the London Symphonies, the clean lines originally so appealing to the Eighteenth-century listener, needed embellishing to be brought into line with new tastes. Even melodic outlines were changed at the whim of the conductors or players with no stronger reason than that they thought they sounded nicer. With the constant improvements in instrumental design, particularly in the brass and woodwind sections, modifications to parts began to creep in which would have rendered these parts unplayable at the time the originals were written. Conversely, the art of clarino horn playing (a term usually applied to trumpet parts, this description was transferred to some of the horn passages written by Haydn, Pokorny and others, and earlier in the century by some of the Mannheim symphonists such as Richter, Fils, and Jan Stamič) had been lost, so that the frequent passages in B flat alto and C alto were lowered an octave. This procedure would have brought the parts into the range attainable by the players, but it wrought incalculable havoc amongst Haydn's orchestral textures.

As the Nineteenth century progressed Haydn's music was elbowed aside by the bigger, heavier symphonies of Mendelssohn, Schumann, Brahms, Tchaikovsky, Dvořák, Bruckner and others. The demand was

for the greatly-increased emotional range which these symphonists were
offering, and no amount of modification to old Haydn's music would
bring it into line with modern trends. Haydn began to be thought
of as an essentially lightweight composer, a pleasing tunesmith of
limited scope, emotionally shallow, and most definitely a far lesser
composer than Mozart, with whom he was frequently compared to
his disadvantage.

It was in this climate of disenchantment at the start of the
Twentieth century, in a period when the description "Papa Haydn"
said all there was to say about the benign, bewigged old gentleman
who used to compose dainty little symphonies, that Breitkopf and
Härtel, the famous and influential Leipzig publishing house, undertook
to produce a new edition of the symphonies. Their first Haydn publications, apart from some editions during the Eighteenth century, had been
at the very start of the romantic era (1800–1806), when twelve volumes
of songs, sonatas for keyboard with and without violin, and trios
appeared, but the order of the works was so hopelessly confused that
even Haydn's preface did little to raise the value of the edition. A
century later, in 1907, the first volume of the symphonies appeared
under the guidance of the Austrian musicologist and conductor Eusebius
Mandyczewski (1857–1929), who was responsible for the numbering
system of the symphonies which is still used today. As Keeper of the
Archives of the Gesellschaft der Musikfreunde in Vienna, Mandyczewski
had access to many valuable Haydn sources, and his three volumes of
symphonies (Nos. 1–12, 13–27, 28–40) brought to light many rare works
and set off the current revival of interest in the composer. A fourth
volume (Nos. 41–49), edited by Karl Päsler, who is remembered for his
editions of the keyboard sonatas, appeared after Mandyczewski's death,
but the project had lost impetus and no more volumes appeared
after 1932.

Although some writers tend to denigrate Mandyczewski by pointing out errors of chronology in his list of Haydn's symphonies, we owe
a great debt to his research into these matters. With evidence which
was extremely flimsy by today's standards, he studied the huge number
of works in symphonic form which had been popularly attributed to
Haydn, divided them between spurious and authentic, and then numbered the latter. Since modern scholarship reckons on close to 150
symphonies as misattributions it seems remarkable that, long before
many autograph scores and authentic editions were available, Mandyczewski was able to sort the wheat from the chaff with such great
skill that his final list did not contain any spurious items whatsoever.
His only omissions were those works now known as Symphony "A"
in B flat (hidden away as Op. 1, No. 5 of the string quartets, with the
orchestral score yet to be rediscovered when Mandyczewski did his

work) and Symphony "B" in B flat, first published in 1955 by Universal Edition Vienna from a manuscript at St. Florian.*

A remarkable achievement: no false inclusions and only two omissions. Although there are errors in chronology these are not numerous enough to throw doubt upon the validity of the catalogue as a whole. When using the familiar numbers, however, one must remember a handful of basic adjustments in the light of later discovery: No. 72 belongs with No. 31, No. 40 with No. 13; and a group of fiery little symphonies, Nos. 26, 49, 58 and 59, just predate No. 41. Any other repositionings argued from the point-of-view of modern scholarship are of no real significance to the music-lover, who may rest assured that his beloved Mandyczewski numberings are likely to remain in standard use.

Despite the new spirit of attempted authenticity which seemed to suffuse the main stream of Haydn symphony publications in the years leading up to the Second World War, there were a number of prints which maintained the dubious Nineteenth century-isms and which served merely to supplement the still current bad old editions. For instance, the Eulenburg issue of Symphony No. 48, edited by Dr. Ernst Praetorius, appeared towards the end of this period. Its inclusion of totally spurious parts for trumpets and timpani, and its mute implication that the horns crooked in C should play in the lower octave, perpetuated a completely anachronistic view of the music, a view which came about through the interference of the arrangers of the early Nineteenth century. Furthermore, it was not just the lesser-known symphonies which continued to be misrepresented. Possibly the most popular of all Haydn's symphonies, No. 94 in G, "The Surprise," carried errors so radical that the tempo of the main part of the first movement might easily be misread through the absence of the authentic phrasing marks and subtle "hairpins." Even today, the pace of performance of this movement is much too fast in the majority of readings. The Menuet of this work has also for many years been misprinted, the shape of the

---

* There was one other symphony—a D major work written at about the same time as Symphony No. 41 and assumed to have been lost; consequently it was given the title Symphony "C." In 1975 a single piece, identifiable as the first movement by comparing Haydn's incipit in his "Entwurf-Katalog," was discovered in the Library of Congress in Washington. There is convincing internal evidence which suggests that this might be the first movement not of a full-scale symphony but of a multi-movement operatic overture (several of these appear in the catalogue, so this would not be surprising). H. C. Robbins Landon, by tying in the date—very likely 1768—with the fact that a known opera of that time—*Le pescatrici*—has its overture missing, concludes that the rediscovered "symphony" is in fact the overture to the opera. He does, however, concede the considerable likelihood that one or more movements of the piece may still be missing. This attractive and immensely convenient theory would in fact solve several questions in one; its only flaw, however, is that the movement to hand includes a repeated exposition—a most uncharacteristic feature in an operatic overture.

second phrase being distorted in defiance of the composer's wishes. Yet editions with these and other gross abuses were in common use between the Wars and even after 1945.

This is perhaps the place to call attention to a man who has done much to create the present interest in Haydn. But for his tireless enthusiasm, solid musicological research, and ceaseless championship, Joseph Haydn might still be considered the relatively unimportant composer of diversions which had been his apparent role in musical history until about 1950. The writer of one of history's biggest specialist books while still in his twenties, Howard Chandler Robbins Landon published "The Symphonies of Joseph Haydn" in 1955 and has since continued researching into Haydn, even at the cost of putting his own published findings out of date. Robbins Landon was one of the first musicologists to realise the value of the gramophone in music research: his energies, shortly after the war, in helping to found the Haydn Society of Boston, Massachusetts, went as much towards the propagation of the music in recorded form as to the printed score, and the early Haydn Society discs brought a quickening of interest amongst the record companies in this rich store of music. This attention has increased and accelerated to such an extent that today there is an astonishing wealth of recorded performances available, including two complete recordings of all the Haydn symphonies and several other series which have made available substantial groups of these works.

In 1950, however, when the first of the Haydn Society releases became known, there was barely a handful of Haydn symphonies on the market and each new Haydn Society disc brought exciting revelations in first recordings to the small group of long-starved enthusiasts. The orchestras included the Vienna Symphony, Vienna Chamber, and Danish State Radio Chamber, and the conductors were Jonathan Sternberg, Anton Heiller, Franz Litschauer, Erwin Baltzer, and Mogens Wöldike. Even by "only available version" standards, it must be admitted that some of these productions were rough, from both musical and textual viewpoints,* but thirty-two symphonies were provided, most of which had never been recorded before, and one of which, No. 50, reached the gramophone at virtually the same time as its first publication in 180 years of existence.†

---

* It is interesting to note that these recordings were sufficiently unusual in their stylistic endeavours for the "World Encyclopaedia of Recorded Music" (1950) to point out the use of "hpsi. and vlc. continuo" in Sternberg's readings of Nos. 1, 13, 28, and 31.

† Some of the performances would still compete fiercely with modern recordings if given enhanced sound. Nos. 6, 7, 8, 21, 42, and 47, for instance, under Franz Litschauer are, apart from the use of a cello rather than a double-bass solo in the Trios of the first three, models of fine Haydn style, while Nos. 26 and 36 have an admirable drive under the baton of Anton Heiller. Indeed, his reading of No. 26 still provides a yardstick for modern performances. Also outsanding to this day are the finely-poised

In addition to the symphonies, the Haydn Society produced a series of Masses, another of string quartets with the Schneider Quartet (now disbanded) which are still highly regarded, and a third series covering many of the keyboard sonatas, along with recordings of concerti, the *Notturni* for the King of Naples, etc., and, outside their main province, an ambitious historical series entitled "Masterpieces of Music before 1750." The Society even went so far as to explore Twentieth-century esoterica, issuing a three-disc set of Schönberg's *Gurre-Lieder*.

In the meantime, three more volumes of symphonies had appeared in print. They were the first in the projected Complete Edition by the Haydn Society: Nos. 82–87 (1949, edited by H. C. Robbins Landon), Nos. 50–57 (1951, edited by Helmut Schultz), and Nos. 88–92 (1951, edited by H. C. Robbins Landon). When the Haydn Society collapsed in the late Fifties, these prints were taken over by Universal Edition in Vienna, the Paris Symphonies (Nos. 82–87) being newly engraved to include the latest findings amongst recently discovered textual sources. The following symphonies, Nos. 88–92, were also re-engraved, and the Concertante was added to the volume, which became part of the complete series of the symphonies, issued in full and miniature score form, together with orchestral parts, by the Haydn-Mozart Presse of the Universal Edition. At last, with the appearance of the final volume, the London Symphonies in 1967, Haydn's symphonic literature was available in complete form for study and performance.

In 1958 the Haydn Institut was formed in Cologne under the guidance of Jens Peter Larsen, who had been involved in the Haydn Society at its inception. The Haydn Institut is engaged in producing a rival publication of the symphonies, as well as the rest of Haydn's music, but its approach, at least to the outsider, seems less methodical, and may well provide problems for libraries. Volume Four of the symphonies, for instance, contains Nos. 21–24 and 28–31 (edited by Horst Walter), and Volume Six (edited by C.- G. Stellan Mörner) comprises symphonies which may be in chronological order but which must also confuse the collector: Nos. 35, 49, 42, 45–47. Georg Feder took over from Larsen in 1960, and the entire series is being published by G. Henle Verlag, Munich.

During and after the existence of the Haydn Society, other recording companies occasionally delved into the vast store of Haydn

---

readings by Mogens Wöldike and the Danish State Radio Chamber Orchestra of Nos. 43 and 50. The recording of the latter symphony is the first example of the use of C alto horns on disc. The Haydn Society had commissioned the building of these horns from Alexander Brothers of Mainz. Sounding a whole octave higher than the traditional Nineteenth-century C horns, these instruments are pitched identically to the Eighteenth-century C trumpets (clarini) and produce the clean, piercing sound which Haydn intended when specifying these high horns in numerous symphonies and elsewhere.

symphonies. With the coming of stereo,* Vanguard recorded a set of the last six symphonies played by the Vienna State Opera Orchestra under Mogens Wöldike. Although Scherchen's performances were largely authentic, Wöldike was the first to record these works with the newly-prepared scores, and they proved to be a revelation of late Haydn orchestral style which could not be accepted by many of the reviewers at the time of their first release. Shortly afterwards, the

---

* If one considers the days before stereo, it is interesting to examine the pointers to authentic style current at the time. Haydn Society apart, what were the chances of assimilating the proper impression of Haydn's genius? To hear Haydn at all, one as likely as not listened to the composer through the prism of the personality of Sir Thomas Beecham—at least, in the United Kingdom. This conductor is regarded from a variety of viewpoints ranging from the one extreme of a cult figure who can do no wrong to the other pole whereby the purist cannot accept anything he did in Haydn as valid. Today Sir Thomas Beecham is not a figure central to the discussion of Haydn performance, but in years past he was one of the few conductors to give considerable attention to the composer. The mystique seems to run along the following lines: he used corrupt scores, one might almost say the most corrupt scores available, and he used the full string body of a modern symphony orchestra; against it he balanced the winds in a manner so musical that the matter of authenticity in numbers became irrelevant and to the music he imparted a swagger and poise that were the prerogative of a great artist. The effect was suave, debonair and delightful: a side of Haydn scarcely to be dreamed of from a study of the scores. Take the lilt he imparted to the second subject of Symphony No. 99's first movement: was there ever such grace of movement, such glorious optimism, such elegance or such poise? Clearly the answer is no, even though Haydn would never have expected the music to be played in this way. This is Haydn as seen through Edwardian eyes perhaps, but it is a facet of the composer worth experiencing. Unfortunately the records never gave the whole story. "Come on," Sir Thomas would shout to his timpanist in the concert-hall—and was rewarded at once by a bellicose roar from the drums. Somehow this never happened on records: tame, remote drums, tepid brass, violins and flutes curling enchantingly round the tuneful melodies, supported by a harmless pleasant mush offering no proper contrast. Yet in the concert hall Beecham largely obeyed Haydn's violent dynamics. On records, the mincing travesty of the Menuet of Symphony No. 100 must surely have been an isolated aberration which the recording team should have scrapped and re-recorded; likewise the ridiculously precious rendering of the Trio of Symphony No. 93. The monstrous cut in the repeat of the Menuetto of Symphony No. 97 should perhaps have been replaced by the appropriate bars from the "first-time-through." The near-inaudible timpani should also have been allowed to reach the microphones far more often. Listen to the terrific impact of these instruments when the Little Orchestra of London recorded, for instance, Symphony No. 93 and then reflect that both here and in the Beecham recordings, the same timpanist (Lewis Pocock) was performing. Beecham, then, left us an interesting, but sadly flawed, recorded legacy.

If the listener of the early Fifties required a different view there were the few Fritz Busch recordings—superbly classical, beautifully proportioned, and instinctively close to Haydn in a way understood by few conductors even today. From about 1950 onwards another Haydn conductor had something very positive to say and, like Beecham, recorded all the London Symphonies: this was Hermann Scherchen. By favouring these one would have been virtually implying the incompetence of most critics of the day, who seemed to take the view that, because Scherchen conducted Haydn in a manner different from that of the ubiquitous Beecham, the former must have been wrong. Sometimes Scherchen was, but not often. His disinclination to make first movement repeats was as damaging to the proportions of the music as it was with Beecham. That apart, Scherchen had a great deal to offer: strong wind playing, powerful timpani, and tempi which allowed the music to breathe. There was true drama in the then rare

American conductor Max Goberman began a project for the Library of Recorded Masterpieces to record all the symphonies.* Goberman's Haydn style matched Wöldike's in vivacity and authenticity, and a new era of Haydn performance had begun. On the last day of 1962, Max Goberman died at the tragically early age of fifty-one, and the days of the Library of Recorded Masterpieces, which he had founded, were numbered. He had recorded forty-five Haydn symphonies in less than three years, but not all were issued at the time of his death, and it was left for American Columbia (CBS in Britain) to release five of these symphonies for the first time. At the time of writing, four symphonies which were actually recorded by Goberman, Nos. 27, 34, 37, and the Symphony "A" in B flat, have never been made available to the purchaser in any form.

The beginning of the Seventies has seen the availability of all the symphonies in recorded form in two separate and completely independent series: Antal Dorati on Decca/London, and Ernst Maerzendorfer on Musical Heritage/Oryx. Thus, at the beginnings of the last three decades, concerted attacks have been made on this literature; the prospect of advances during the Eighties seems exciting.

Symphony No. 80, weight in No. 93, proper grace-notes for the first time on record in No. 94, realisation of the significance of the timpani in No. 97, a really military No. 100, and a Beethoven-like No. 104. These were revelations, and if there were eccentricities such as a monstrously slow opening movement to No. 98 or a virtually static variation movement in No. 103, such miscalculations were never for want of an enquiring mind on Scherchen's part.

* Similar items in their wildly ambitious plans were to record the complete works of Corelli and Vivaldi, and all the operas of Haydn. Substantial inroads were made into the first two of these projects.

Haydn the Man

Joseph Haydn was born in 1732 in the village of Trstnik on the river Leitha. The parish register shows that he was baptised on April 1, making his likely birthdate March 31, and it gives his name as Franciscus Josephus Haiden, son of Mathias Haiden.

The village was sizeable and also gave its name—known more widely in its German form as Rohrau—to the surrounding district which was adjacent to Pressburg (Požun), then the second largest city in the Austro-Hungarian Empire. Mathias Haiden was a wheelwright and earned his living through tasks allotted to him by Count Harrach. They consisted largely of coach repairs. He was also the local Marktrichter, an appointment which required overseeing the repair of hedges and ditches, the marking of boundaries, the settlement of any disputes arising from such problems, arranging fire duties and other such tasks as befell a servant of a rustic community in those times. His wife, Anna Maria Koller, at one time a cook to Count Harrach, was by all accounts an expert housekeeper who brought up the six surviving children of her marriage in exemplary fashion, the more so in view of the very simple standard of living to which the household was committed.

It is certain that life offered the family little more than the necessities. Rohrau was far from being a prosperous neighbourhood and the farmers' crops were under constant threat, in this low-lying area, from the floods which occurred from time to time. The people were a closely-knit group, although it is certain that there was a great mixture of Slavonic and Germanic races, and the ancestry of the Haiden family (probably known commonly but not, at that time entirely, in the conventional Viennese form: Haydn), together with its environment, makes Franz Joseph Haydn very much an Austrian citizen, influenced by Austrian customs but with a Croatian background that would be virtually self-evident in his music even if no documentation were available. Three-quarters of a century ago (when writers had none of today's irrational fear of admitting that racial characteristics cause people to differ from one another) Sir Henry Hadow wrote a book which investigated the Croatian aspect of Haydn's make-up. The clues are less in the factual research than in the folk aspect—in Eisenstadt the Croatian saying comes down to us: To je lovac i ribar kao Haydn (As good a marksman and fisherman as Haydn). No better accolade of brotherhood could be imagined. Clearly, Joseph Haydn was of peasant stock, was raised in simple rural surroundings and knew nothing, in his younger years, of luxury.

The first signs of musical inclination were evident through his good voice aided, significantly, by his excellent musical memory: a point worth bearing in mind when writers casually dismiss music of arguable authenticity from Haydn's own catalogues on the grounds of faulty memory. There seems no reason to regard this faculty as suspect in Haydn until his late old age.

Haydn, goes the apocryphal story, had watched the village school-master playing the fiddle and had imitated him by using two pieces of wood. One must beware of apocryphal stories, otherwise one becomes regaled with eternal fairy-tales such as that in which Haydn wrote his "Toy" Symphony regardless of its actual composition by someone else. Nevertheless, it is clear that either by this incident of the violin or something similar, the schoolmaster Johann Matthias Franck, a cousin of the family, took young Joseph to nearby Hamburg to teach him the rudiments of music and to sing in the local choir—all this at the age of about six (an age when Mozart was to be capable of playing key-board sonatas and writing his first slight compositions).

Because the Franck household had a small orchestra, there was every opportunity for practice upon various instruments, and soon an opportunity occurred whereby young Joseph (known at this time by the Viennese diminutive Sepperl) was able to study the timpani. His enthusiasm for these instruments is reflected not only in his daring use of them in very many works but even extends to his London visits half a century or so later, where we know him to have played the timpani in at least one performance of a late symphony. Some two years later Johann Adam Karl Georg von Reutter (1708–1742), Kapellmeister to the Court and, in addition, Kapellmeister at St. Stephen's Cathedral in Vienna, visited Franck, with whom he had been friendly for some years. The immediate result was for Reutter to recruit Haydn for the cathedral choir. This was wonderful news for the Haydn family since, subject to their son reaching the age of eight (the minimum age for appointment to St. Stephen's choir), it meant that his everyday needs together with his general education at the choir school were assured.

Musically the next ten years or so were invaluable to Joseph Haydn; educationally they left much to be desired. He had instruction in Latin, arithmetic, writing and religion, with violin and singing lessons from Finsterbusch. As far as we know he received only two lessons from Reutter himself and practically no guidance was given in musical theory. Nothing daunted, the young Haydn pored over such theoretical treatises as Fux's "Gradus ad Parnassum" and even attempted to compose: in later life Haydn told Georg August Griesinger, his friend and biographer, of the occasion at St. Stephen's when he set out to compose a twelve-part *Salve Regina*, certainly unsingable and unplayable but, as Haydn said, "I assumed that all would be well provided that the paper were filled up."

During the period at St. Stephen's, Johann Michael Haydn (1737–1806), Joseph's junior by five-and-a-half years, joined the choir. Two years later Michael's extraordinary ability began to endanger his brother's position, for the time had come when Joseph's fine soprano voice was beginning to break. There are numerous versions of the story which tells that Reutter had sought to preserve Joseph's voice by the barbaric operation which was none-too-uncommon at that time, and it is suggested that Haydn's father, in Vienna at the time, arrived miraculously at St. Stephen's to prevent such an occurrence. Rather more likely is the less coloured account which says that parental consent was sought and firmly refused. Inevitably the choirboy with no voice had to be dismissed and in November 1749 the seventeen-year-old Haydn was turned out of St. Stephen's to spend his first night in the open air in Vienna, penniless. The next day he chanced upon a fellow chorister, Spangler, who to his undying credit took Haydn to his already crowded home and gave him the attic to live and sleep in.

Haydn's adulthood had begun—starting with a long, frustrating period of poverty before any significant appointment was obtained. It is an aspect of Haydn's life which is little-discussed in the biographies. The sudden burgeoning forth of genius from about the age of thirty was so striking that it is no wonder that commentators are fascinated by that aspect of Haydn's creative life, yet it would be wrong to overlook the dozen or so years which helped shape the man's destiny. This is a greater length of time than that which he spent at St. Stephen's and during it the sheer dedication to the absorption of musical knowledge was remarkable. When he could find no employment (which was a frequent circumstance) he devoted himself to study. He took on a few pupils, played as a musician for local bands and open-air serenade-groups, and wrote music for such ensembles. When Spangler moved, Haydn was saved from near-destitution by an interest-free loan from a rich and important figure in the city called Buchholz. The sum was 150 florins and with it he was able to rent lodgings and buy a few more books, including some sonatas by Carl Philipp Emanuel Bach whose influence Haydn always freely acknowledged ("those who know me well, understand what I owe to Emanuel Bach").

On another floor of his lodging house lived an Italian Abbé by the name of Trapassi; on the lower floors of Viennese houses there dwelt the more successful. Haydn's room was an attic at the fifth floor; Trapassi had six rooms on the third floor. The Abbé's appointment was at court as poet and opera librettist, and he educated the two daughters of an ecclesiastical friend, one of whom, Marianne de Martinez, was to become a pupil of the famous theorist and teacher Niccolò Porpora (1686–1766). Haydn had often accompanied and taught Marianne for the sake of a good meal, and hence fortune smiled on him by the poet —better known to history books by his translated name Metastasio— recommending him as accompanist and (unofficial) manservant to Porpora. Haydn could never have hoped to pay for lessons from Porpora, but his position was such that he received guidance and help—including knowledge of the Italian language, invaluable to one so sketchily educated as Haydn—and for this he was more than willing to perform the many menial tasks that fell to him in Porpora's *ménage*. A significant event at this time was in 1751, when the actor Kurz was so delighted with Haydn's *Nocturne*, commissioned for Kurz's wife, that he at once fetched Haydn into his house. Before he left a bargain was struck whereby Haydn was to compose a Singspiel: *Der krumme Teufel*.

Clearly then, Haydn's talents were appreciated in a modest way at this time of study and effort. There is no treasure-house of undiscovered works during this period. Sundry small divertimenti or serenades may be placed here; certainly the *Missa Brevis* in F (two sopranos, chorus, two violin parts and basso continuo) is from the early Fifties. The first organ concerto dates from the mid-Fifties, and Haydn also wrote keyboard sonatas for his pupils, limited naturally in the demands made upon the performer's technique. To his disadvantage several of these fell into the hands of Viennese publishers who made a reasonable profit from their publication whilst the composer received nothing.

Around 1754 Haydn's circumstances changed a little—his mother died and his father remarried a year later. Haydn was now more self-sufficient and was able to afford a new apartment at the Seilerstatte. Matters improved further when he made the acquaintance of the Countess Thun, who engaged him as her keyboard teacher. This recognition enabled Haydn to increase his charge for lessons to all his pupils, but it was still necessary for him to go serenading of an evening. His Sundays were no less full: acting as violinist for a religious order in Leopoldstadt, travelling swiftly from their service to Count Haugewitz to act as organist, and later singing in the Cathedral choir—his voice being once again presentable though less remarkable in manhood than it had been in his boyhood. It is likely that during his brief appearances for isolated services Reutter never noticed him.

A further modest appointment came after a year or two, that of music master to the family of Baron von Fürnberg, who invited the young musician to join him from time to time at his country property near Melk, sixty miles away, where local musicians formed a chamber group. This encouraged Haydn to compose sundry simple trios and was the obvious spur which led him to develop his talent for string quartet composition.

Two years passed, during which Haydn's music made a great impression upon those around him, and in 1759 Baron Fürnberg recommended him to Count Ferdinand Maximilian von Morzin, whose castle was at Lukaveč in Bohemia. It was here that Count Morzin's court remained for most of the year and Haydn was appointed Kapellmeister. His fee was two hundred florins per annum, an adequate though hardly remarkable sum for the time. At twenty-seven Haydn had at last a major appointment to his credit; his security was assured from now on, though it is interesting to note that Michael Haydn had already reached this happy state in 1757 (at the age of only twenty) as Kapellmeister to the bishop of Grosswardein.

The chronicles of the stay at Count Morzin's establishment are by no means detailed, except that musically we know Haydn prospered. It was here that Haydn's first five symphonies were composed and, more importantly in view of the modesty of numbers in that musical establishment, Haydn composed many divertimenti and Feldparthien for the Count's wind band. In 1760, whilst the Count was away, Haydn met Dittersdorf—an historical meeting-point rather than one of musical significance. The exchange of knowledge between the two young court musicians (Dittersdorf, then twenty, was at the court of the Prince of Hildburghausen) was, as far as we understand it, by no means a technical affair, consisting more of an exchange of knowledge about the most interesting Viennese taverns.

On November 26, 1760, Joseph Haydn made the gravest error of his life by marrying Maria Anna Aloysia Apollonia, daughter of Johann Peter Keller, a hairdresser. Haydn had taught both Maria Anna and her sister Thérèse some four years earlier, and had, it seems, fallen in love with Thérèse before she elected to enter a convent. Haydn was all too soon aware of his sad misjudgement; it was clear that his new wife was to be a hindrance and a bringer of sadness—how curious that he, a notably good judge of character in musical and business matters, should have made such a grave and damaging mistake. "She cares not whether her husband be an artist or a cobbler," he said none too soon after his marriage. It seems that Maria Anna was not even a good housekeeper, had a spiteful tongue and a strong streak of jealousy—this last defect being a prime quality, as so often happens, in causing her husband to be (as he put it himself) "less indifferent toward the attractions of other women."

On top of this unhappy situation, Haydn was thrown out of work the following year when Count Morzin fell upon hard times and was forced to disband his court orchestra. Momentarily, therefore, despite his earnest endeavours supported by an ever more apparent streak of genius, Haydn's career was at its lowest ebb: a shrewish wife to encumber him and no appointment at all. From this point, however, he never ceased to progress. From the darkest moments, his life's work advanced—diligence was rewarded when Prince Paul Anton Esterházy heard of Count Morzin's difficulties and, realising that the court composer, sixty-five-year-old Gregorius Joseph Werner, was rather past his prime, offered Haydn the position of Assistant Kapellmeister.

The Esterházy family was of great importance—a high-ranking, immensely powerful example of Hungarian nobility, greatly devoted to the arts. Their first member to be elevated to the rank of Prince from that of Baron was Pál (Paul) (1635–1713), himself an excellent composer. He it was that had the family seat built: the castle at Kismarton (Eisenstadt), a two-hundred-room residence set in an immense and beautiful park. Werner had been Kapellmeister here since 1728 and had at his disposal some outstanding musicians, although at the time of Haydn's arrival on the first day of May 1761 the orchestra, which was to become so famous under his direction, was of very modest proportions, its wind complement being borrowed from the court military band. It was Haydn's immediate influence that enlarged it soon after his new appointment was confirmed—a flute, two oboes, two bassoons and two horns became a permanent part of the ensemble. The string section, previously only three violins, a violoncello and a violone, was also enlarged.

Haydn's new master, Prince Pál Antal (Paul Anton) Esterházy, was an excellent musician and played both violin and violoncello. His wise appointment of a new Assistant Kapellmeister was looked on none too kindly by Werner, who must have suspected that the intention was for himself, in due time, to be replaced by this young man who had at once taken control of the orchestra and already begun to revolutionise its importance in the context of musical life at court. Werner and Haydn had certain bitter encounters, but there is little doubt that the Prince was well-pleased with his new musician, despite disparaging reports which filtered through via Werner.

Rather less than one year after Haydn's appointment, Paul Anton died, on March 18, 1762. His successor was his brother, Prince Miklós (Nikolaus) Esterházy, known later as "Der Prächtige" (The Magnificent). Musical interest was retained, in fact enhanced, by the new master. Significantly he had a favourite instrument—the baryton—which accounts for over 160 works for this curious instrument* being written by Haydn.

The final turn of events which was to settle Haydn's existence for the greater part of his life happened in 1766. Prince Nikolaus had been perfecting a great castle in the swamps of Hungary near a lake (the Neusidler See). Why, apart from his family owning a hunting lodge in the region, the Prince was so taken with the area is difficult to understand, and certainly the insects which lived freely in the swamps must have been no little deterrent. As an engineering project, which cleared swamps, dug canals, and raised a castle clearly influenced by the magnificence of Versailles and indeed worthy to be mentioned in the same breath, it could only be described as a triumph. Though the language is colourful, the book on the subject, published in 1784 and

---

* The most lively description of this odd hybrid is provided by Burney's "General History of Music": ". . . this ungrateful instrument, which has the additional embarrassment of base strings at the back of the neck, and he [the celebrated barytonist Lidl] accompanied himself with these; an admirable expedient in a desert, or even in a house where there is but one musician, but to have the bother of accompanying yourself in a great concert, surrounded by idle performers who could take the trouble off your hands and leave them more at liberty to execute, express and embellish the principal melody, seemed at best a work of supererogation." There are, in fact, examples of the baryton being used in concerted music—notably in Haydn's divertimenti (from Group X of Hoboken's catalogue)—but significantly the original scoring of baryton, two violins, viola, cello, double bass and two horns was altered in three sets of arrangements of six of them published in Haydn's time. Haydn certainly approved the first of these by Artaria of Vienna in 1781, where baryton was replaced by flute, as indeed was the case with the Forster publication of a few years later, whilst Longman and Broderip issued an arrangement which they described as being "Simphonies in eight parts for Hoboys, Horns, Tenor and Bass." In such circumstances one need not fear that Haydn's genius was being wasted merely because so much of his time was spent in writing works—largely Trios—featuring the baryton, for he was not afraid to re-use some of the material if he thought it at all suitable.

thought to be the work of the Prince himself, does give some idea of the incredibly lavish scale on which everything was set.

These then were the surroundings to which the entourage moved and indeed stayed for the greater part of the time. The musical arrangements were more than ever in Haydn's hands; Werner had died in March 1766 and the post of Kapellmeister had passed to Haydn automatically. It was a job of fearsome size, with events to organise in the music-room, the opera-house and, by no means least, the puppet theatre, the function of which was perhaps more important than is usually recognised. The castle was basically Haydn's home and place of work for over a quarter of a century: he and his wife were permitted three rooms as compared with the bachelor musicians who had to share rooms with one another. Haydn, though certainly privileged, was still no more in the hierarchy of the court than a senior and respected servant with special talents and sufficiently cultured to be introduced to and converse with the distinguished visitors to Eszterháza. His financial situation was adequate, he was never again to be poor, yet it was necessary for him to supplement his income by selling works in Vienna, usually to the publisher Artaria. Nevertheless, it is unlikely that, even with this additional income, his finances were acceptably comfortable until after his fiftieth year.

The distinction between master and servant remained rigid in the Eighteenth century. The Kapellmeister would be referred to as "he," the normal manner of referring to any servant. Even as late as 1797, when Nikolaus II had become Prince and Joseph Haydn was, if for no other reason, worthy of respect as Doctor of Music at Oxford, the reference was still the bald, uncomplimentary "Haydn." (This last discourtesy was, in fact, corrected at court by the Princess Marie Hermenegild at her express direction.)

The greater part of Kapellmeister Haydn's stay at the Princely court is of immense importance to the musical world because of the number of great symphonies composed there. The history of their composition (most of those numbering between 6 and 91) forms the majority of the history of the composer's years between 1761 and 1791. Their nature is discussed elsewhere, but despite the overwhelming significance of the symphonic aspect of Haydn's output, the compositions in other forms would in themselves have been enough to single him out as a quite extraordinary composer. His operas were composed at regular intervals, and sometimes, as in the case of *L'infedeltà delusa*, at short notice: the Archduchess Catherine put in an unexpected appearance at an Eszterháza ball in her honour in 1773, and although Haydn's "short notice" must have been modified by privileged advance information it is hardly likely that he had long to compose this two-act burlesque. It was this opera, too, that prompted the

Empress Maria Theresa to make her famous remark to the effect that if she wished to hear a good opera, she would have to come to Eszterháza.

The account of the celebrations in 1775 for the visit of the Archduke Ferdinand and the Archduchess Beatriz gives some idea of the true magnificence of the court at the height of its glory. The guests were greeted with cheering crowds of villagers, waving flags and beating drums. Their arrival at the castle was announced with a military fanfare of trumpets and drums and—most significantly—the account proceeds to list those drawn up at the doors in the order whereby they had been arranged, *viz.* the Grenadiers in dress uniform, the servants in livery, six couriers, six lackeys, the Hussars, the musicians and their Kapellmeister, the hounds and their handlers, the household officials, six German and six Hungarian pages. So there we have it: Haydn and his musicians presented after the soldiers and servants but at least favoured in precedence before the hounds and the pages.

The entertainment which followed was on this day extraordinarily lavish but far from untypical of the Prince. A drama in German was performed for the guests soon after their arrival, the gardens were illuminated, and a banquet held outdoors. The next morning the Archduke and Duchess were serenaded outside their windows and subsequently taken on a guided tour of the palace. Lunch was another feast followed by a drive in the grounds and a visit to the temples. The evening featured Haydn's new opera *L'incontro improvviso,* and there followed a dinner and a masked ball attended by some 1,400 people. Throughout the stay the scale remained lavish. The theatre was visited again for Regnard's "Le distrait" (incidental music by Haydn). There were further dances—the last preceded by a display by Hungarian and Croatian folk dancers—and when the nobility retired to the final ball of the visit, the peasantry ate, drank and made merry at the Prince's expense on the lantern-lit lawns. This was the type of visit which would oblige Haydn to compose a major work and it is reasonable to suppose that the greater part of his operatic output was prompted in this way. The Seventies and early Eighties were rich years for such compositions, nor must one forget such operas written for the Marionette Theatre as *Das abgebrannte Haus* (significantly dating from the year of the serious fires at Eisenstadt in 1777 in which certain of Haydn's scores were lost).

By 1777 Haydn had composed about a dozen operas and an incredible amount of other music, including half his output of over sixty keyboard sonatas, about the same number of string quartets and all his compositions for baryton, the Prince having given up the instrument in 1775. Nearly seventy symphonies were to his credit, and half a dozen masses. The interesting gaps in his life's output lay at this time in the absence of published songs (the first of fifty were published in 1781) and of keyboard trios, of which only one (No. 26 in F) predates 1777. All this leaves aside innumerable divertimenti, string trios, wind partitas and a group of divertimenti for harpsichord and strings (effectively miniature keyboard concerti).

Haydn, now in his forties, had enormous responsibility at court. He wrote relatively few operas mainly because of the demands on him as conductor of operas by others; these were generally Italian—a reflection of the taste at court. His last opera for the Prince was *Armida* (1784) but in fact the early Eighties showed a great increase of interest in this art form at court. Even the fire of 1779 which destroyed the theatre in which the operas were housed did not halt the performances, which were merely transferred to the Marionette Theatre. Examining the programme for 1786 one finds that operas were performed at an average rate of more than one every three days.

In Haydn's circumstances his attraction towards the young wife Luigia of the court violinist Antonio Polzelli is none too surprising. Antonio was ageing and consumptive, Luigia was nineteen and vivacious. She was a mezzo-soprano and Haydn wrote many parts which we know her to have sung. Hers was never said to have been an exceptional voice but, clad carefully in colourful orchestral clothes by the Kapellmeister, it must have sounded rich indeed. Haydn never denied the affair though today's evidence is largely circumstantial. In some circles it is even accepted that Haydn was the father of Luigia's younger son, Aloysius Antonio Nicolaus (born in 1783), and indeed Aloysius's daughter nearly a century later described herself publicly as "Haydn's granddaughter." Whatever the truth of the matter, Haydn neither confirmed nor denied anything; we simply know that at this time in his career he was blessed by the companionship of an attractive woman, such as had been denied him the greater part of his life.

In this period Haydn also met Mozart—an event less meaningful in matters of artistic influence the one upon the other than is often supposed, but a friendship immensely important to both men nevertheless. It sometimes needs to be stressed that men of true genius recognise one another's gifts unstintingly. Many are the stories of their genuine appreciation of one another, as in Mozart's rejoinder to Leopold Koželuh's remark concerning a daring keyboard passage in a concerto by Haydn: Koželuh declared that he would never have written such a thing, to which Mozart replied, "Nor would I, because neither you nor I would have had so excellent an idea."

Haydn's fame had by now spread far beyond the confines of Eszterháza. In 1781 he had been presented with a golden snuff box by Charles III of Spain, via the secretary of the Spanish legation who was sent specifically to Eszterháza for the purpose. The director of the "Concerts Spirituels" in Paris approached Haydn: an encounter which culminated in the six grand symphonies published in Paris under the description *Repertoire de la Loge Olympique*. For Cadiz Cathedral Haydn composed his *Seven Last Words of Christ*,—consisting of an introduction, seven slow movements and a two-minute "earthquake" at the close. Each ten-minute piece followed a discourse upon the "word" or sentence uttered by Christ upon the Cross. As Haydn so aptly commented: "It was no easy matter to compose seven Adagios each lasting ten minutes and succeeding one another without fatiguing the listeners." The work nevertheless became a great success and a string-quartet arrangement was even made—although it has always seemed something of a misconception to have numbered the movements among the string quartets proper as Nos. 51 to 57 inclusive.

As the Eighties wore on Haydn's thoughts began to turn outside the confines of Eszterháza and to the rare breaks in court routine when the Prince moved to Eisenstadt or the staff went to their homes, a great many of which were in Vienna. In 1787 Haydn, in writing to the English violin-maker and publisher William Forster, mentioned that he hoped to meet him in London. One can by no means be sure, however, if this were anything more than an idle whim on the part of the composer, who was certainly tied contractually to Eszterháza for an indefinite period and could never have hoped to obtain leave of absence for the huge period required for such an enterprise as travelling across Europe. An important set of compositions about this time was the group of eight *Notturni* written in 1786 for King Ferdinand IV of Naples. The principal instrument involved was the lira organizzata (a curious cross between chamber organ and hurdy-gurdy). It was the re-scoring of this music for more conventional instruments which made it possible for Haydn to achieve no little success with the music in London some years later.

As the era of magnificence at Eszterháza drew towards its close Haydn's frustration began to show beneath the surface. He became acquainted with the wife of his friend, a Doctor Peter Genzinger, at whose home he was often made welcome during his visits to Vienna. Marianne Genzinger was an excellent singer and keyboard player; her children were also musical and their friendship continued by correspondence on Haydn's return to Eszterháza, where a hitherto unencountered note of bitterness begins to creep into his letters. In particular he complains that he does not know whether he is "Kapellmeister or Kapell-servant." In 1790 any taste, however mild, of the outside world —a world in which the fifty-eight-year-old composer was famous and yet had scarcely been seen—began to make him less satisfied with his position. His delightfully blunt complaint to Marianne of having to eat at the local tavern "a slice of a fifty-year-old cow instead of your admirable beef" is significant enough. The correspondence was always

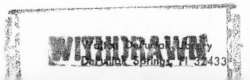

warm though there seems little enough evidence to suppose that Haydn was more than merely attracted to a woman who took an interest in his professional visits. The mood of Eszterháza may be gathered clearly from these communications, and in particular when Princess Maria Elisabeth, the mistress of Eszterháza, died on February 25, 1790, the subsequent pall of gloom over the castle was reflected in Haydn's letter, notably in his reference to "my poor prince who on hearing my Adagio in D, was affected by such deep melancholy that it was difficult to dispel it by other pieces." At the end of the letter Haydn confides that his faithful coachman had also died on the same day as the Princess. That Haydn had someone to whom, as he put it, he could pour forth all his sorrows much have been a comfort in those dark days. Joseph II of Austria—who had succeeded his mother the Empress Maria Theresa in 1780—died in the very week Princess Esterházy had died and so for the court servants life must have seemed particularly tragic at that period. Haydn now desired change, longed for the cultured company of the Viennese and in particular that of his great friend Mozart, and yet remained faithful to the court and the Prince, whom he held in genuine respect and who was now seventy-seven years old.

*

Suddenly events changed with a swiftness unheard of in all Haydn's thirty years' sojourn at Eszterháza. Prince Nikolaus died on September 28, 1790, after a brief illness. The young Prince Anton succeeded him and at once dismissed the whole orchestra except for the Kapellmeister, his leading violinist Tomasini, and a mere handful of others. Nikolaus had bequeathed Haydn a thousand florins a year, Anton added a further four hundred to retain his services nominally but left him free to order his own affairs. With amazing haste Haydn was in Vienna, omitting even to take most of his belongings with him. Hardly had he arrived and taken lodgings than offers of the post of Kapellmeister came to him: at Prince Grassal Kovics's court at Pressburg, at the court of the King of Naples, and an offer from the English impresario Johann Peter Salomon who, with incredible acumen, had made himself aware of Haydn's situation and announced immediately on meeting him that he had come from England to fetch him. His offer: three hundred English pounds for a new opera, another three hundred for six symphonies, another two hundred for their copyright, another two hundred for twenty smaller works and a minimum of two hundred pounds from a benefit concert. An advance on these sums was also proposed. Naturally there were problems but this was clearly the offer Haydn had waited a lifetime to hear—at last he would no longer be a servant, as he would certainly remain if he took the appointment at either Pressburg or Naples. The choice he made is part of musical history: he at once sought and was granted Prince Anton's permission to leave for England —and though forced to retract his promise to the King of Naples, the matter was settled amicably.

If one considers the circumstances leading to Haydn's London visit it seems almost more than coincidence that his greatest triumphs occurred through such a seemingly inevitable sequence of events: Salomon had read of the death of Prince Nikolaus in November when in Cologne, had hastened to Vienna, found Haydn, made all arrangements and planned to leave on December 15. Many of Haydn's friends tried to dissuade him—Mozart in particular: "You were never meant for running about the world and you do not have sufficient languages," to which Haydn replied, "My language is understood by all the world." Nevertheless, the parting was not an easy one and Mozart, with tragically prophetic accuracy, said to the older man: "I fear we are saying our last farewell." The journey took place on the appointed day nonetheless. Haydn and Salomon spent Christmas in Bonn and made the crossing of the English Channel on New Year's Eve. There was a violent storm and Haydn was fascinated, staying on deck to observe, as he put it, "that huge monster—the sea." At five in the afternoon of New Year's Day 1791 they arrived in Dover and the composer's subsequent triumphs lay in the history of the culmination of his symphonic art.

The enormous acclaim, the winning of genuine friendships, and not least the amassing of more money that he had ever held at one time in his life, must have made London seem like some bewildering fairyland to Haydn. His valuable notebooks, though not well-ordered chronologically, give some superbly frank insights into the life which surrounded him. He always gave due credit to the hospitality of his hosts and though he never really mastered the English tongue we find no complaints of problems arising from his unfamiliarity with the language. We do, however, have some delightfully tart observations on the English way of life. One of his earliest notes relates to "Milord Chatham, Chief of the General Staff and brother to Minister Pitt" whom, he observed, "has been so drunk the last three days that he has not been able to sign his name, which is why Lord Howe could not leave London and why, in consequence, the fleet could not set sail." His observations on English womanhood were also often disconcertingly frank: "In France women are virtuous before they marry and promiscuous after. In Holland they are promiscuous before they marry and virtuous afterwards. In England they are promiscuous all their lives."

The first of the great Salomon concerts took place on March 11, 1791, at the famous Hanover Square Rooms; thereafter life became a whirl of professional engagements, during which Haydn somehow found time to compose. He was given the Doctorate of the University of Oxford in July—a famous occasion which featured the Symphony No. 92 —although the thrifty Haydn noted in his book that he "had to pay a guinea and a half to be made a Doctor at Oxford, another guinea for the gown, the whole journey has cost me six guineas."

He spent the summer at the country home of a Mr. Brassey, a wealthy banker. Returning to London he was genuinely charmed by the personality of the Prince of Wales whose friendliness was an aspect not too often encountered by Haydn in his dealings with nobility. We may assume that sympathy between the men would have been enhanced by their being able to converse in German, and Haydn was very complimentary about the Prince's abilities as a cellist.

One notable impression made on him was the magnificence of Handel's oratorios, and this could well have influenced his concentration upon choral music in his later years. His love of nature is also noted in terms of no less feeling, and it would seem that a picnic on an island in the Thames at Richmond delighted him greatly as a result of the glorious surrounding scenery.

A touching encounter about this time was made possible by the Prince of Wales, who arranged for Haydn to meet the seventeen-year-old daughter of King Friedrich Wilhelm II of Prussia, currently on her honeymoon with her husband the Duke of York. She and Haydn had met before and his admiration for her highly musical father drew them closer. Haydn remarks on the beauty of her voice, the excellence of her piano playing, and her fine memory for his music which she had heard at her father's court. Above all he mentions her charm and intelligence. Clearly, when not inundated by work, Haydn's leisure time gave him a joy he had rarely had the time to experience before.

After about a year in England, Haydn met the widow of Johann Samuel Schröter, who had been music-master to the Queen. We know of the closeness of this relationship mainly through her letters to him, copies of which she kept in her notebook; in his last years, however, Haydn revealed that he had retained his own copies. His correspondence with Marianne von Genzinger was maintained with warmth, and his willingness to tell of his successes and describe his concerns remained. The relationship with Mrs. Schröter, if we are to accept her writings (none of Haydn's replies are preserved), was rather closer. She started as his music pupil but this was clearly not the only matter which brought Haydn often into her company.

Amidst many joyful events in his full life in London, there fell a shadow: the news of Mozart's death on December 5, 1791, at the age of only thirty-five. At first Haydn would not believe it (reports had circulated some years earlier concerning his own death) and so he was by no means prepared to accept such news about a dear friend, especially one who had yet to reach middle age. Eventually, however, the truth had to be accepted and he could not conceal a feeling of guilt at having been so far away when the event took place. He wrote at once to Johann Michael Puchberg, a mutual friend, asking for a list of those Mozart compositions as yet unknown in England so that he might seek their publication. When persuading the music-dealer Broderip to buy a Mozart manuscript, he insisted, according to Burney, that "friends often flatter me for having some genius, but he stood far above me."

Haydn returned to Vienna in June 1792 and bought a house where his wife might live. Their relationship was scarcely less bitter than before, particularly since Haydn discovered that she had been spreading malicious rumours about him. It was to Marianne von Genzinger that Haydn turned for friendship and hospitality but there is little documentary evidence of their continued relationship; they could now meet whenever they wished and we know of only two more letters at this time. Haydn was certainly always a welcome guest and her cultured friendship remained a valued part of the composer's life.

At this time, too, Beethoven became Haydn's pupil. He had originally intended to study with Mozart and it is curious that, although Haydn willingly instructed him for a nominal fee (eight groschen per hour), he did not have an easy relationship with the headstrong, impatient musician, despite undoubted sympathy with the younger man's "revolutionary" musical ideals. It could also be that Haydn, at the height of his fame, had no more than modest enthusiasm for correcting exercises in counterpoint and musical composition. Despite their strained musical relationship, their personal friendship was a little warmer and in a long letter written to the elector of Bonn, asking that he might support Beethoven and recommending several compositions, Haydn gave the view that "Beethoven will one day be one of Europe's greatest composers and I shall be proud to call myself his teacher."

In January 1793 a further tragedy occurred: Marianne von Genzinger died at the age of only thirty-eight—the one genuine confidante on whom Haydn could rely, as well as being a very dear friend. It was this sad event which proved to be the main factor in deciding Haydn to return to England. True, the process took some time: the agreement with Salomon was concluded in the summer and was based on the composition and performance of six new symphonies. This time, Haydn arranged for his copyist, servant and great friend Johann Elssler to accompany him. In Haydn's circumstances it is clear that he sorely needed attention in domestic matters; that Elssler* was a friend as well made Haydn's hard domestic lot all the easier to bear.

---

* Johann Elssler (1769–1843) was, in fact, Haydn's godson, and the father of the famous Nineteenth-century ballerina Fanny Elssler. It was he who in 1805 helped Haydn compile his catalogue of works—much as Johann's father Joseph had helped Haydn with his "Entwurf-Katalog" in about 1765.

Haydn and Elssler set out for England on January 19, 1794, in Baron van Swieten's coach, travelling via Wiesbaden. It was unfortunate for posterity that there was no longer a Marianne von Genzinger to whom Haydn could write, for we know less of the details of this visit than of his former one. Haydn's own diary was more factual than descriptive. We know that he made a friend of the great double-bass virtuoso Dragonetti : it is a shame that no double-bass concerto resulted from this meeting, although the interest which Haydn took in the instrument is reflected not only in his use of this (or the violone) as a solo concertante instrument in five of his symphonies but also in a lost double-bass concerto of unknown date. A further bar to our knowledge of this second visit lies in the loss of one of Haydn's notebooks. We believe that his warm friendship with Mrs. Schröter continued and that she received the scores of his last six symphonies when he left. Haydn, despite the unfamiliar language, made more friends, remained on excellent terms with the Prince of Wales, and was asked by the King and Queen to stay in England and settle there with his wife. However, it was not to be, and he left in August 1795 on a somewhat sad journey via Hamburg, where he hoped to meet Carl Philipp Emanuel Bach who, unbeknown to Haydn, had died as long ago as seven years before.

On his return to Vienna Haydn was both a famous man and one of reasonable financial substance. His works were now performed frequently and in many places in Austria, but particularly in Vienna. He bought another house in Gumpendorf and the following summer dwelt again at Eisenstadt, although his duties were very light. War was threatening, however, and in just such an atmosphere he wrote the *Paukenmesse* (*Missa in tempore bello*). Here began the rich Indian summer of Haydn's late works: the great masses (virtually one each year until 1802), *The Creation, The Seasons*, the short but magnificent *Te Deum*, and the choral version of the *Seven Last Words*. All to say nothing of the glorious quartets Op. 76 Nos. 1-6, Op. 77 Nos. 1 and 2, and the unfinished Op. 103.

Though his output lessened in sheer quantity and he began to fail in his later years, his creativity never dried up. One matter that remains a mystery, however, is the completion of his symphonic work relatively early: nothing at all after the last year of his second London visit (at the age of sixty-three, fourteen years before his death). Haydn's symphony-writing span was, therefore, thirty-eight years in length— exactly half his life. Why, then, did he cease to write in a form which came so naturally and permitted him to pour out his greatest creations? It is perhaps a greater mystery than at first appears. Landon suggests that the masses themselves are indeed symphonic; accepting this, the formal symmetry of Haydn's structures is still satisfied, along with his natural instinct for shape and flow. This theory is attractive and logical, a reasoned explanation of Haydn's development in his last creative years, but it does not actually try to account for the absence of true symphonies. Those who feel that a close study of the form of the masses (for the sake of relating their construction to that of the symphonies) is a demanding project may find an easier verification by examining the brief but magnificent *Te Deum* in C major of 1800, which Haydn composed for the Empress Maria Theresa—consort of Franz II (Franz I of Austria). Here in microcosm is the formal similarity to which Landon refers, with a majestic opening section, a reflective central part, a joyful yet grand peroration and finally a superb, triumphant fugal episode to close the work amid a blaze of brilliant C major brass and timpani. This above all is the writing of the Haydn of the symphonies—the link being taken even further in that the old Gregorian *Te Deum* melody is to be heard wraith-like moving among the complex writing of the fully-scored music. Despite such a ready short-cut to understanding, the question as to why no more symphonies were written by Haydn remains unanswered. It seems he simply did not happen to write them, and no more dramatic explanation is to be found. Indeed, the romantic conception of death taking a composer's pen from his hand as he builds toward the climax of his last and greatest symphony is delayed in actuality until the day of Bruckner's death.

The end of Haydn's symphonic career marked a point at which he turned towards a new and rather different era. There is just one indication that Haydn's domestic unhappiness might have been alleviated at this time, for we know that between the two London visits the young Pietro Polzelli, the elder of Luigia's two sons (born 1777), had come to stay at the Haydns'. Whilst one may imagine Frau Haydn's mixed feelings over welcoming the son of a rival, by Haydn's own account she was kind to him and Pietro was friendly and dutiful to them both. "Papa" Haydn's naturally fatherly nature was put to good use late in life and he obtained for Pietro an appointment as piano teacher to the Countess Weissenwolf and her family. The talented young man next obtained a post as violinist with an orchestra in Vienna. Tragically, he died of tuberculosis before the end of 1796—a sad occasion for Haydn. His contact with more youthful friends was becoming less and the only close link with the younger generation remained in his true friendship with the pupil Sigismund Neukomm. In 1799, however, he became acquained with Georg August Griesinger, sent to Haydn initially by Härtel the publisher but destined to become his biographer and friend through his last years.

In 1798 Haydn completed his great oratorio *Die Schöpfung* (*The Creation*) and the *Missa in angustiis (Nelson Mass)*. The following year *Die Jahreszeiten* (*The Seasons*) was begun and the two string quartets Op. 77 for Prince Lobkowitz completed. The music composed at this time, though less in quantity if larger in scale than of years past, shows not the slightest sign of waning powers, but Haydn was in fact over-stretching himself. He knew that work on *The Seasons* was taking its toll and in April 1800 a fever made his friends worry about his condition. He recovered only slowly, though he was looked after well at Eisenstadt. Two years before there had been a lesser sign of overwork but this one was clear and it may not have been entirely wise of him to have collected subscriptions personally in order to publish *The Seasons* himself. After his recuperation Haydn resumed his ordered day (delightfully set out in detail by Elssler as late as 1805)—a day which included his pupils playing to him—and he still improvised and sketched compositions. This bachelor life had not been too dissimilar since about 1799 and was in no way altered by his wife's death in 1800, except for a mild flurry caused by Luigia Polzelli's domicile in Vienna and her un-disguised hopes of Haydn's renewed attention. Nearly twenty years had passed, however, since the fires had died between them and this had altered the situation. The slightly embittered Luigia married elsewhere, went to Italy, and out of Haydn's life for ever.

The Seasons was at last finished and proved to be a triumph. It was, however, his last major work—"*The Seasons* has finished me off," said Haydn—and in the summer of 1801 he drafted his will. This document throws some light on the composer—a man of substance in his later years, he distributed his wealth to even the most distant of his relatives. Historians have also been intrigued by bequests to women who scarcely seem to have featured in his life. Elssler was to receive a sizeable sum, as were Haydn's two brothers Michael and Johann. Most intriguing of all, however, was the bequest of one hundred florins to Fräulein Anna Buchholz because, as Haydn put it, "in my youth her grandfather loaned me 150 florins when I greatly needed them."

*

The closing years of Haydn's life found his failing health a severe technical handicap to his creativity. He did perhaps exaggerate the in-firmities of old age in his letters but this seems forgivable in one who had been so accustomed to hard, accurate, and copious toil all his life. He complained in 1802 that he was "working most wearily" on what was to be his last mass—the *Harmoniemesse*. In 1803 the quartet Op. 103 was written—two marvellous movements were completed and neither shows any enfeeblement of musical thinking, though it is legiti-mate to see a quiet, dark sadness in the music which is certainly nos-talgic in feeling, for the composer had by this time begun to see the shadows lengthening. His last appearance as a musical director was at an 1803 performance of the *Seven Last Words*. Thereafter he rarely appeared in public and in any event walking became somewhat difficult for him. Though he knew that physically he was beginning to age, Haydn's sense of humour did not desert him and, when in 1805 it was reported in England that he had "died at the age of ninety-seven," causing Cherubini to write a Requiem in his honour based on melodies by Haydn (what price its resuscitation today?) and for a performance of Mozart's Requiem to be planned in Paris, Haydn wrote to the publisher Thomson saying: "If I had known in time, I should have come to Paris to conduct the Requiem myself."

Even in his declining years, Haydn's inbred passion for tidiness and cleanliness remained and he always dressed with care, indeed splendour, including wig, waistcoat, dress coat and silk hose—even keeping his white gloves by him. This is the splendid figure that his guests encountered, although by the time he was seventy-three he was plainly on the verge of becoming an invalid. The Princess Esterházy visited him frequently and her husband not only increased his salary but also paid all the doctor's bills. On March 27, 1808, a famous performance of *The Creation* took place at which the master appeared before a multitude for the last time. The auditorium was full of great musicians, with Beethoven, Gyrowetz, Hummel and Salieri acting as a welcoming party. He entered to a flourish of trumpets and general jubilation. Salieri directed the historic performance and at the words "Let there be light" applause broke out and Haydn lifted his arms toward heaven, declaring that not from him but thence had come this moment of inspiration which had so moved the hearers. As he left, people crowded around him, aware that this might be the last time they saw him. Beethoven knelt and kissed Haydn's hands.

A year remained to Haydn and one matter with which he concerned himself was his will. His two brothers having died, Johann in 1805 and Michael in 1806, much needed redistribution. As little as six weeks before his death he read his will to the main benefactors and asked if all were satisfied.

These last years of Joseph Haydn were certainly sad. He was comfortably off and well looked-after but it is clear that a creative brain was still housed in a body too weak to give it written expression. The greatest tragedy for him must have been the unfinished quartet. Even the two miraculous fragments that exist remain a rich experience, but it must have been deeply frustrating for the composer to hear the material for its completion flowing through his brain whilst not being able to gather it in order to complete his important task.

The end came shortly after Napoléon occupied Vienna in 1809. Elssler tells of a French officer who called upon Haydn, talked with him, and sang an aria from *The Creation* with extraordinary feeling and style. Haydn was much moved and later that day played to the members of his household his great *Emperor's Hymn*—three times over. The following day he was unable to rise from his bed, and was rapidly becoming exhausted. Some four days later, on May 31, 1809, he fell gently asleep to wake no more.

1: Early Development

Unless one understands a little of the nature of the orchestras for which Haydn wrote his symphonies, a chronological survey of his work in this *genre* will seem to show certain inconsistencies. Logic comes into play provided one remembers that the instruments of his day sounded different not merely to modern ears but even between one country in Europe and another. Very relevant, too, was the availability of instrumentalists. When Haydn wrote symphonies for Count Morzin, his wind band would have consisted at most of no more than two each of oboes, horns and bassoons, and he is unlikely to have had more than eight strings—only one of which would have been a viola player. The lower line would have been taken by a violone, the player being capable of using a cello as an alternative, and the remaining bass harmonies would be supplied by the harpsichord strengthened by a bassoon or two.

Haydn's orchestra at Eszterháza was soon increased at the behest of the new assistant Kapellmeister, and for the famous trilogy of Symphonies Nos. 6, 7 and 8 he probably had a dozen strings. Supplementary musicians available in the early Eszterháza days would have been the two violinists and bassist who more usually accompanied the church choir, and he could always borrow trumpets and timpani from the band of the Prince's private army. Even when the orchestra expanded so that four horn players were available for special occasions, it seems two of the hornists were violone or cello players and were more often used for the latter purpose. It was a decade and a half after Haydn's arrival at Eszterháza before two clarinettists were engaged and even then they were never used in the symphonies. Prior to the London period, Haydn is unlikely to have used more than twenty-seven players even for his biggest symphonies. True, the special occasion of the Paris Symphonies being performed by a massive orchestra was a famous exception, but we know that they were played by the normal Eszterháza orchestra without supplement and so it would be misleading to assume that Haydn had anyone other than his own players in mind when composing the music and hearing it in his mind's ear.

The original sound of the earliest symphonies, then, was probably rough-hewn by the standards of the suave playing heard today—although the stringed instruments would have been gut-strung and hence given a more mellow tone. It is the winds that would have made more impact than the blended sounds of today's players, and it is possible that the more primitive key-systems on the woodwinds of the day might not have permitted some of the high speeds which are currently applied. This is not to say that Haydn's men were not virtuosi in their own right: clearly they were, as the incredibly difficult horn parts in, for instance, Symphony No. 5 indicate, but one must still bear in mind the nature of the limitations imposed. Haydn, early in his symphonic output, wrote thoroughly worked-out viola parts despite the fact that he had only one or two players to perform them. The continuo line would normally have consisted of harpsichord with celli and violone and/or double bass. Even if there were no written bassoon part, at least one such instrument would also support the bass line. There is some misunderstanding over this matter, as when, for example, Haydn notes a bassoon part in Symphonies "B" and No. 9 only when it has a solo in each Trio. Unfortunately one still encounters recorded performances where this instrumentalist seems to sit silent except for his brief moment of glory. Another perversity, mercifully dying out, is a similar treatment of the bassoon in the "Farewell" Symphony, where it is marked only a few bars before its final disappearance in the Finale: to sit doing nothing except for those few bars, so that the listener may suddenly realise that the instrument has made its exit, is perhaps one of the most crass of all modern misconceptions.

Two last points need to be made in respect of tonal differences in Haydn's orchestra. The violone is given extended solos in Symphonies Nos. 6, 7, 8, 31 and 72. This instrument was superseded in due course by the double-bass, but whereas the modern double bass only reaches a low E, Haydn frequently wrote down to a low D and C—an excellent example being the low C which rounds off the Trio to Symphony No. 48 so effectively. There are recordings available in which it is obvious that no instrument is available to obtain such a note and so the bottom harmony is allowed to leap an octave upward—to disconcerting effect. It need hardly be added that the simple expedient of ensuring that there is one or more five-stringed bass in the orchestra is all that is required to enable Haydn's bass parts to be performed properly. The last problem concerns the timpani. Haydn used these instruments in a very individual manner and being a timpanist himself was often very clear in his directions. A glance at the scores soon reveals that he sees them not as the equivalent of organ pedals, as sometimes is the case in Brahms's orchestration, but more as a higher voice, always with a distinct *timbre*. In the Eighteenth century shallow hand-tuned instruments were employed, normally struck with plain wooden sticks; the sound emphatically did not resemble the modern chromatic timpani struck with large woolly-headed drumsticks. The additional resonance of the big modern drums would (and all too often does) muddle Haydn's lucid textures, although skilful timpanists can and do avoid this by altering their technique to represent the drier, essentially military, tone of the older instruments.

Unless, at the very least, most of these matters are attended to, a recording of a symphony can mislead the modern student. There is, however, an encouraging side to present-day Haydn performances—especially those elements which are preserved on disc. I refer to an enlightened awareness of the importance of Haydn's formal *da capo* markings. The more one looks at these, the more obvious it becomes that there can be no suggestion that this was a mere formality which can be happily ignored. Haydn's earlier symphonic movements are frequently in binary form, i.e. that of a Scarlatti sonata. To leave out either of the two repeats in a movement such as the Finale of Symphony No. 22 is to misconceive the nature of Haydn's formal design, and this comment can be extended to cover every first movement exposition repeat, however lengthy. That Haydn knew exactly what he was doing by demanding double repetitions in so many of his early works is proved conclusively by Symphony No. 26 (c. 1768)—something like the forty-fifth symphony that he composed. Formally this is similar to its companion works of the period, but dramatically something quite extraordinary happens in the development section of the first move ment: abrupt modulations through foreign keys and angry changes of instrumental colouring to give effect for a special occasion. The occasion will be referred to later, but concerning the formal design this gripping drama means that the listener has been subjected to a musical experience far more dramatic and emotional than is normal for the period, and so Haydn, for the first time in a symphony of conventional format, does not require the second half of the movement to be played twice. How right he is. To have done so would have undermined the whole impact of this wonderful piece of dramatic writing.

Only much later may one query the wisdom of following the *da capo* markings to the very letter. The clue comes from comparing the contours of Symphonies Nos. 83 and 87. Observe all repeats of the first, third and fourth movements and the proportions of the two works are identical. In the respective slow movements, however, No. 87 has no repeats, whereas both halves are marked for repetition in No. 83. Taking an average timing of several recent recorded performances, movements 1, 3 and 4 take 9, 4 and 6 minutes respectively (where all repeats are made). If no repeats are made in the slow movement of No. 83, then, like that of No. 87 where no repeat is required, it becomes another 6-minute piece, i.e. both symphonies are timed at 9, 6, 4, 6. It seems, therefore, that No. 87 must be one's criterion since the observation of the slow movement repeats in No. 83 would give the extraordinary contour of 9, 12, 4, 6.

Certainly this is an aspect which the modern performer must treat on the merit of each individual case if anomalies such as the above are to be avoided. There does, however, seem to be an awareness of formal design nowadays and, since this was such a large part of the compositional method of Eighteenth-century music, it is as well that we have at last experienced the inevitable reaction against the "personalised" interpretations stemming from the Nineteenth century. All that is required is an inventive realisation of the written parts. The shedding of the traditional lines of thinking is probably one of the chief reasons why music of the Eighteenth century has had such a staggering revival in recent years: a score of that period is not simply more "correct" for being played as written rather than imposed upon, it is also infinitely more exciting aurally.

*

Scholarly research cannot tell which was the very first symphony penned by Joseph Haydn, but then scholarly research may sometimes take itself rather too seriously. To remain perplexed about this small but interesting point would be to ignore no less than the composer himself. He, at least, firmly believed that the D major work which we know as SYMPHONY NO. 1 was indeed the first symphony he ever created. The archives of Count Morzin have never been located and there is no autograph copy of this work; nevertheless, there are plenty of authentic manuscripts of the period, the earliest of which are to be found in the collection from the Library of Count von Fürnberg, supported by an excellent copy of c. 1770 at the Monastery of St. Florian.

To find a Haydn symphony in that collection is a good guide to the nature of the symphonies composed for the Lukaveč court. No problems arise as to the nature of Symphony No. 1, though one cannot be too sure of the date—not earlier than 1757 and not later than 1759 is as much as can be assumed with certainty, the former date being the more likely. That this first symphony begins with a crescendo means that current Viennese styles, as influenced by the great court composers at Mannheim, were well known to Haydn. The slow movement—a central Andante—owes much more to the dance than to the after-dinner drawing-room concert and, as is typical of the period, there are strings and continuo only. To put winds in a slow movement was a measure for which Haydn was not yet ready. The colouring of the oboes in the outer movements largely reinforces the violins, while the horns strengthen the middle parts and the cembalo provides the remainder of the harmonic interest. An original work for the period, though certainly not remarkable or exceptional—merely the work of a composer far more skilled than his lowly position at that time might imply.

SYMPHONY NO. 2 in C (two oboes, two horns, strings and continuo) is an oddity—the only Haydn symphony with no repeat signs. In some ways it is like an operatic overture and thematically the first movement is reminiscent of the Finale of the First Horn Concerto. Once again no autograph exists and in some ways this work sounds more archaic than Symphony No. 1 Closer examination, however, shows a forward-thinking approach to structure and the long winding theme of the Andante has harmonic daring. Haydn's sense of colour, though, is as yet undeveloped: horns in low C carry out a function in the outer movements little more adventurous than that of the bassoon supporting the continuo group. Nor do the oboes (missing from several early sources but certainly authentic) do more than add a slight touch of rusticity.

In order to obtain a glimpse of later glories in microcosm, one must turn to SYMPHONY NO. 3 in G, perhaps the earliest four-movement work, again dating from the Morzin period and scored like Nos. 1 and 2. It is often noted that both formally and thematically the fourth movement bears a resemblance to the Finale of Mozart's last symphony. No less of an advance, however, is the extremely long lyrical first-movement string/oboe melody over a rapid, restless bass. Oboes begin to assert themselves by becoming occasionally divorced from the surrounding strings. One could scarcely mistake this music for that of any other composer: the dancing Andante Moderato seems to be the only movement where Haydn is content with existing forms, and even this has the occasional unexpected syncopation—a tendency destined to be dormant not for very long.

SYMPHONY NO. 4 in D springs no surprises of scoring and reverts to three movements again. The first movement is in Haydn's best "driving" style but does not step outside the confines of its period. The central Andante, however, is highly original and the composer's use of syncopation is extraordinary. The theme is shared between first and second violins, each lying across the beat in relation to one another.

The restless effect can well be imagined, the more so since the whole movement is required to be played *piano*. The lower line on second violin is marked rhythmically by the continuo.* The Finale is marked *tempo di menuetto*, but has no Trio: with a time signature of 3/8 instead of 3/4 the diminution of the bass rhythms gives the required rhythmic spice to a movement in which the instrumentation is content to blend rather than to impose.

Symphonies "A" and "B" may be mentioned together since, apart from sharing late discovery, both are in B flat and neither can be dated with any certainty. They are from somewhere between 1757 and 1761 —in any event later than No. 1 and earlier than No. 6. SYMPHONY "A" was mislaid largely because the publication of the music in the form of a string quartet (as Op. 1 No. 5) discouraged researchers from looking further. It should, however, have seemed obvious that this three-movement work merited enquiry since all its companions of Opus 1 had five movements and the real candidate for inclusion—the five-movement string quartet "Opus O" discovered in 1931 by Karl Geiringer and Marion Scott—was waiting patiently on the sidelines. Its first publication as a symphony was in 1955 as a supplement enclosed with H. C. Robbins Landon's book "The Symphonies of Joseph Haydn." Needless to say, the three simple movements take on a new dimension in full orchestral dress, with adventurous oboe writing in the Finale of which the bare string parts could give no inkling.

Mandyczewski may have overlooked the four-movement B flat symphony now called SYMPHONY "B" since it is listed in some authentic sources as "Partita." It was first printed by Adolf Sandberger in 1934 and provides no revelations apart from breaking the general rule by

---

* In Max Goberman's recording this disturbing a-rhythmic effect is made even more remarkable because of this conductor's separation of first and second violins to left and right of the orchestra. The deliberate muting of the harpsichord to allow the gentle violin entries to seem the more pointed is a further example of insight.

placing the Menuet second. As with No. 9 there is an independent bassoon part in the Trio which verifies yet again the existence of such an instrument as *basso continuo* in the works where Haydn does not bother to specify it. In some ways this is the most advanced of the movements, with high thematic ideas given to the horns—a sharp contrast to the simplicity and bare harmonies of the hushed string-and-continuo Andante which follows.

The SYMPHONY NO. 5 in A is the last of those popularly thought to have been composed for Lukaveč (though the Fürnberg collection shows that several others date from this period and were unlikely to have been composed at Eszterháza). Its form needs a little explanation, for it begins with a complete slow movement, a procedure signifying something special in Haydn's output. It can be termed a church-sonata work, each such composition having the characteristic of a slow first movement; in all but one case the marking is *adagio*, something deeper in feeling being implied than in the conventional *andante* (with its roots in the dance). The symphonies in this form are Nos. 5, 11, 18, 21, 22, 34 and 49. Quite why every one of these works seems to stand out in emotional impact amongst its contempories is difficult to assess—of these darker works few others in conventional layout have similar dramatic effect, although Nos. 44, 52 and 64 do come very close. In No. 5 the power of Haydn's thought is already manifest: the bass lines in the fast second and fourth movements take on that rhythmic, pounding character which is soon to become a notable fingerprint of fast movements in Haydn symphonies. In the second movement there is tremendous nervous tension, and in the Menuetto 2do (as Haydn prefers to call the Trio of the third movement) the horns ascend to very great heights,

although the spectacular element of such writing is probably even more obvious in the ethereal opening movement.

Doubtless the horn players at Lukaveč were considerable virtuosi.

Several other early Haydn symphonies of which the dates are uncertain are possibly from the Lukaveč period, and Nos. 10, 11, 15 and
18 belong to this group. On the whole these are fairly slight works in
terms of instrumental originality but time and again elements of tragedy
come to the surface. SYMPHONY NO. 10 in D does not really progress
much further along the paths of development than No. 1, although
some of the thematic echoes are taken up by oboes and horns across an
octave. There is one further technique, however, which has not been
noted before—the effect of sudden dynamic change. Loud rhythmic
chords strike across the melodies in the outer movements of this three-
part work.

SYMPHONY NO. 11 in E flat opens in a purposeful way. The solemnity of No. 22 ("Der Philosoph") is foreshadowed but as yet Haydn still
does not choose to shake off the habit of answering phrases violin to
violin, or violins against continuo. This device is not too far removed
dramatically from those in a Vivaldi concerto, but Haydn chooses to
tie these effects to a clear-cut sonata form; one would only think this
were ancient music if one forgot the form—and few who listen to
Haydn are likely to do so. In this opening Adagio the oboes remain
silent and it is only in the angular Allegro which follows that they
appear for the first time—mainly acting as sustaining power to
strengthen the textures. The Menuet is driving rather than elegant, and
even the Finale does not spare one's nervous energy.

SYMPHONY NO. 15 in D, which, because of the convenience of recorded couplings has tended to be regarded as part of a trilogy comprising Nos. 15, 16 and 17, is in fact similar to previous works in style,
the intervening change of Court not being sufficiently early to have any
strong effect. In terms of form, however, it is unlike any other symphony. Yet again the key is D (infinitely the most favoured for symphonies written in the Eighteenth century). The form is that of a past
era, with a French overture for a first movement (slow-fast-slow) in

which the middle section (in *kolo* rhythm) has a theme suspiciously like that which opens Symphony No. 4.

15

4

The Menuet is stately, almost Handelian (except that Michael Haydn has written minuets in similar style), and there is a chamber music Trio with either solo cello (Göttweig manuscript) or two concertante violas (Lambach manuscript). The Andante dances happily along and the Finale is in an unusual form which includes a "trio" section with a coda for good measure.

SYMPHONY NO. 18 in G is yet another exception to the rule—a church-sonata work with only three movements. For some reason it is one of the most neglected of Haydn's compositions. The opening Andante Moderato is far less searching than other church-sonata openings and has a cheerful rhythmic spring about it. There are, in fact, some interesting gaps between chords, with plenty of improvisatory opportunity for an imaginative harpsichordist. The *staccato* weight of the bass properly requires a bassoon to double the continuo here, even though such an instrument would normally remain silent during a slow movement.* The second movement is similar to other early driving movements but the bass line moves more freely; further, there are horn fanfares, a Haydn fingerprint more familiar in later works. The symphony ends with a minuet and trio—a device which works in the context (given solidity in performance) and is a tribute to the sturdy

---

* The extremely stylish recording by Charles Mackerras includes both bassoon and harpsichord and the latter gives a clear view of the improvisatory possibilities in music of this period.

nobility of Haydn's earlier style and a forerunner of more glorious minuets to come.

*

I have outlined above a combination of symphonies which stem probably from the Lukaveč period. The scoring is identical in every one: oboes, horns, strings, bassoon and keyboard continuo. The favourite key is D, the tonal contrast within the orchestra is modest, but certain features—such as the high horn writing in No. 5 and the insistent rhythmic force of the underlying bass—anticipate later styles. This seems a good point to switch the attention to those of the earliest symphonies which were definitely written at Eszterháza, where already the availability of additional instruments gave Haydn the opportunity to expand his orchestral palette. The first three symphonies to be composed for the Prince were almost certainly the "Morning," "Noon" and "Evening" trilogy: No. 6 in D, No. 7 in C, and No. 8 in G. At once the difference can be seen to lie in the exploitation of instruments. All three works are notable for their many concertante features: demanding solos are given to flutes, bassoon, leading violin, cello and violone. There are even solos for the leading second violin. The flutes appear for the first time in any Haydn symphony. The actual nicknames ("Le matin," "Le midi," "Le soir" are among the few that are authentic.

SYMPHONY NO. 6 in D, "Le matin," tells a small rustic story, some parts of which are obviously pictorial—the opening "sunrise," and the "music lesson" in the slow movement where the Konzertmeister plays his scales for the delectation of his pupils. The concertante parts are nominally for violin, cello and violone but the bassoonist has a part in the Trio which is almost as important as that of the bassist, albeit less demanding. It seems likely that the transposition to cello of the middle part of the bass solo in some reliable manuscripts was occasioned by the more limited range of the double bass when the violone was superseded.*

SYMPHONY NO. 7 in C, "Le soir," has many interesting features. This time there are two flutes, which have leading parts following a curious recitative-like Adagio. First violin, second violin, cello and violone have solos, and the oboes and bassoon also have isolated and far from easy episodes to cope with. This symphony has been known to suffer (along with its two companions) from the misconception that the violone solo in the Trio (playable on the modern double bass) should be transferred to the cello and taken to the higher octave. This simply will not do, and those orchestras (including, unfortunately, some professional bodies relayed over the radio) which have hitherto ruined this

---

* In Maerzendorfer's recording the whole line is taken by the lower instrument—the ear tells one that this must have been the composer's intention.

episode by such inartistic procedure would do well to refer to W. H. Hadow who, in "The Viennese Period" (part of the Oxford History of Music series), referred to the Trio of the Menuet to "Le midi," saying that "even the double bass has its obbligato." Since Hadow wrote this as long ago as 1904, it seems reasonable to argue that it leaves little room for misconception today.

SYMPHONY NO. 8 in G, "Le soir," is the only symphony of the three which does not start with a slow introduction. Again there are copious concertante parts as in No. 7, and the slow movement is virtually a sinfonia concertante between two violins, cello and bassoon. In the Trio there is the most glorious violone solo of all, and even at so early a stage in Haydn's career there seems to be an element of nostalgia in the music. The Finale is a straightforward storm—nothing over-literal, but more on the lines of a Vivaldi scene or one of Dittersdorf's programmatic symphony movements.

After these symphonies with "special effects" Haydn returned to more conventional structures, but the inspiration of the new surroundings and improved orchestra remained much in evidence. SYMPHONY NO. 9 in C, composed about 1762, is notable for a slow movement which includes two flutes; moreover, the Trio of the final Menuetto contains a solo bassoon. This is by no means a developed work but it does underline the fact that Haydn was becoming more sensitive to orchestral contrasts and instrumental differentiations.

The scale of a symphony is never the most cogent point by which to judge Haydn's inventiveness and SYMPHONY NO. 12 in E, one of the shortest he ever composed, is also one of the most truly original of the early pieces. Lasting scarcely a quarter of an hour it conforms to the well-established three-movement pattern. In addition, there is a now familiar fervour and drive, with the lively influence of C.P.E. Bach never far away and Haydn's own brand of enormous optimism. E major is a rare key but it attains a curious radiance which grows from the opening bars; even those are unconventional in that they allow a rapid movement to commence quietly. The Adagio is no dance, more a meditation; nor is it in romantic vein. Rather it reflects the melancholy of a shepherd left to his thoughts in an Eighteenth-century landscape. Bucolic joy returns in the Finale, a traditional and suitable culmination. The scoring is the standard early Haydn group of two oboes, two horns, strings and continuo.

With SYMPHONY NO. 13 in D we have something strikingly different. Haydn had the use of four horns—a luxury he permitted himself in only four of his symphonies (Nos. 13, 31, 39 and 72)—and there is also an invigorating timpani part and some quicksilver writing for flute. Drama and humour are inextricably mixed in the first movement, with hammer blows from the timpani followed at once by squeals of protest from the flute. As with No. 12 there is a dated autograph manuscript of the music from 1763.

The very opening is enormously imposing, with powerful wind harmonies filling the textures as the strings and continuo drive relentlessly forward. The timpani punctuate the proceedings nobly, the part being particularly interesting in that it was written into the autograph score in another hand—so quite obviously Haydn approved of it (it also appears in contemporary copies of the symphony). It is more than likely that the timpanist at the first performance had created it under Haydn's supervision. It is certainly a most interesting part and could possibly have been written by Adamus Sturm—a pensioned timpanist available to Haydn on request but no longer a permanent member of the orchestra. The support for this undocumented theory comes only from the part itself, for clearly it is the work of an orchestral musician rather than a hired military bandsman; since the old percussionist lived for another decade he may be considered the most likely person to be credited with the realisation, not only of this part but also of those which are linked to other symphonies without being in Haydn's own hand or that of his copyist. The slow movement is virtually a cello concerto and the Menuet has a striding nobility which anticipates the middle-period symphonies. The Finale, too, is fascinating. Where that of No. 3 showed signs of parallel to that of Mozart's "Jupiter" Symphony, that of No. 13 is not only fugal but even uses the identical four-note theme (traceable to Gregorian chant) that Mozart made so famous.

HAYDN

MOZART

SYMPHONY NO. 14 in A returns to conventional scoring but has the forward-looking intensity of No. 12 with the additional bonus of a sturdy Minuet. The powerful repetitious notes which typify the bass-line are part and parcel of Haydn's early style (if one ignores the more spectacular timbres of No. 13 one can hear the very same feature). The melody of the Andante had been used previously in a divertimento but the symphony provides an opportunity for Haydn to spice it with syncopations. The Menuetto is peasantish and conventional enough in basis, yet the use of the horns high in their register is pure Haydn, as is the winsome oboe solo in the Trio. Once again the Finale is a fugue—curiously this device appears early in the symphonies but not until the Seventies does Haydn make it a feature of his string quartets.

SYMPHONY NO. 16 in B flat is the work which might well confirm that to Haydn at this period the unusual was usual. There are three movements only, and again there is the standard oboes-horns-strings-continuo scoring, but the composer fashions something immensely lyrical here. The yearning Mozartian theme with which it opens lies low in the orchestral register, with the violins having only the accompaniment, yet later in the movement, theme and accompaniment swap instruments. Again there is an unconventional occurrence for the period: a fast movement opening quietly. A simple central Andante, with the melody doubled in the bass, is succeeded by a jolly hunting Finale with much use of high-horn writing, yet the suggestions of darkness evident in the opening movement are not entirely dispelled.

By comparison with this music SYMPHONY NO. 17 in F sounds rather primitive. The Fürnberg manuscripts, which tempt one to think of symphonies Nos. 10, 11, 15 and 18 as being Lukaveč works and therefore automatically earlier, now add some confusion, for whilst No. 17 is not included in that group, Haydn does not seem to be searching even as deeply as in the simple Symphony No. 9. The central Andante ma non troppo is a plain, solemn little piece. evoking its period but showing none of Haydn's forward-looking character. The Finale starts each sequence with an affirmative chord; a primitive device by Haydn's standards and one where it is necessary to return to the beginning of the Trio of the early Quartet Opus 1 No. 4 to find a definite parallel.

If one divides off those "early" symphonies which, No. 13 apart, do not stray too far from conventional instrumentation of the time, then this group can reasonably be said to include the first nineteen numbered symphonies, plus "A" and "B." SYMPHONY NO. 19 in D is a pleasant enough little piece but it certainly breaks no new ground, the points of interest really being confined to technicalities such as the interesting (though far from original) device of throwing the theme from first violins to seconds and back again). The Andante is charming in a J. C. Bach-like manner but has sufficient syncopations to make it clear that Haydn is indeed the composer.

2: The Early Festive Symphonies

One particular type of sound is unique to Haydn—unique, in fact, in Eighteenth-century music. It is the type of scoring which he used when constructing C major symphonies on a large scale. Such symphonies often indicated some special occasion and inevitably they stand apart as the most brilliant and exciting, the best known being No. 48, the famous "Maria Theresia." The central common factor about these works is Haydn's use of the horns in C alto, whereby the instruments play the notes as printed and not, as was the Nineteenth-century custom, transposing to the octave below (C basso). It is well to keep in mind that the horns crooked in C alto had the same tube-length as the Eighteenth-century trumpets in that key and therefore the *timbres* would be similar in all the brass instruments of the period. Sometimes (as in Symphony No. 82 or the Overture to *Il mondo della luna*) the score simply asks for horns in C alto *or* trumpets in C. No doubt both would have been welcome if available, but when performing such music today there seems little point in merely doubling high horns with modern trumpets unless they have independent parts to play; by so doing one adds anachronistic tone colour, today's trumpets no longer being in an eight-foot C but producing different harmonies with valves to provide the same notes from a four-foot brass tube. The fanfare writing and the extremely strong underpinning of the bass line makes it quite obvious that Haydn knew the massive sound that this high brass writing would achieve and this style cannot for one moment be likened to the use of high horns in C by other composers such as Mozart (Symphony No. 18), Salieri (Concerto for flute, oboe and orchestra) or Sammartini (Sinfonia dell' Academica No. 2); in these cases the employment of the horns is essentially lyrical, filling in the high parts in a manner little different from that employed in other music in the "high" keys of B flat or A. With Haydn the C major symphony was a grand, majestic affair, brilliant, even martial, in effect—and fanfares played a big part.

It is worth noting the features of all these celebratory pieces but chronological sequence is best served by looking initially at only Nos. 20, 30, 32, 33 and 37, the high points of Haydn's early years.

SYMPHONY NO. 20, though striking enough in the outer movements, is not as developed as other works in this style, the charming Andante Cantabile being written in the earlier fashion with *pizzicato* accompaniments reminiscent of the early quartets. It cannot be dated accurately, although if one looks beneath the exciting fanfare-laden brass and timpani writing it is plainly not a developed work. The Menuet, however, has that confident stateliness that was to become a hallmark of Haydn's grander style. Certain passages would sound rather bare without continuo and the use of *pizzicato* is obviously intended as a weighty supplement to the lower lines. The Finale is in the same A-B-A form as that of No. 15.

SYMPHONY NO. 30 has many interesting features. Its subtitle "Alleluja" stems from the use of a Gregorian *Alleluja*

which lies dormant in the second violins and wind until its final statement by the wind unaccompanied.

Corno I in C and Oboe I (written)

The catalogue belonging to Kees—a Viennese friend of Haydn—mentions timpani and trumpet parts even though these are missing from the autograph manuscript. The trumpet part can be taken with a pinch of salt since symphonies with timpani in the Kees catalogue always have trumpets noted too, more by convention than any other reason; and since, in a contemporary copy in the Monastery of Schlierbach, trumpets are noted against the horn part, it is clear that the horn parts as written were one and the same as those for trumpet, the latter used for convenience when horns were not available. So, whilst there is not likely to be a separate lost trumpet part—a pair of horns in C alto being all that is required for the brass complement—it is necessary to reconstruct a timpani part for modern performance since no contemporary one has been preserved.* Haydn adds a flute in the slow movement and in the first of the two Trios of the Minuet-Finale. Clearly it requires a separate performer, since at one point it plays together with the two oboes; why he should have to remain silent throughout the first movement is, however, rather a puzzle.

Symphonies Nos. 32 and 33 were written at much the same time. It has long been suspected that this was early in Haydn's career, and the existence of the manuscripts in the Fürnberg collection seems to confirm this, although it is interesting to note that in Haydn's own "Entwurf-Katalog," in which he listed and numbered the symphonies he had composed up to about 1769, they appear rather later. Certain "symphonies" as specified in this "Entwurf-Katalog" are not numbered among the standard works in this form, since Haydn included the occasional three-movement overture and all six of his *Scherzandi*. The latter are indeed miniature symphonies and only the terminology employed inhibits modern performers from giving them the attention these delightful little pieces deserve. Symphonies Nos. 32 and 33 can at least be said, therefore, to be approximately the thirty-second and thirty-third symphonies that Haydn chose to list.

SYMPHONY NO. 32 is remarkable for its sound. True, there are contemporary manuscripts which omit the all-important trumpet and timpani parts but above all this is a Festive Symphony and the attack

---

* This should cause little trouble to an intelligent conductor (or timpanist) because similar treatment is required in the case of several of Mozart's symphonies (notably Nos. 20, 22, 23, 26, 28 and 30)—the simple tonic and dominant of the timpani strokes leaves far less room for harmonic conjecture than, for instance, the creation of a harpsichord continuo. A glance at the appendix of Recommended Recordings, however, will reveal that not a single available version of Haydn's No. 30 has attempted a reconstruction of the timpani part, and all have transposed the horns to an octave below the printed notes. The incongruity of this becomes obvious as early as bars ten and eleven where, when played on modern low horns, the brass fanfares make no impact, and for some notes the second horn is actually playing an octave below the violas, celli and bassoon.

of the high brass with its percussive underpinning could only have been created by Haydn. The Menuet comes second, and again there is a glorious sonority in the brass worthy of Bach in his most triumphant church music. The Trio is mere thoughtful relief and the Adagio ma non Troppo—for strings and continuo alone—has a Handelian simplicity. The 3/8 time signature of the Finale is a measure of the music's relatively early composition.

SYMPHONY NO. 33 is different but not necessarily later in concept. The very first thematic subject is unusually extended and has a strongly independent viola part in the melody which follows—in other words the brass and drum onslaughts grow from the inner complexities rather than being superimposed upon them. This time the slow movement—an Andante—lies second: a deliberately bare movement, in which Haydn maybe left the harmonies simple to enable the harpsichordist (perhaps himself) to improvise at will. The Minuet is a subtle affair with even the brass and drums playing softly at certain cardinal moments; the Finale is a sweeping conception, powerful and fully-worked—the most advanced movement in any Festive Symphony mentioned so far.

SYMPHONY NO. 37 is certainly an early composition—early enough to be considered a misnumbering except that its exact position is unclear. Sufficient to say, however, that it must surely have been a Lukaveč symphony. The trumpet and timpani parts were almost certainly added later and the latter, from the internal evidence of its writing, is so stylish and of such merit that Haydn is by far the most likely creator. The pounding rhythms of the early Haydn style are accentuated by the impact of the brass and timpani, and the twist to a remote minor key for the second subject of the first movement is a tribute to the young composer's originality. Again the Menuet comes as the second movement: a very simple piece on the lines of a rustic Leopold Mozart dance but taken from the fields by the brass and timpani and placed firmly at court. This is another example of there only being one set of brass parts, and an authentic sound is obtainable today by the use of horns in C alto. The Kees collection gives only a pair of trumpets but since they have the same notes as the horns it is clear that once again they were intended as a substitute rather than as an addition.

3: Pre-Sturm und Drang

Perhaps such a grouping puts the cart before the horse, yet the deepening of compositional intensity from about 1764—the year in which Haydn composed SYMPHONY 21 IN A—is strikingly evident. This work is a key composition in his development, church-sonata in form but with all manner of Haydn fingerprints, not least the spectacularly high horns and the extremely plaintive and beautiful oboe writing which in the opening Adagio reaches a point of almost unbearable poignancy. There are no repeats—indeed the movement is something of a *Fantasia*, built on a single theme.

By contrast, the succeeding Presto is one of those devilish pounding pieces—that curious contradiction, a piece of music that is both fast and heavy—its sheer weight giving it an incredible impetus. The Menuet brings an old friend—the melody which is familiar as the Menuetto of Mozart's *Eine kleine Nachtmusik* and appears also (with some rhythmic alterations) in the Menuet alla Zingarese of Haydn's Quartet Op. 20 No. 4.

The Finale is another dashing piece marked *allegro molto*, the note-for-note switch between first and second violins at its opening an exciting aural experience.*

Where No. 21 retains the conventional oboes, horns, strings and continuo orchestration, the SYMPHONY NO. 22 in E flat, "Der Philosoph," is an example of Haydn's searching outlook in respect of orchestral colour—something he pursued all his life. His flirtation with cors anglais was more than a passing fancy and although this is the only symphony in which they appear, there are chamber works, operas and choral compositions where their individual tone is used. The term "Philosoph" is one of the most appropriate of all the many nicknames applied to Haydn's symphonies and dates from the composer's lifetime. Although the most striking aspect of this, another church-sonata symphony, is obviously its orchestral *timbres*, it shows its period through its forward-moving eagerness. Where in No. 21 there were repetitive bass figures in the fast movements, here in the opening Adagio of No. 22 are legions of quavers in the bass, marching unswervingly forward beneath a brooding, thoughtful theme on cors anglais and horns.

---

*Especially in a recording such as that by Max Goberman, where the separation to left and right of the two groups makes for thrilling listening—a solution which stems directly from sheer musical thinking.

A fierce Presto follows and a strong Menuetto with some spectacular horn-writing in its Trio section. This has a structural purpose as well as one of ear-catching splendour since it prepares the listener for the hunting Finale, with its horn fanfares taken up no less enthusiastically by the cors anglais.

There is an alternative version of this symphony in which the cors anglais are replaced by flutes—a three-movement piece comprising the swift second and fourth movements between which is inserted an entirely new slow movement. The original "philosophical" Adagio and the Minuet are thus omitted. This revised version, originally printed in Paris, is but a pallid reflection of Haydn's first conception. There is no documentary evidence to show that the new slow movement is by anyone other than Haydn, but its brevity, colourlessness and lack of inspiration must put its authenticity in doubt.*

The four-movement SYMPHONY NO. 23 in G, though not perhaps the most remarkable of its period, could well be taken as a typical example of Haydn's developmental achievement up to the mid-Sixties. Scored for the standard orchestra, the first movement is grand, regardless of how the interpreter chooses to read the term *allegro*. The Andante is really a dance movement for strings and continuo, with delighted upward sweeps in the bass urging the music forward every few bars. The very simplicity of the themes gives unrivalled opportunity for cembalo improvisation on repeats, thereby adding to its period charm without detracting from the line. The Menuet is one of great stateliness: the answering of upper strings by lower was often used in the latter part of the Eighteenth century and there always seems something special about such a piece—in Mozart the style is more abrupt and culminates perhaps in the question-and-answer drama of the Menuetto of his Symphony No. 29 in A. Haydn's approach is more flowing and leads eventually to his most famous minuet in this style: the *Witches' Minuet* of the "Quinten" Quartet Op. 76 No. 2. By this time question-and-answer has developed into full-scale canon, although in the Trio of the symphony there is canon in inversion. All such thoroughly-worked-out detail is swept aside by the fierce directness of the Finale, with slashing chords interrupting the theme when it is scarcely begun. The ending is gently uproarious: the music having quietened to what could be the final chord, there is an indeterminately spaced single *pizzicato* note. The interpreter may choose whether this is to lead to the fierce onslaught of the repeat of the second half of this tiny movement—so that the listener will be amazed that the returning *pizzicato* note is in

* Antal Dorati has recorded this revision—for those musicologically inclined it is a useful source of study, for the music-lover it is one of the experiences which he need not regret having missed.

fact the last stroke of the whole symphony—or whether to omit the *da capo* in order not to risk the surprise ending being anticipated.*

A great outcry of oboes and horns, holding the melodic line against the fury of the driving strings and continuo, makes for a thrilling opening to SYMPHONY NO. 24 in D. Haydn often eased the rhythms in No. 23 but here the drive returns redoubled. By sudden but apt contrast the slow movement turns out to be a virtual flute concerto. Melodically one cannot help but recall the *Dance of the Blessed Spirits* by Gluck; in accompaniment one hears the Haydn of the concertos. There is even ample room for a fully-fledged cadenza—though Haydn leaves its composition to the performers. The strong Menuetto has yet more force allowed the winds. As throughout the work, the horns in D are written low in their register (even in the Menuetto) and the solo flute returns in the Trio section. An echo of the earlier symphonies appears in the Finale, except that the top line is now reflective and the repeated notes in the bass are more subtle and varied than hitherto.

SYMPHONY NO. 25 in C is curiously unsymphonic in the terms of the neighbouring symphonies. In dramatic thought, however, the work develops more purposefully than those three-movement overtures which may lay claim to be, at least superficially, symphonic. There is a long Adagio introduction, but this is no church-sonata; the taut Allegro Molto into which it leads shows the contrast. A Menuet is placed second, but not as a return to an earlier style, for this is in fact a central movement (the introduction apart, there is no slow movement). Indeed, this symphony is full of exceptions, with some very low C basso horn writing. Although the key is C major this is not one of the *Festive* symphonies: the horn soli in the Trio are modest and tuneful but in no way spectacular. This leaves a simple two-part Finale. It is as eager in spirit as any of the period although dramatically it is rooted to the spot.

SYMPHONY NO. 26 in D minor, "Lamentation," is somewhat misplaced in order, but even by bringing it to join other symphonies of its period—such as No. 39—it becomes obvious that it is well ahead of its time. The theory is advanced by H. C. Robbins Landon that this music was inspired by a Passion play which previously had been set to music in the Middle Ages. The identification of events with thematic fragments—which almost makes the first movement a pictorial documentation of the Crucifixion—has often been explained, so suffice

---

* Of recommended recordings Goberman takes the former alternative, Dorati the latter.

it to compare part of the second violin line in the first movement

with the music for the passion play, copies of which are to be found in certain Austrian Monasteries.

The dynamism of the first movement is breathtaking and worthy of the timeless drama to which it relates. The headlong pace, the violent syncopations, the cutting edge of the oboes, and the whole lashed forward by the incisiveness of the cembalo which gives added point to the jaggedness of the bass-line, all make this a very advanced movement which takes the best of Haydn's fierier nature and crystallises it in one short piece. The flying upward scales for violins and the violent cross-rhythmed horn entry near the end all make for a mood of darkness and gripping tension. Earlier I mentioned the absence of a second-half repeat to this movement, since the development does not bear hearing twice. H. C. Robbins Landon clarified the point in succinct terms twenty years ago in "The Symphonies of Joseph Haydn" when he said: "It is to be expected that the second part of the movement contains no indication for repetition: the drama of the Cross cannot be repeated."

Over a never-ending succession of quavers in the first violins the main theme of the Adagio emerges: derived from plainchant, the *Lamentations of Jeremiah*.

To Haydn this must have seemed an important theme, for it reappears in several of his works; only in the Trio of Symphony No. 80, however, does it have an effect of similar poignancy. In Mozart's *Masonic Funeral Music* it can be seen again—a voice from the past which grows from within the music as if only in the deepest and most tragic of compositions should such a sombre creation become manifest. In Haydn's

Adagio, the accompanying string figures are all the purer for being unphrased throughout, and the few great performances of this music have in common the conductors' refusal to add spurious slurs.* The Menuet is a sad movement and even its major-keyed Trio is fierce. This is not an unfinished work; the Minuet simply happens to be the Finale also. There is, nevertheless, a Sibelian abruptness to the final chords' fall into silence.

The composition date of SYMPHONY NO. 27 in G is unknown but it is certainly an early work. None of the feeling of crisis and turmoil evident in No. 26 is to be heard here—hardly surprising, since No. 27 could perhaps date from as much as seven years earlier. The jolly opening Allegro Molto, slight but fully-worked-out with delicate punctuation from the horns, is very much a dance movement, whereas the Andante which follows is more thoughtful despite its *siciliano* rhythm. The Finale is no more than a typical 3/8 Presto of its period —a peasant *galop* rather than a full-scale hunting piece, despite the time signature.

SYMPHONY NO. 28 in A begins quietly and nervously. Why a Leipzig critic of the time disliked the work so much is difficult to understand. That the slow movement is perhaps disproportionately lengthy cannot have been the problem since it was of the Minuet and Finale that he largely complained. The dash of the opening movement grips the attention from beginning to end: *allegro di molto* is the marking, and even the Menuet is marked *allegro molto* while the Finale is *presto assai*. The slow movement, though long, is not languorous and takes the form of a withdrawn march. The harmonies are deliberately bare, but keyboard decoration needs to be subtle if it is not to obtrude. The Minuet is notable for its "gypsy" Trio—silent and remote, with the camp-fire embers barely glowing and every phrase ending on a question-mark. There are no such problems in the country-dance Finale, though here for the first time in the symphony the high horns speak out.

The Trio is also the point of departure for the SYMPHONY NO. 29 in E. Over an oompah accompaniment in the strings

----

* Unquestionably Heiller's is one of the great Haydn interpretations. He leaves the accompanying figures in the slow movement entirely unphrased and the all-important chorale melody is the more clearly etched as a result. Perhaps because he is himself a violinist, Tátrai adds just a few slurs. Maerzendorfer, though his performance lacks authenticity on account of his omission of bassoon or keyboard continuo, is otherwise almost as textually pure as Heiller.

the horns play:

Corni in E (written)

But what about the tune? Unless the harpsichordist provides one it simply has to remain absent, and no keyboard player has dared to provide such a thing for a quarter of a century.* The grand opening of the whole work, the deft switches from first to second violins and back in the Andante, and the flying scales of the Finale show Haydn in a variety of moods from the majestic to the furious.

The two D major symphonies Nos. 31 and 72 are hunting works without a shadow of a doubt and many of their horn phrases are traceable to genuine hunting calls. The hunt was an integral part of Eighteenth-century court life and it is hardly surprising that it is reflected strongly in the music of the time. Two other points lie in common between the two works, quite apart from the use of four horns in both. There is a return to the concertante principles of the early Eszterháza symphonies, and further, the design of the music is very similar, each work having sets of variations as a finale. There are various slightly different arrangements dating from the Eighteenth-century, with sometimes a pair of trumpets replacing one of the pairs of horns. We also know that timpani were sometimes added.†

SYMPHONY NO. 31 is slightly the more complex of the two, with exceptionally demanding horn-writing. The Konzertmeister leads the proceedings with a florid part in the Adagio and all the other movements have a solo flute. Whilst the concertante parts are predictably shared between the various principals by the division into variations in the Finale (including one for all the horns), it is interesting to note the inclusion of the violone as a soloist once more. Even more interestingly, this selfsame pattern is held in SYMPHONY NO. 72, though instead of the violone solo coming just before the coda to the variations, it is placed approximately halfway through the movement.

---

* The last time was in Loibner's recording when Christa Fuhrmann gave the outline of a melody.

† The two best recordings of No. 72 available at the time of writing (see Appendix) employ a spurious but contemporary timpani part. It is not, in fact, a badly written addition, except for the Trio section of the Minuet where it is merely a crude, intrusive disruption to Haydn's elegant writing. Provided, therefore, that the timpani are omitted from this Trio, there seems no harm in employing them elsewhere in modern performances.

These two works do need to be studied together in order to appreciate their similarities and differences.*

The SYMPHONY NO. 34 in D minor starts with the utmost intensity but somehow the inspiration is not fully sustained. It is church-sonata in form and the opening Adagio is sternly tragic. This is the "Sturm und Drang" period to all intents and purposes, and the subsequent Allegro with its wide melodic intervals almost holds the drama at the same level. In the Menuet, however, the grip slackens. Its Trio is certainly fascinating with its elegant horn syncopations but Haydn subdues his orchestral contrasts elsewhere in the movement.. The Finale is the most unlikely of pieces to act as a culmination to the strong opening Adagio: skipping happily along, it seems as if it were dashed off in the one hour remaining before Haydn had to rush it into the copyist's hands. It is a three-part piece with a quiet central section; the coda is very slight. a mere twelve bars of jollification to sum up the previous country dance. The *da capo* mark at the end—which would require the whole of the repeated section of the theme plus the coda to be stated twice—is surely a miscalculation, and no recorded performance has observed it.

SYMPHONY NO. 35 in B flat is outstanding in terms of the originality of its part-writing. Oboes join and leave the string consort as the dramatic situation demands and the horns are given virtuoso parts of terrifying difficulty. At the recapitulation the first horn has a hair-raising upward double-triplet run to a^2 (sounding g^2)—sufficient to account for the work hardly ever being given in live performance.

Corno I in B♭ Alto (written)

There are few more charming Andantes of the period than this one, the broken rhythms giving it a lightfootedness which still shows its roots as being fixed in the dance. The Menuetto soon makes one aware of the golden brilliance of the horns, with exposed passages to keep them on their toes, while the Finale is weighty enough to be worthy of this fine symphony yet sufficiently brilliant to maintain the sense of tonal originality.

SYMPHONY NO. 36 in E flat—a slightly earlier work than No. 35— has the familiar elements of drive but with concertante soli for violin and cello in the Adagio. Even in the fast movements there is much

---

* Unfortunately no gramophone recording has yet paired them.

ornamentation (of a type which sometimes gives problems to performers not specialising in the period), but the music makes an impact
through its symmetry on the one hand and its subtlety on the other.
The insistent oboe *timbre*, a certain sternness in the bass resulting
from the presence of the bassoon in the continuo group, together with
an equable flow across the double bars, all clearly make this the
product of Haydn's most skilled "pre-dramatic" years. The Adagio is
something of a recitative but with cello and violin sharing the lime-
light equally. The Menuetto e Trio is very baroque in conception, with
gentle echoing horn fanfares. Even the Finale, though rapid and with
flurries of notes in the strings, never reaches the pitch of anger.

Haydn's standards for the period have already been set, so when,
after an interval, there appears another C major Festive Symphony, one
may reasonably anticipate an advance in his thinking. That this has
indeed taken place at once becomes clear, for the SYMPHONY NO. 38
opens with a dashing, joyful movement in which the high horns and
trumpets have parts which are quite independent of one another. The
old pulsing eagerness is there, but the brass are used not merely to
punctuate the melodic line but also to aid it. The thinking is not too
far removed from that of Symphony No. 35, for orchestral colour is
important but soul-searching is not attempted. The Andante Molto of
No. 38 remains a strings-and-continuo affair but Haydn has by now
assimilated his own inventions in syncopation and echo effect. The
answering between first and second violins is the more fascinating since
only the seconds are muted and the tonal contrast is obvious to even
the most untutored ear. That Haydn has six clear bars of Menuet
before timpani and percussion enter is a sure sign that the composer
has the whole design in mind, for even after a pause the full orchestra
would have seemed too abrupt a change from the peace of the closing
bars of the previous movement. No such need for graciousness in the
final Allegro di Molto, however, although Haydn still keeps back the
glory of his greatest C major writing a little while longer. There are
some excellent soli for oboe, and menacing passages from the timpani
which threaten to burst forth every time. The oboe part is extraordinary and in the second half of the movement there is even room
for a cadenza at a fermata: the old concertante tradition dies hard.

4: *Sturm und Drang*

Somewhere in a book on Haydn this heading has to be employed. In a more or less chronological survey of the symphonies it is not essential to stress outside influences, yet this term is used with such frequency that its application must be examined if only because it is so often misconstrued. Traditionally "Sturm und Drang" (literally, "Storm and Urgency") is simply the description applied to Symphonies Nos. 44 to 49 inclusive. This is perhaps the kernel of Haydn's changed style but certainly not its be-all and end-all. The earlier symphonies demand examination because, despite a similarity of orchestration, Haydn is formulating his style and they are extraordinarily varied. After writing some forty symphonies this style crystallises and forms the basis for his thoughts to progress on secure technique. "Sturm und Drang" need not concern us in detail except to say that it was a movement culminating around 1772 in European art, literature and music, stemming from the naturalistic outlook of Jean-Jacques Rousseau and taken further in Germany with more romantic connotations by Goethe. Composers, even those as relatively isolated as Haydn, could not avoid such powerful influences and the stress which crept into his music paralleled that which pervaded all the arts throughout Europe at the time. It would be easy to suggest that Haydn studied the style and decided to apply it to his own art because it seemed the right thing for the period and added something to his expression. Such a conscious espousal of an artistic faith is highly unlikely; far more possible is the gradual infiltration of drama into a technique which had had the seeds of such ideas lurking beneath the surface for some years. Already one symphony (No. 26) has been described which has all the ingredients of "Sturm und Drang," and regardless of period or grouping it must be included. In terms of the accepted meaning of the description Nos. 26, 39, 44, 45, 46, 47, 48, 49, 50, 52, 56, 59 and 64 must certainly be included, but it would not be unreasonable to say that the last fifty symphonies written prior to Haydn's London visit bear influences of that style. The arbitrary baker's dozen shown above is the nucleus but there are many other excellent candidates for inclusion in the list. The keys seem influential: C major, A major and various minor keys account for almost all of them. Haydn was not searching for expression; he already had the means and was using it. There are few experiments in form, and even the church-sonata bids farewell with Symphony No. 49. This is the only one of the group to begin with a complete Adagio movement, but since form is no longer subject to experimentation, Haydn is free to widen the scope of his dramatic inventiveness.

SYMPHONY NO. 39 in G minor, scored for two oboes, four horns, strings and continuo, brings one sharply back to the world of the "Lamentatione." The drama is less in matters of pace—the Allegro Assai is at least in common time, which makes the pulse relatively measured—rather it lies in the breathless, asymmetric pauses at the opening.

The splendour of the four horns is as yet held back and the Andante, though no longer a mere ballroom piece, is concerned with melody rather than orchestral adventurousness and so strings and continuo suffice. The new intensity returns for the dark Menuet e Trio, although still the horns are used sparingly—two in G for the Minuet, two in B flat alto for the Trio. The bass-line is entirely uphrased and the striding, separate crotchets add severity to the Minuet, thereby setting off the optimism of the Trio to good effect. This leaves a dynamic Finale, *allegro di molto*, in which Mozart's Symphony No. 25 is certainly recalled (another G minor work with four horns); the fierce downward scales and questioning returns to the tonic must surely have left self-searching doubts in the minds of the audience at court even if the new waves of influence were not yet stirring in the theatre and opera house. It would be surprising, however, if certain disturbing influences were not at work there too.

SYMPHONY NO. 40 in F is a highly original work but of a different period (1763); it properly belongs with No. 13 and has some connections with styles to be found as early as No. 4, where the withdrawn mystery of the slow movement finds a parallel. The Minuet of No. 40 is also sturdy and unyielding, with a Trio giving full rein to the winds: one authentic edition from the collection of the Archduke Rudolf actually marks the strings to be silent. The Finale is fugal—an obvious link with its close contemporary No. 13—yet the writing in No. 40 seems so advanced and "un-baroque" that Mandyczewski may at least be forgiven in part for his listing it so late in Haydn's *oeuvre*.

SYMPHONY NO. 41 in C is one of the important Festive Symphonies, a composition of no little magnificence which opens with broadly-spaced chords and expressive woodwinds. At this stage in Haydn's development the high horns and trumpets join the timpani as part of the texture. This is one of Haydn's store of fully calculated ensemble-sounds and the punctuation of the rushing figures which soon sweep in is as much a matter of contrasting colour as of rhythm, the oboes being asked to penetrate like trumpets. Only in the underlying sense of hectic rhythm are the earlier years recalled. The slow movement has an important flute obbligato, reflecting Symphony No. 24, although the oboe melody is no less important, the solo flute providing decorative material over the gentle muted strings. The fullness of the Menuet e

Trio is highly impressive—a piece early in style, with an unhurried *galant* air, yet too complex to have graced any ancient ballroom. The Finale begins with a descending melody for second violins—the accompaniment being in the firsts (an excellent test for satisfactory balancing in a performance—particularly if it is recorded*). At the first brass fanfare, however, there is a foretaste of Haydn in his later C major glory, with the fantastic joy of the close of No. 56 several strides closer.

SYMPHONY NO. 42 in D is the latest symphony to be considered so far: 1771 is its date—two years later than No. 41. It is, in fact, not possible to place a single Haydn symphony as dating from 1770, although evidence of life at the time gives no concrete evidence as to why this should be. Symphony No. 42 does not lay claim to being of the "Sturm und Drang" variety, being in an optimistic major key and with no more than the (implied) use of two bassoons rather than one to distinguish it in scoring from earlier works. Its lyricism is new and the wind writing, except in the final rondo, is not so rustic. The sweeping first movement has an elegance and symmetry that makes one wonder which cultured visitors were being borne in mind. After a song-like Andantino the Minuet is all sunshine, with the violins delicately imitating trumpet fanfares in the Trio. The Finale is the first use of rondo in a style which is to become familiar in the later symphonies.

SYMPHONY NO. 43 in E flat was given the name "Merkur" ("Mercury") during the Nineteenth century. A good reason to draw attention to a work which, in view of the surrounding "Sturm und Drang" spectaculars, might be overlooked, since, despite its lyricism in the style of No. 42, it speaks more soberly. The effect of grandeur is perhaps cumulative, with Haydn's witticisms subtly technical rather than back-slapping: note the false reprise at the beginning of the development—having hesitated in order to show that it is really a joke, Haydn then continues at some length with his deliberate "error." The gem of this work is the Minuet: dogged, severe and utterly winning, with tremendous momentum. At this period, Haydn's music becomes more dependent on stylish interpretation: for example, a conductor's sympathetic sensitivity, which could make the muted Adagio beautiful, would not be sufficient unless the performer held the Menuetto e Trio in a metronomic grip right up to its final note, for Haydn's contrasts are ones of mood as well as of colour. Similarly, the complex line of the Finale cannot by its very nature be rushed, but without good

---

* One might have assumed that Goberman's recording would clarify this matter well since only his version has first violins to left and second violins to right, yet the effect is less clear than in those recordings where all the violins are grouped on the left. The really avid discophile might value the information that the mono pressing of Goberman's performance is balanced more satisfactorily in these few bars than the equivalent stereo.

impetus it will not act as a satisfactory conclusion to a work which, for all its sparkle, has weighty things to say.

SYMPHONY NO. 44 in E minor, known as the "Trauer" ("Mourning") Symphony, is very much church-sonata in mood but not, in fact, in form. Its opening Allegro con Brio is tragic and fiery but the hectic pace of the earlier bi-partite movements has gone: the plaintive oboes do not follow the biting violin line but make their own way once they have supported the initial onslaughts of thematic ideas. This is a symphony which, as far as the admirable Universal Edition is concerned, stands at the further side of the Haydn crossroads—the point at which the use of keyboard continuo is not recommended. This need not be regarded as an arbitrary instruction.* True, there are points when it can contribute little—notably in the Trio section where it might disrupt the *legato* of the lower lines—but it certainly helps the thrusting bass of the Finale when it is included. The tragic Menuetto lies second, with horns giving a soft ray of light in the Trio. The Adagio is one of the most sadly beautiful ever composed and one which responds to a broad interpretation—the movement that Haydn is said to have asked to be played at his own funeral.

This suggestion is understandable when one hears the grave beauty of this movement but these are not the thoughts of an ageing man looking back on a full life: Haydn was approaching forty and his more serious music was by no means nostalgic. There is perhaps a certain yearning in the opening phrase but when, in the main body of the movement, there is a firm, repeated figure followed by a sheerly beautiful wind-band afterthought, it is clearly the work of a musician rising towards his greatest achievements. Haydn attains a clear-eyed sadness which the composers of the Nineteenth century rarely permitted themselves, preferring always to invoke tears. This emotional purity fits Haydn's Adagio admirably for use as funeral music, and few symphonies have been more appropriately named. The abruptness of contrast is the more striking in view of the fierceness of the Finale, which in its very repetitiveness of rhythm builds a tension scarcely dreamed of before the "Sturm und Drang" period.

SYMPHONY NO. 45 in F sharp minor, "Farewell," has a story attached to it of which few can be unaware. The curious thing is that for once it is actually true: the Prince *did* wish to stay at Észterháza for longer than usual, which meant that the musicians, who largely lived at the castle away from their wives and children, were certainly becoming restless as 1772 wore on. Haydn *did* write a Finale in which the instruments stopped playing one by one, and at the first performance the musicians indeed blew out their candles and left as their

---

* It is interesting to note that Leslie Jones, who has conducted an excellent recording *without* harpsichord, has in fact given a public performance *with* it.

individual parts ended, the *dénouement* being that only Haydn and Tomasini were left to play the two remaining violin parts at the close. The Prince took the hint and history was made. If posterity chose the incident to typify Haydn's wit and to stress his concern for his colleagues, then on both counts it may be considered accurate. One must not forget, however, that at the centre of this legend, which happens to be so delightfully true, there lies a quite extraordinary symphony in a most unusual key: F sharp (special crooks in that key had to be constructed for the horns). Structurally it has many unusual features, not least a fierce first movement which actually delays the second subject until after the repeat of the exposition: a strong reason for performers to observe both repeats.* The highly romantic Adagio, with a yearning muted violin line, is set off by a strong Menuet e trio marked *allegretto*—a timely warning, since too fast a tempo can bring an unsuitable air of levity. The horn melody of the Trio is a close relative once more of the *Lamentations of Jeremiah* and so matters should not be hastened. The Finale speaks for itself: beginning with fire and brimstone but ending in beauty and gentility. The joke was against the Prince certainly, but there is never a hint of malice: how could there be when Haydn was writing one of the world's greatest symphonies?

SYMPHONY NO. 46 in B major is again an example of an extraordinary key. The work has some of the drive and tragedy of No. 44, with Haydn using the bass line in a *legato* manner. The textures, however, are more like those of No. 39, with high horns† brightening the texture rather than being used to spectacular effect. The Poco Adagio uses muted strings to contrast the power of the opening movement, and the warm Menuet is stately and unaccountably sad. The latter matches the gypsy-style Trio, which has much of the mystery of Symphonies Nos. 28 and 29 but is interrupted by violent *sforzandi*, so leaving a disturbed impression. The answer to why Haydn placed a relatively important-sounding Menuet at this point rather than affording light relief comes in the Finale, for here the dark-hued jollity is interrupted by a return of the Menuet proper just at the point where one might have expected a bright coda. This arrives in due course, but not until the air of sobriety has been firmly re-established.

For anyone unaware of the delights of middle-period Haydn SYMPHONY NO. 47 in G should be one of the first to be explored. Commencing with a movement which is more of a march than a symphonic

---

* Only John Pritchard has recorded it in this manner, although Rudolf Barshai always observes both repeats in performance also.

† All recordings available at the time of writing contradict Universal Edition by transposing the horns down an octave further than that of the interval of a second shown in the published score.

piece, an imposing chord leads to some wonderful horn dissonances, after which all the supporting instruments fill the texture until a strutting second subject is reached—never has the hardening of the bass line by bassoon been so clearly justified as here. Mozart admired this symphony and it is surely more than coincidence that his great *Serenade* for thirteen wind instruments, K361 of 1781, includes a theme straight out of the slow movement of Haydn's No. 47.

HAYDN

The Menuet e Trio al Rovescio is famous, for it is an exact palindrome —ten bars of Minuet with repeat are followed by the same ten bars backwards with repeat; the Trio is written in the same way, and so a *senza repetizione* playthrough of the Menuet forward-and-back is all that remains to satisfy classical form. An uproarious idea that in practice provides a formally perfect Minuet and Trio: assuming that the conductor keeps in strict tempo to the very end the mirror image remains perfect. The Finale goes at a furious pace—an excellent reason for it not being performed too fast, for there are subtleties of key change which are lost with a hasty approach. The thrusting bass chords give all the pace needed and the curiously unphrased oboe part adds spice to this, one of Haydn's most Hungarian movements.

By repute, the visit of the Empress Maria Theresa to Eszterháza in 1773 was celebrated, among other things, by the performance of the SYMPHONY NO. 48 in C which is now subtitled "Maria Theresia." There is a manuscript of the work by Haydn's copyist Joseph Elssler in Uhroveč, Slovakia, on which there is a pencilled date 1769. This was discovered only in the last few years by Dr. Pavel Polák and makes it clear that the various trumpet parts of the period are spurious. With the scoring problem clarified (two oboes, two horns, timpani, strings, continuo) it remains only to place this important work, not only in the context of "Sturm und Drang" music (where its optimism makes it sit uncomfortably) but also in terms of date. H. C. Robbins Landon has concluded, in the light of the Slovakian manuscript, that the date 1769 is valid, thus placing it scarcely later than Symphonies Nos. 38 and 41—to name the two most mature C major symphonies prior to this time. However, if the pencilled date in an unspecified hand is to be accepted, what trick of inspiration caused No. 48 to move so far ahead in style of other works of this type? This is very much a matter for conjecture, for here already is a summit of achievement: the very opening with its thrilling melodic use of high brass, making the previous fanfarish methods seem primitive, is a revelation in itself, with horns and oboes taking the tune entirely on their own.

The rhythms no longer repeat tensely but sweep the music forward: music for Kings, Queens, Emperors and Empresses indeed. Nor is the plaintiveness of the Adagio with its demanding horn writing (this time in F) any the less in stature; and the glorious Menuet e trio is the epitome of chandelier-hung pageantry. Every facet of the music shimmers with a majestic inner light. Even if it could have been proven that the Empress did not after all enjoy the glory of this music during her visit, it would scarcely matter, for as a result of the supposition the work has obtained the most apposite title imaginable. The Finale shows the hysterical joy encountered in the Finale of Beethoven's last symphony, wild desperation entering the composer as he strives to convey the utmost in optimism. The horn octaves do not fall in their military affirmation but, towards the double bars, actually leap upwards. Here is the most advanced thinking of all the symphonies examined so far.

SYMPHONY NO. 49 in F minor dates from 1768. It is the very last of the church-sonata works and its opening Adagio is perhaps the most solemn and moving of them all. The Allegro di Molto which follows has wide intervals and an insistent bass line which, when the other strings become more lyrical, follows behind threateningly in smooth canon.

The sobriety continues into the Minuet. The work was, like the "Trauer," reputedly written for performance during Holy Week and, though no Gregorian melodies are used, the more serious mood of these celebrations is captured in a style which is unmistakably liturgical. The Trio offers the only moments of major-keyed repose with a gentle, shining horn rising above the oboe melody. The feverish power of Haydn's conception returns in the Finale, which is driven forward by a most incisive bass-line: the sense of propulsion is almost unnerving. This symphony was copied many times in the Eighteenth century and excellent contemporary manuscripts abound in the courts and monasteries of Europe.

SYMPHONY NO. 50 in C again raises the unresolved question of the visit of the Empress Maria Theresa in 1773, for this was the year in which Haydn set his autograph upon the most authentic manuscript of Symphony No. 50. It is the only symphony to which the year 1773 can be ascribed with certainty and this prompts H. C. Robbins Landon to suggest that it might have been the work presented before the Empress. The style is in fact different from that of No. 48. In No. 50 the brass writing is a little more military—as one might expect from the specification of trumpets in the score—yet the trumpet parts are, save for a few bars in the Finale, a mere doubling of the horns. Indeed, it would be quite possible to perform the work with only a pair of horns as the brass complement: the trumpets have only two minims in the whole symphony (bars 51 and 52 in the Finale) which are not unisons with the horns. Since the horns are silent at this point they would have little trouble in replacing the trumpets.* Haydn's first movement starts with a slow introduction of almost baroque splendour. Thereafter a lengthy theme, less direct than those of No. 48, makes clear that this is to be a work of majestic solidity rather than brazen excitement. The slow movement looks back to an earlier period, with a solo cello doubling the melody and the brass omitted. Grandeur returns in the Menuet, although the theme is extremely simple. The Trio leads on thematically—a most unusual feature, and the *presto* Finale has a somewhat complicated melody which begins quietly but is soon punctuated by fanfares. Somehow the furious optimism of the "Maria Theresia" is missing but a sturdy forcefulness takes its place. All in all, No. 50 is the natural if more complex successor to the earlier Festive Symphonies up to No. 41, but the advanced thinking of the "Maria Theresia" is not achieved. Those who feel compelled to accept the implication of the pencilled inscription which lies beneath the theory re-dating No. 48 have, it would seem, no little problem in proving its style to be four years earlier than its previously supposed time. Research sometimes makes legends a little suspect but the "Maria Theresia"

---

* Of our recommended recordings, that by Wöldike omits these two notes in any case, presumably since the illogicality of requiring the C trumpets to play the note D twice at a point where no dramatic effect is created makes these bars suspect.

legend seems to withstand the ravages of musicology exceptionally well.

SYMPHONY NO. 51 in B flat is a concertante piece featuring the two horns, which are given parts of staggering difficulty. Is this a "Sturm und Drang" symphony? Yes and no—certainly it is revolutionary and its originality goes far beyond many earlier works, but Haydn does not conceive it in terms of dark drama. He certainly enjoyed writing for two solo horns and there is a lost two-horn concerto (the one commonly attributed to him is so unlike Haydn in style, with passages which vary between the unsympathetic and the unplayable in the terms of the horns of the period, that it is unquestionably spurious). Symphony No. 51 has scarcely begun before the horns begin to creep up into the stratosphere; beneath, the strings thrust aggressively into fugal textures which incorporate wide dynamic contrasts. Over muted strings the horns, crooked now in E flat, commence the slow movement, first horn reaching written f^3 (sounding a flat^2) in bar 6.

Corno I in E♭ solo (written)

and second horn plumbing the uttermost depths between bars 9 and 12.

Corno II in E♭ solo (written)

The Minuet has two Trios,* the second of which is again geared to spectacular horn writing, with a yawning chasm between the first horn high in its register in B flat alto and the second horn again exploring subterranean regions. After so much virtuosity Haydn pleases the ear with a little light relief in the form of a Rondo-Finale, one section of which has a rollicking, bubbling effect that has to be heard to be believed—take note, for such an effect never occurs again in the symphonies.

---

* Haydn marks the movement Menuetto e Trios.

SYMPHONY NO. 52 in C minor is *echt*—"Sturm und Drang," commencing in the same tenebrous mood as No. 44: the strong bass line, supported by the bassoon (preferably with *staccato* emphasis in performance), gives a sombre effect, as does the bite of the oboes low in their register together with the dark hue of the second horn in E flat. There is, however, a gleam which breaks through frequently—the first horn crooked in C alto and used in a lyrical manner in such a key for the very first time; its striking high tone in a closely-knit texture has a subtly strong dramatic impact. The Andante is dark enough in all conscience but must certainly not be lingered over in performance. Rhythmically it is lighter than the first movement and it is left to the muted but largely non-*legato* strings to keep the sense of poise. The horns are here in C basso and merely support the textures. The same is true of the Menuetto e Trio, more a prefatory shadow of that in Mozart's Symphony No. 40 or Schubert's Fifth. As in the Trio of No. 46 there are *sforzandi* to drive home the tension in this section of the C minor work. The Finale is laid out in much the same way as the first movement: one horn in C alto, the other in E flat, but the strings take on a new fierceness, the oboes become more independent—and also more soulful.

5: From Revolution to Resolution

True, one has yet to say farewell to the "Sturm und Drang" muse, but Symphony No. 53 in D is laid out in such a way that another look at Haydn's orchestral style is essential before moving on. It is important in that it is the first to look forward to the solid, substantial scoring of the London Symphonies, with the hints of the richer textures of the Nineteenth century. In those considered so far there have been in the main only two types of scoring—the majority of symphonies have been for two each of oboes and horns, with strings and continuo, the latter always including a bassoon. Even No. 52 retains this pattern, although Haydn did go to the trouble of writing out the bassoon part separately. Secondly, there have been the C major Festive Symphonies which add timpani and occasionally trumpets. Only in the special case of No. 13 with its four horns is there an accepted timpani part in a work in any key other than C, and so far Haydn has not written a symphony with trumpet parts in a key other than C despite the enormous number of D major works at this time. He only broke this "rule," when composing a symphony as late as Symphony No. 86 in 1786 (the trumpet parts for Nos. 70 and 75 were added after the initial composition of the works).

However, in SYMPHONY NO. 53 in D, "Imperial," there is a solidity in the D major writing. The scoring is for one flute, two oboes, one bassoon, two horns, timpani and strings—one of the examples where the richness of the texture makes it possible to omit harpsichord continuo in modern performance (though its inclusion can never actually be wrong). It was one of Haydn's most popular symphonies and was very widely circulated, achieving especial popularity in England at the Bach-Abel concerts and being performed in such provincial cities as Leicester. Haydn did not write the slow introduction until later and the British performances almost certainly took place without it. Manuscripts also suggest that the timpani were missing from all but the first movement, but it is unlikely that any timpanist would sit idle for the rest of the work. Again there is the complex problem of the Finale, of which there seem to have been no less than four different versions used in Haydn's day. Following Helmut Schultz, H. C. Robbins Landon and the Universal Edition these are now called Finales "A," "B," "C" and "D." "B" and "D" are the Overtures Nos. 7 and 4 respectively, "C" is by the publisher Sieber (or one of his house composers). Why then is Finale "A" not the accepted finale, since it is both symphonic and genuine Haydn? The trouble seems to be that it was usually one of the other three that Haydn and his contemporaries used. In fact Finale "A" was not actually printed until 1951. The first to be employed was probably Finale "D" (certainly in England), yet this lacks the required timpani part together with the formal sonata design. The same applies to the widely-favoured Finale "B" which has flute and timpani parts in the published version that are patently not by Haydn. In short, the most reasonable finale to use is "A," it being fully acceptable from the points-of-view of both form and authenticity. Performers, however, are generally unwilling to do this. The slight oddities of the timpani part elsewhere need not give cause for worry. The Universal Edition score adds (in square brackets, let it be said) some drum notes to the Menuetto which do not seem very convincing, and the music sounds rather better without them.*

The opening of the first movement's Vivace is an interesting look forward to the Nineteenth century with the spirit of the Cherubini of *Anacreon* looming large. The remainder is fully-worked and fully-scored but a new richness is in evidence.† The Andante variations are not searching (maybe a contribution to their considerable popularity)

---

* A thought which may also have occurred to the excellent timpanist in Neville Marriner's recording, who omits several of these strokes together with the occasional unbracketed crotchet.

† Is there something deeper than meets the ear in the fact that Leopold Stokowski has recorded this symphony but no other by Haydn?

and Haydn's solo flute weaves in and out of the texture—no longer is the concertante element present.

SYMPHONY NO. 54 in G is from 1774. It could be similar in date to the initial part of No. 53 but the completed "Imperial," especially with the Introduction and Finale "A,"* can be said to be later under the law of averages. No. 54 is in much the same form and has an *adagio maestoso* introduction which begins with a strikingly forceful chord. The Universal Edition score also shows trilled minims in the timpani which seem strangely out of style. Superficially, the presence of trumpets implies a revolutionary departure since the symphony is not in C; a moment's examination, however, shows them to be safely in that key, and their brilliance is such that they tend to cut very forcefully through the textures if care is not taken in performance.† The dash of the fiery Presto is exciting indeed and both halves really need to be repeated in view of the great length of the succeeding Adagio Assai. Even with both repeats observed in the first movement and neither in the second, the Adagio Assai remains the longer movement of the two. The Menuet is a light Allegretto, with spiky trumpet punctuations which are entirely independent from the horn parts. The insistent grace notes give punch to the rhythms and the military attack of the shallow timpani of the day‡ must have made for an exciting evening at court. The bassoon is promoted to soloist in the Trio and the jollity ends with a racy Presto in which the trumpets ram home the tonic and dominant aspects in no uncertain manner. This is very full scoring—two each of flutes, oboes, bassoons, horns, trumpets and timpani, plus strings—which scarcely needs keyboard continuo: the orchestra is second in size only to that used in five of the London Symphonies.

SYMPHONY NO. 55 in E flat, "Der Schulmeister," is a relaxed, happy work, in which Haydn is largely content to rest on the laurels of his felicitous style, incorporating concertante elements without underlining them. It is a popular symphony nowadays but this could perhaps be due more to its nickname (which does not appear on the autograph) than anything else. The first movement is taut and precise, with not a note wasted, nor are there the shadows of the early Seventies—the composer seems to be reserving himself for the Adagio ma Semplicemente, a movement schoolmasterly enough to have earned the nickname. Its dry humour comes out best if played with a clipped, strutting rhythm.§ The Menuetto is earnest rather than dark, with interesting *sforzando*

---

* Which is probably as late as 1780.
† In Jones's slighty thin recording the trumpets do indeed cut through piercingly, yet this performance has a satisfactory and welcome brilliance.
‡ Well represented in Maerzendorfer's recording.
§ Maerzendorfer is exemplary here.

flourishes from the second violins. Two bassoons support the bass, but only in the Rondo-Finale do they detach themselves from the continuo. Even there both instruments have the same notes to play.

If Haydn relaxed slightly in the delightful but eminently sane No. 55 his SYMPHONY NO. 56 in C is a return to the glories of the mid-classical period as epitomised by the "Maria Theresia" Symphony. The onslaught of high brass and timpani is compelling—a unique sound in which Haydn opens out the textures by giving penetrating parts to the oboes, they in turn standing clear of the strings which are mainly concerned with giving *ostinato* support. Haydn also writes a separate bassoon part in the slow movement (it joins the continuo for the remainder) and the trumpets are occasionally independent of the horns. Here is an advanced symphony with fierce counterpoint striking through from the string band whilst the other more brilliant *timbres* delight the ear. The Adagio uses in the main the open-air tones of oboes and bassoon. A serious but not a sad movement, though still one which has something to gain from the use of a harpsichord, especially since it helps to give bite to the bass. The need for harpsichord continuo is not solely dependent upon the necessity for extra harmonies—that is true only of the earliest symphonies—but Haydn's music is above all a conception of tonal colour and though often, as in this Adagio, there is a harmonic structure which is perfectly self-sufficient, tonally speaking the light, percussive impact of the harpsichord can enhance the total sound in a most satisfying way. Where with Vivaldi, for instance, a full harmonic basis is needed and an organ can often be employed to excellent effect, with Haydn an organ would represent an unthinkable intrusion of foreign colour. The harpsichord is never unwelcome and Haydn probably always heard its sound in his mind's ear—he either directed from the instrument himself or had another performer to take his place whilst he took the violin.

The stateliness of the Menuet has a martial air (Haydn actually permits the more lyrical horns to play higher than the trumpets in their fanfares) but in context this atmosphere suits the music; the simple Trio, led by solo oboe, provides momentary light relief. The Finale is full of lengthy themes crushed into the bars at high speed: there is scarcely one common-time bar which Haydn does not divide into twelve notes. Another point which shows something of the nature of orchestral *timbres* in the Eighteenth century is the taking over of the brass fanfares by the oboes when the key sequences make it impossible for the brass to play the open notes. Clearly the oboes had scarcely less impact, otherwise the line could not have been carried by them. Because today we tend to think in terms of elegant woodwinds, we accept all too easily unauthentic re-orchestrations (notably in Beethoven) which give brass instruments parts which originally lay in the woodwind.

If only the original *timbres* were noted and reproduced, many current misconceptions could be swept away.*

SYMPHONY NO. 57 in D is a large-scale work and dates, like Nos. 54, 55, 56 and 60, from 1774. It is scored for a standard orchestra of two oboes, two horns, strings and continuo, but as with No. 53 there is a timpani part, perhaps added later but in view of the scale of the music indispensable. The expansive nature is obvious from the outset, with a powerful adagio introduction—a clear parallel with the fully-scored Nos. 53 and 54. The main part of the movement has no tempo marking in the autograph score—*allegro* is the sensible suggestion in the Universal Edition edited by Helmut Schultz. The old idea of a strong, fast-moving bass line reappears here but the subtle cross-rhythms of the beautifully-written timpani part also attract the attention. Rhythm is also the essence of the slow movement. A simple three-note figure forms the basis of this set of variations, and by beginning and ending every six-bar group it gives a subconscious unity to the whole movement.

The Menuet has a superb lilt, with gloriously heavy emphasis on the first beat of every bar contrasted by crossed turns off the beat. The *Ländler* influence is large, but Haydn is also concerned with structural tightening: just as he used three notes in the Adagio, so the Menuet has a rising figure of four to form a summarising motto. The same rising figure serves as an introduction to the otherwise quiet Trio which includes no wind instruments (unless the bassoon chooses to join the bass line).

---

* Listen, for example, to Ernst Maerzendorfer's recording of No. 56 when, at bar 62 of the Finale, oboes take over a three-note figure from the horns and trumpets—there is a changed *timbre* but no lessening of force.

The *Finale* is a whirlwind *moto perpetuo*, stirred forward by rushing semiquavers and crushed triplets. The timpani part is again subtle, accentuating the rhythm even when playing softly. Note the unusual title of prestissimo for this movement.

SYMPHONY NO. 58 in F is a misplaced work in Mandyczewski's listing; together with No. 59 it dates from somewhere between 1766 and 1768. The curious thing is that where No. 59 is clearly in the "Sturm und Drang" mould, No. 58 has no such pretensions. Scored for the usual small orchestra, it does not strive to create dramatic situations; indeed, the solid metre of the opening movement has a comfortable optimism which is hardly typical of Haydn at this period. The oboes, however, have some interesting holding notes high in their register and for once it seems that the composer is not very interested in giving difficult passages to the horns. In this combination of the importance of the winds together with subdued brass writing, the symphony is similar to No. 24. No winds at all appear in the Andante, which dances gaily along leaving decent gaps for the harpsichordist to add ideas of his own. The Menuet alla Zoppa is much more daring: irregular rhythms abound and in the Trio the gypsies are again present—a quiet, static piece, more a landscape in fact—or an encampment with no gypsies to be seen. By some unfortunate consensus of opinion, conductors frequently allow the rhythmic impetus, so carefully built up in the Menuet, to collapse entirely at this point; perhaps one day there will be a performance which comprehends Haydn's objective with such interplays of rhythm. The myriad syncopations of the Finale should at least make it clear that this is a very important element in the symphony, yet all recorded performances to date virtually ignore it.

SYMPHONY NO. 59 in A, "Feuersymphonie," is a strong contrast to its contemporary No. 58. The stormier aspects are not concerned with explorations of minor keys but more with vivid juxtapositions of loud and soft. There is also horn-writing far more adventurous than in No. 58, and this together with devices in the first movement such as the sudden halving of note-values gives an added intensity to a method not normally employed at this period. That the work was thought of very much as a whole, despite its possible use as incidental music in the theatre at

Eszterháza, is clear when the equable Andante o Più Tosto Allegretto suddenly darkens before a sombre rising phrase.

The structural reason for this remains in question until the following movement, where it turns out to be virtually identical to the opening flourish of the Menuetto.

In the second half of the slow movement Haydn even goes to the trouble of forcing this figure into the listener's memory by putting an unexpected horn fanfare across it. Where, in the slow movement, the phrase was minor-keyed, the Menuetto shows it to have a major-keyed outcome with the horns becoming yet bolder.

There is little sadness in this delightful work and the title is justified by the fury of the Finale, introduced by horn-calls of a hunting nature. The flying string scales are all the more effective for being set against square, bold wind chords with the horns holding the upper line to brilliant effect.*

SYMPHONY NO. 60 in C is a magnificent exception among Haydn's symphonies. It is drawn from his incidental music to Regnard's comedy "Le distrait" which won great acclaim when Karl Wahr's theatrical group performed the play at Eszterháza. The symphony was created later, probably in response to the popularity of the original music. There are no less than six movements, yet they form a superb entity; the

---

* In his excellent recording David Blum makes a most convincing amendment by omitting bars 131 to the end on the first statement of the repeat. This equates the form to finales such as that of Haydn's "Mercury" Symphony and Mozart's "Jupiter." The explanation given by Mr. Blum himself is: "My reasons were as follows: the repeat as it is in the score, following the horn signals, seemed forced and lacking in spontaneity; the horn signals themselves seemed to lose something through another statement. Believing that the change would render the music stylistically correct, I chose to follow my instinct rather than the letter of the score. I know there are some similar examples (in other symphonies)—but of course this would not be sufficient justification in itself. Had I not felt that the passage was intrinsically conceived as a coda, I would never have made the change." (Letter to the author.)

dramatic references are delightful bonuses with all manner of reminders of the absent-minded nature of the principal character. The C major key is used not for splendour or tragedy but for high spirits throughout. The scoring is for two oboes, two horns, timpani, strings and continuo. Various sources show trumpets (their parts being exact duplicates of those of the C alto horns) but usually as an alternative rather than an addition. There is certainly no good reason to add trumpets in modern performances since horn players of today need no such helping hand and the modern trumpet, being divorced in *timbre* from that of the horn, would introduce a tonal split, into the unison passages.

The slow introduction (one of only two in any pre-London Festive Symphony) gives way to a most joyful theme—either *allegro di molto* or *presto* according to the source used. In the second subject Haydn seems to forget where he was going and the theme peters out indefinitely; a little later he even forgets which symphony he is writing and there is a readily recognisable chunk from the "Farewell."

60

45

The second movement is quiet and march-like with sudden horn and oboe fanfares breaking in from time to time, one theme appearing in the latter part which has no relation to any other. The Menuetto is very peasantish and in the Trio the absent-mindedness again creeps in with the string *tutti* crashing in before the oboes have completed what they have to say. A furious, shadowy Presto follows, oboes, strings and continuo starting in whirling Slavonic Dance style; these are hurled aside by still more peasant elements as the brass and drums erupt. The jubilation becomes uncontrolledly wild. The subsequent Adagio at first seems out-of-place, yet the symphony's great diversity of style easily accommodates the poignant melodies. In its midst there is a great military brass and drum outburst with a further powerful brass fanfare; soon all is quiet again, until the first chords of a final Prestissimo burst in after a bridge-passage with an insistent rhythm, the shortened note-lengths giving the effect of a written-out *accelerando*. The movement has only gone a few bars, however, when everything stops, the violinists having apparently forgotten to tune the G strings of their fiddles. This is now done (with the bows on the strings!) and the orchestra moves off at a great gallop, including another Slavonic Dance before the final paean of jollity.

6: The Middle and
Pre-Paris Symphonies

Haydn enters the group of symphonies numbered from 61 equipped to strike out in any direction. His originality is proven, his ability to handle the orchestra is beyond question and no facet of drama is left unexplored, yet it is this group of twenty works written over ten years from the mid-Seventies which seem to be among the least-often performed today. The reason is difficult to understand since they contain so many riches. Occasionally one symphony is a little similar to another, but this happens very rarely; one wonders if the lack of nicknames is connected with their relative neglect. In addition, these symphonies are well and clearly authenticated: there is nothing to prevent the enthusiast getting to know them, and the problems of text which sometimes stand between a performance and the truth no longer provide difficulties here.

The first of the line is SYMPHONY NO. 61 in D—an excellent, large-scale example with flute, two each of oboes, bassoons and horns, plus timpani and strings, to which a keyboard continuo can contribute little. The first movement opens with a violent crash and after a few moments when a gracious theme is stated, the full orchestra grasps the initial

chord and hammers it out again and again with furious insistence.*
This is a long movement and the rich development is full of surprises
in tone-colour, with lyrical string passages pulled up short by driving
rhythms supported by winds. Haydn also has some fun with the second
horn by putting it low in its register. The scoring of these D major
works up to this period simply does not take into account the potential
of trumpets—indeed, there is no place for them in such music, so
carefully manipulated are the other instruments.

The Adagio is ineffably peaceful. The youthful fires still glow but
this is clearly the writing of a mature composer—as one might expect
from a man by now in his mid-forties. The recognisable fingerprints
are there: gentle *sforzandi* giving shape to the line, dynamic contrasts
and flowing accompaniments; the wind instruments always encourage
the shadows. Needless to say, there are no timpani in this movement.
The Menuet features the wind ensemble in concertante solo sections
over timpani, a very rustic movement with a contrastingly gentle
Trio—again a concertante featuring a solo oboe with lightened accompaniment. The fermata in the second half provides the opportunity for
the oboist to build a miniature cadenza.†

The Finale is a jolly *galop*. *Prestissimo* is the marking and 6/8 the
time signature. The oboe afterthought to every phrase is doubtless a
deliberate minor "irritation" that must have seemed hugely amusing
to the early audiences. The same thoughtless approval is provided by
the horns in their approbatory toots after the main phrases of the
Finale of Symphony No. 99—very similar to today's "yeah-yeah"
choruses backing our less advanced popular music.

SYMPHONY NO. 62 in D—scored as No. 61 except for the absence
of timpani—opens in a very familiar style with our old friend Overture
No. 7, otherwise known as Finale "B" to Symphony No. 53. The
opening phrases are different but it is very much the same piece. There
is no longer any need for a timpani part to be added since it does not
have to be matched to more fully-scored movements, and Haydn wrote
his own flute part (one which conductors might consider adapting for
Finale "B" in preference to the unauthentic one). In the form used for
Symphony No. 62 it makes a good opening movement (now with the
conventional *da capo* markings). The Allegretto which follows is, however, an exception to several rules, being in the tonic major of the
symphony. It is a quiet, flowing piece which does not fall naturally
into any particular pace, and a slow tempo and broad phrasing can

---

* The shock of the brilliance and power displayed in Guschlbauer's recording at
this point makes an unbelievable contrast with the weak, ill-defined mildness of the
recording under Dorati's conductorship.
† In Guschlbauer's recording the slightly different flourish on the repeat of the
section is an excellent touch of super-authenticity.

bring out aspects that a conventional *allegretto* would miss.* The Minuet is different too—an extraordinarily weighty piece (for the salon rather than the ballroom) and far removed from the peasantry which inspired so many of Haydn's other dance movements. The Trio is splendidly light with the bassoon holding the melody and demanding (and today usually obtaining) a reduction of string strength in accompaniment. Again the Finale stresses that there is something less than ideally cohesive about this symphony. It makes a useful conclusion but its main theme starts in doubt, rather as if the exposition had been missed and the movement started partway through the development. What, too, of those joyful chords that dispel the gloom? They are all but identical to those which gladden the melodies in the first movement of Mozart's "Linz" Symphony, written some three or four years later.

HAYDN

MOZART

SYMPHONY NO. 63 in C, "La Roxolane," defies any simple description. In the first place there are two versions of the work, the reasons for this being extremely complex. Harry Newstone and H. C. Robbins Landon have, as a result of their separate researches, come to the same conclusion concerning the four movements which Haydn very likely intended to leave for posterity. This is called version "A." The other work, which was collected together, revised and performed in Haydn's day (albeit some time after the initial concept), shall be called version

---

* Almeida adopts an extremely slow tempo but is able to sustain it with conviction. Dorati, who conducts the other recommended version, is much swifter and treats the movement more as entertainment music. In view of Almeida's breadth of tempo his omission of the exposition repeat in this movement would have been acceptable since this is such a lengthy piece (Almeida observes the *da capo*), whereas Dorati's swifter approach would be given point through his making this repetition (Dorati omits the *da capo*).

"B." Haydn first constructed the music by taking the Overture to the opera *Il mondo della luna* (scoring: oboes, bassoons, horns or trumpets, timpani, strings and continuo); he then composed the "Roxolane" variations and took two other movements—a Minuet and Finale already composed—which were copied in part by an unknown hand and in part by Haydn himself. Plainly they are of earlier style since the bassoon plays along with the bass line.

Whatever the reason for the availabilty of the spare movements, this group of four—version "A"—can be thought of as a complete Festive Symphony. The horn parts for the Minuet and Finale are marked C alto—an obvious point since the ex-Overture of a first movement with its horns *or* trumpets implies that pitch without question. The manuscript full score, however, does give both instruments but again this is a mere matter of consistency since the Menuetto and Finale also have both. A close examination of the opening Allegro shows the brass to be completely in unison except for a series of held horn notes after the double bar—since the timpani were silent at that point, there was no reason to double horns with trumpets. At no point are the trumpets given notes to play which are not also in the horn parts.

The famous variations are tuneful and jolly, a delightful movement in popular style but with another oddity of text: alone among the movements it has a flute part. The Menuetto has a C major grandeur, with the expected sharing of brass parts to give the horns the *legato* moments with the trumpets joining them for the fanfares. The Finale is obviously much earlier than the conjectured date of 1777, though the delicacy of only first and second violins giving out the main theme is a refreshing little touch.

Version "B" is an even more makeshift assemblage than the conveniently constructed "A." Here Haydn simply left the trumpets and drums out of the first movement—the earliest authentic manuscript marks the horns specifically C basso—added a flute and removed one bassoon. No alteration was made to the variations (there are tiny differences concerning flute and bassoon which need not concern the listener). Haydn then wrote a new Minuet for the symphony, again including a flute; and if an early authentic manuscript is to be believed, he marked the horns C alto. After some time he also replaced the Finale with a very trite affair written to please the public and sell the music more quickly in its reduced orchestration. After all this reduction and alteration, the symphony had become little more than a shadow of its old self. Doubtless Haydn did well enough out of the sales of this version but musically the listener may be forgiven for bothering only with the four original movements.

SYMPHONY NO. 64 in A has many strange shadows. It dates from not later than 1775 and could be as early as 1773. Scored for the normal small orchestra, it has the urgency and disturbed undertones of the "Sturm und Drang" period, and also one extraordinary passage in its lightly-scored first movement where Schubertian darkness closes in so suddenly that the blood momentarily runs cold.

A major is an excellent key for Haydn since it allows his horns to ride high but with elegance over the oboes; given a firm bass-line, the transparency of the basic orchestra becomes manifest. The little upward runs seem to bring in a sunny glow—not the fierceness of No. 26 but instead a prophetic romanticism which, miraculously, touches only this work of all those in its period. It is difficult not to believe that some dramatic event in Haydn's life had inspired such perception, but there is nothing known.

The tragic, infinitely remote Largo which follows is amazingly modern and is not even in sonata form; rather, it has a beautiful theme, interrupted by other ideas, sombre or elegant as the mood leads, with highly original key sequences. It would seem almost impossible to write a movement to follow the two just described since, like Schubert's "Unfinished" Symphony, they are virtually self-sufficient. Haydn chose a questioning type of Menuet, not consciously dramatic but in fact rather peaceful. The Trio is all sweetness, the horns soft, high and effectively distant, give a comforting warmth. The Finale is a rondo which does not take the usual high-spirited form. The vivacity is there, the second strain is forceful too, yet the basic theme continues to pose unanswered questions. Even the standard rondo form is broken from time to time—in the subtlest possible way.

SYMPHONY NO. 65 in A, similarly scored, could be a little earlier —certainly it is not later than 1773 and it may be considered alongside Symphonies Nos. 45, 46, 47 and 52. The difference is that No. 65 is consistently major-keyed and optimistic, and this mood can often be heard in Haydn through the brightness and flexibility of the wind writing. Here is typical untroubled composition, with the violins taking the mid-range melodies in the first movement leaving horns and oboes to add high sustained lines. The Andante is something of an enigma—a homely theme, repeatedly interrupted by wind fanfares, almost as if a dramatic sequence of events were in the composer's mind. By now one might well expect the unexpected in Haydn, and this is borne out by the revolutionary Menuetto, driven strongly along by accented ornaments until by a conscious misplacing of the accents Haydn tricks the ear into believing that it is in 4/4 time. It is indeed possible to beat three 4/4 bars in place of four 3/4 bars at two points in the Minuet; doubtless a composer of today would have written the passages in changed time signature. The Finale is pure hunting jollity with a great many fanfares and whirling string figures in support. 12/8 is the time signature and the hidden imaginings of Symphony No. 64 are a world away from such merrymaking. No. 65 would have been the ideal work for performance after a good day's hunting—and there were certainly many such days at the Court of Nikolaus the Magnificent.

SYMPHONY NO. 66 in B flat is a later work; together with Nos. 67 to 69, 1778 is accepted as its approximate date of composition without having ultimate documentary proof. B flat is a key of which Haydn made some use in his earlier works ("A," "B," 16, 35), exploiting the wind writing and—in No. 51—turning the horn parts almost into a concerto. Symphony No. 66, being rather later in years, is the first of a group in a new B flat style where the virtuosity of the horns may be taken for granted, their bold tones ringing out whilst the remaining instruments engage in thematic problems worked out at greater length than hitherto. An examination of the sheer sound of the music seems to indicate that Haydn may have been at this time exploiting not merely the instrumental potentialities of his instruments (identical to the earlier B flat works except that there are now two bassoons to add to oboes, horns and strings) but also the effect of broad chording on the ambience of the hall. In the first movement there is some busy string writing, but instead of repeated notes forcing the movement along, each one now has a part to play in the development of the thematic material. The rich chords, notably at the final double-bar, are so strong and full that the sound would be sure to be ringing around the hall whilst the repeat of the development was under way. The slow movement starts as if it were all to be sheer elegance, but the hushed atmosphere later wells up into grand, sombre organ-like chords towards the close—a far cry from the flailing bass lines of the music of a decade and more earlier. The Menuetto is powerful and the strings even break off to display the new-found fullness of the winds; the Trio is this time no more than an interlude. The Finale, *scherzando e presto*, has one of those extensive and complicated rondo themes which, the moment the full orchestra enters, becomes crystallised, Haydn taking only the elements he needs for the essential forward motion. Again there are sudden outcries from the wind band, with the strings falling softly away to allow the resonance to override and impress. Did Haydn have particularly fine wind players at this time? Did the venue for the concerts change? One cannot be sure, but certainly the overall sound is now changing.

SYMPHONY NO. 67 in F, scored again for two each of oboes, bassoons and horns, with strings and a rather less essential keyboard continuo, begins happily with repeated notes lightly touched in. The winds hold chords across these or punctuate the smoother elements. This is a *presto* movement but it makes its best effect when not hurried, the insistence of the detached notes giving all the speed that is necessary. The delicate, syncopated theme of the Adagio, which uses muted violins, has a tunefulness and elegance which must have delighted the nobility, and the answering figures between first and second violins make the most cultured dialogue. When, however, Haydn seems to be living up to the ill-founded traditional view of an Eighteenth-century gentleman of impeccable manners, the melody is played for the last time with the backs of the bows—an isolated example of *col legno*, thrown off quietly as if of little importance. We are into the stately Menuetto before the shock has fully struck home. The latter is almost predictable in its nobility, and inevitably it is time for another shock: this occurs in the Trio—another Hungarian country scene where two first violins play the melody whilst a single second violin, deliberately mistuning its G string, holds a hurdy-gurdy-like drone-bass. This passage fails in modern performance if the second violin merely plays its held F by conventional fingering. What Haydn requires is a drone on an open string, and since the violin does not possess an open F it has to be created: the composer really does mean what he says. The Finale is also an exception to the rule; the Allegro di Molto having been expounded, yet another slow movement is inserted: an extensive Adagio Cantabile for two violins and cello which brings in the world of the late quartets—a remarkable feat, since in the late Seventies Haydn's work in that field had yet to reach Opus 33. The strings are followed by the winds, which carry the slow section forward reflectively before sonorous orchestral chords at length herald the reprise of the Allegro di Molto.

SYMPHONY NO. 68 continues the new B flat revolution: commencing softly, the repeated notes impinge only gently upon the consciousness. The oboes have smooth lines—an echo of the melody

1: *Joseph Haydn's birthplace in Trstnik*
(from an oil by Wilhelm Kröpsch, 1829, ÖNB)

2: *St. Stephen's Cathedral in Vienna, with the house where Reutter and his pupils lived at the front (Vienna City Museum)*

3: The Esterházy palace at Eisenstadt (lithograph after a steel engraving by C. Rohrich after L. Rohbock, Budapest National Museum)

4: The Esterházy winter palace in Wallnerstrasse, Vienna (engraving by Johann Ringlin after Salomon Kleiner, H. C. Robbins Landon)

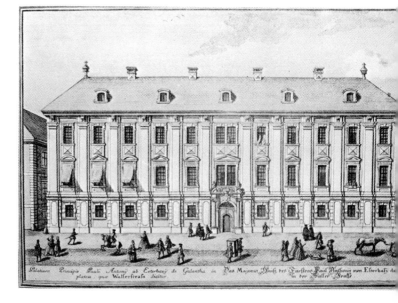

5: Haydn's house in the Windmühl district of Vienna where he lived for the last decade of his life (engraving by Vincent Alloja after Elisabeth Vigée-Lebrun, Salzburg Mozarteum)

bildung des Haufes in der Vorftadt Windmühle in Wien, in welchem **HAYDN** den 31. Mai 1809 starb, und in welchem am 1. Juni 1840 die Trauer- u. Erinnrungsfeier Statt fand.

6: *Prince Pál Antal Esterházy*
(Esterházy collection)

7: *Prince Miklós Esterházy in 1770*
(Budapest National Museum)

8: *Haydn in 1791*
(aged fifty-nine)
(ÖNB)

: Empress Maria Theresa in 1770
(Budapest National Museum)

10: *Johann Peter Salomon*
(by courtesy of the Trustees of the British Museum)

11: Joseph Haydn, Mus. D. (Oxon)
(by courtesy of the trustees of the British Museum)

but omitting its *staccato* implications—and although the newly-found independence of the two bassoons provides some brief solos of a different hue, Haydn is very sparing on the horns with no more than a series of high chords to round off the return to the tonic key. In the Menuetto the colour of the wind ensemble is more evident. It is an unusually smooth movement, all the more unusual for being placed second at this period. The winds retain equal importance in the Trio, a nostalgic piece of simplicity, but the lack of complexity is now the result of Haydn writing a specifically urbane piece—there is nothing gauche here. The extensive slow movement, marked *adagio cantabile*, is based on a markedly *staccato* rhythm and looks forward to the "Clock" movement of Symphony No. 101. Given a springing rhythm, the halving and even quartering of note-lengths has a wonderfully fierce effect. This idea is used sparingly and hence with great impact. The quaint violin grace-notes are also an indication of a desire to keep an element of the unexpected running through the music. The final Rondo races in with emphasis; line upon line of jolly repeated notes give way to the bassoons, handling the same material in their own comic but never crude way. This is a prelude to a grand circuit of the instruments, each contributing their colours to the material—the strings being largely employed upon expounding the many alternative tunes. The horns only come into their own towards the end and even then as equals. Each instrumental group finally throws out an angular fragment before all is swept away in the dash of the coda.

*

Ernst Gideon Freiherr von Loudon (1716–1790), the great Field-Marshal who defeated the Turkish army, was commemorated in a large-scale work at this time. The tribute was probably more to ensure good sales for the music than for any nationalistic reasons. A piano reduction of the score was compiled but the copyist made a poor job of the Finale—undismayed, Haydn simply suggested to his publishers Artaria that the movement could be left out of the transcription altogether since "the word Laudon would do more for selling it than would ten Finales." "Laudon" note, rather than "Loudon," since the former seems to have been the name by which the Field-Marshal was generally known at that time. In its way this is a Festive Symphony and yet there is a difference. The joy is perhaps implicit in the conscious striving for majesty, but regarding the music in the terms of orchestral sonority it is difficult to reconcile it with what has gone before. The very first theme of this SYMPHONY NO. 69 in C is similar to that of the "Maria Theresia" (indeed, it has been confused with it in old thematic catalogues) but the conception is different, the furious eagerness being no longer in evidence.

The scoring is for two oboes, two bassoons, two horns, two trumpets, timpani and strings. The immediate question is: at which octave do the horns play? The answer is not so immediately forthcoming. If, as is generally accepted, they are intended to be in C basso, it is the first symphony in this style that has any such requirement. Even close examination of the score does not make for a firm conclusion since although, if played alto, the horns would cross above the trumpets on several occasions, it would not be the first time that this had happened and certainly there is nothing unplayably high. Circumstantial evidence is more helpful, and since, of C major symphonies of the Seventies, this is the only one where the trumpet parts are written in such a way that they could not be dispensed with, together with the fact that no contemporary manuscript actually has the inscription "alto" (or *hoch*, as Haydn sometimes wrote), there is some probability that "basso" may have been intended. This certainly is how it is always performed but there are musicians who would not concur; the ultimate test, in the absence of absolute documentary proof, would be to compare performances in both styles.

This is not one of Haydn's greatest creations, but an air of spaciousness can be created by the adoption of broad tempi and sturdy rhythm in performance. It is a curious phenomenon that the finest music can withstand misinterpretation, but an unsympathetic performance of the "Laudon" creates an impression of superficiality in the listener's mind which does unfair discredit to the composer.*

After the opening of the work with its superficial similarity to the

---

* Dorati and Maerzendorfer, both excellent Haydn stylists, take an eccentric view of this symphony, expounding it in an ultra-lightweight fashion and, in the case of Dorati, recessing the brass and drums to the extent that the violin lines become over-insistent. In the Menuetto this conductor imposes a foreign elegance and delicacy

"Maria Theresia," it soon becomes obvious that instead of nervous, racing energy and the quickening of the blood in the veins—elements which are the very essence of the earlier work—the "Laudon" is a creation of more conventional build, the repeated fanfares being an affirmation of success rather than a striving towards it. Nor are the minor-keyed episodes full of cloudy mysteries; rather they are a formal modulation *en route* to the home key. Having set out for once on a conventional course, Haydn continues by writing a slow movement without any unsuitably thoughtful ideas creeping in. He does this by starting deeply but, for the sake of unity, repeats certain figures before returning to the home key. Many slow movements are like this but for one important difference—the muted sound of elegant violins is often clouded by seriousness before a return to the home key via a tonal wanderlust of the kind inimical to Haydn. Here, however, there is no such diversion. He does not forget how to write a triumphant Menuetto, even though this is a *pièce d'occasion* (or perhaps because of it). For once one is pleased to be bathed in a bright C major, yet the textures are less brilliant than hitherto and the jolly Trio is a shade perfunctory. The Finale is an exciting Presto, light in touch and searching in spirit. Just as the old battle-pieces used to end with a celebration, so too this battle-piece must be joyful and not too deep; the brass parts are conventional but the string counterpoint is inventive.

SYMPHONY NO. 70 in D, written shortly after the disastrous Eszterháza fire of 1779, is a D major work with a difference. Haydn added the trumpet and timpani parts later but they are moulded into the texture in an eminently skilful manner and their omission would be unthinkable (although, unfortunately, not unheard-of). The scoring is for flute, two oboes, bassoon, two horns, two trumpets, timpani and strings. All of these are thrown at the listener at the beginning of the lively opening Vivace con Brio which drives its way along in a heated fury, the jagged phrases forced together to form one erratic angular theme to which scarcely anything is added as the brief movement progresses.

which eliminates all majesty. He does this with such consistency, however, that although Dorati's is an interpretation which misses all the grander aspects, his eccentrically mild view of the music, though sadly unexciting, is carried through with greater conviction than is to be found in the pale, negative interpretation by Maerzendorfer.

The bite of the trumpets, the furious whirl of strings and the cutting edge of a bass line which takes on an old assertiveness leaves the listener all the more ready to welcome the lengthy suppressed beauty of the slow movement—"a type of canon in double counterpoint," as Haydn somewhat forbiddingly called it. There is nothing difficult, however, in this sustained example of other-wordly grace; the only problem is what to do for a succeeding dance-movement in the circumstances. In such movements Haydn is never short of ideas; this time it is scherzo-like with a driving first beat to each bar—the very negation of the relaxed lilt of the Menuet in Symphony No. 57. After each phrase there is a wind echo of the theme and the bucolic effect is complete: a fast *Teutsche* rather than a graceful *Ländler*—the latter mood is reserved for the bitter-sweet Trio which foreshadows the Viennese waltz school. The return of the Minuet also includes a surprise, for it adds a brief coda which is immensely affirmative. The Finale, built on five statements of the note D, breaks into a rare flurry of counterpoint—a wonderful triple fugue ("three subjects in double counterpoint," said Haydn) of the sort of writing evident in the chamber works as early as Op. 20 (1772) but never allowed to flower in the symphonies until now. A mass of complexity is here poured into the shortest movement of the period. The ending is devastating—twice the violins ponder over those five notes, the full orchestra defiantly crashes out the same five, and the music ends.

SYMPHONY NO. 71 in B flat has one flute, two oboes, a bassoon, two horns and strings, but breaks with convention by beginning with a slow introduction which tries the same rhythm in various different ways without settling on an actual tune—an idea very similar to the opening of Haydn's *Seven Last Words* (Mozart unwittingly gave the solution when writing the opening of his "Haffner" symphony). After only a few bars the music sets out on an Allegro con Brio which after only a few notes echoes the opening theme of Symphony No. 51—was it the key of B flat that tripped the composer's memory?

71

This is still a very different work, however, much in the new B flat style of No. 68 though certainly more questioning in contour. A theme and variations follows with copious use of winds setting it well in period while the overall hush makes it quite clear that the soft dance movements which once served as slow interludes in the earlier symphonies are now forgotten. It is not that Haydn *could* not utilise that style once again, but rather that he *would* not. The Menuetto is colourful; the master orchestrator, having delighted the listener with musical technique, does not forget that the ear needs satisfaction as well as the mind and it is noteworthy how the winds, as never before, stand clear of the strings in this movement. The Trio is for two violins and *pizzicato* bass—full of doubt and comical mock-hesitation. No surprises in the Finale except to wonder how the strings can possibly play those swirling, rushing torrents of notes. The woodwind have their share of thematic material with some surprisingly delicate writing —touching-in the ideas rather than stating them. The development could scarcely be more divorced in key from the original. The wind band humour before the coda remains decorous, however: these are aristocrats enjoying peasant revels rather than the personification of bucolic people themselves.

SYMPHONY NO. 73 in D, "La chasse," was, and still is, one of Haydn's more popular symphonies. It is scored, in the first three movements, for flute, two oboes, two bassoons, two horns and strings. These movements were added to the Overture to *La fedeltà premiata*, which makes a splendid Finale, and the appropriate halfway bars included to make the movement symphonic from the *da capo* point-of-view. A problem of orchestration remains, however, since this Overture included timpani and a brass line which asked for horns *or* trumpets. The addition of trumpets *as well as* horns—suggested in some modern editions—can have the effect of brass adding an unnecessary coarseness to the texture, so it is not surprising that many conductors content themselves with the usual D major Haydn scoring which has horns and timpani but no trumpets. In the light of several authentic Eighteenth-century scores, it is clear that many performances took place without timpani also.

Following a slow introduction, the theme of the first movement Allegro is unusually long, yet overall Haydn develops a melody which might seem unwieldy in other hands. The second movement is the melody of the song *Gegenliebe*, a recipe for immediate success. The Menuetto swings gladly along, with an elegant Trio brought down to earth by the rusticity of the prominent bassoon part. The Finale opens with hunting calls (genuine ones, not the fruits of Haydn's fertile imagination) and the only departure from the high spirits comes in the development, where the angriness of the strings in unison is to be assuaged only by a restatement of the happier melodies that form the greater part of the movement.

SYMPHONY NO. 74 in E flat, for flute, two oboes, two bassoons, two horns and strings, opens with three sharp chords and strides along confidently—the only hesitancy being afforded by deliberate uncertainties in the second subject for momentary humorous effect. No depths are plumbed, and minor keys are employed merely as a simple expedient to contrast major ones. The point about the movement is its impetus: even when Haydn plays to the audience by going round in quiet circles near the close, the ending is still obviously in sight. A smooth violin over a jerky cello accompaniment represents the start of a tuneful Adagio Cantabile which, for all the implication of its title, never quite achieves repose. Geiringer has suggested Mozartian influence in this work—a theory which seems to have no more than superficial merit. In the first place Symphony No. 74 dates from 1780—the year before the two composers met—and Haydn's opportunity for hearing any of Mozart's music would have been restricted in the extreme. In Mozartean terms it could perhaps be suggested that the Mozart of the Serenades is hinted at in the calm, smooth Menuetto of Haydn's symphony, but even this is probably putting the cart before the horse. Much more likely is the notion that Haydn was writing a symphony with which he intended to please his audience through its tunefulness; the passing resemblance to a contemporary composer is no more than an inevitable coincidence. In any event the Minuet is danceable, rhythmically speaking, in a style which is very much Haydn's own, and the smoother-than-usual contours of the winds are a mere offshoot of melodic intentions as opposed to dramatic ones. The Finale is not so strong a movement—here the jollity of the 6/8 rhythm has no great thematic inventiveness superimposed; instead, a happy *dénouement* to a none-too-serious symphony is provided and Haydn does not even bother to provide the half-expected changes of orchestral tone. The string body makes the ideas seem more *legato* in concept and for once the wind band plays a relatively subsidiary role.

SYMPHONY NO. 75 in D has a story behind it, vouched for by no less than the composer himself. The music was written at the end of 1779 and became very popular, a fact which no doubt encouraged Haydn to add trumpets and drums to the score (Eszterháza being without a set of timpani at the time of composition due to the great fire earlier in 1779). England took to the music from the time of its publication in the early Eighties. When Haydn visited London ten years later he found its popularity undimmed and in his diary wrote of a performance at which an English Protestant minister became deeply depressed on hearing the beautiful Poco Adagio (which Haydn in his diary calls an Andante) since the previous night the clergyman had dreamed that the music represented a premonition of death. After the performance, the cleric took to his bed and, just one month after the performance, Haydn heard that the worthy gentleman had died.

The slow introduction leads to a furious Presto, full of snapping rhythms, enhanced by the fierce, short notes of the trumpets, with fanfares which become ever more insistent during the second half of the movement and take on a new air of Beethovenian strength. If one compares this work with its contemporaries in terms of its sound, it is clear that the additional instruments make it so very different tonally. The Poco Adagio has every ingredient necessary to support the veracity of Haydn's story—a most moving set of variations, measured in concept to an extent that too lively a tempo in performance would prove disastrous. The pointing of the Menuetto, with its abrupt ornaments, calls to mind the equivalent movement of No. 54; flute and violin have a concertante role in the Trio. The Finale foreshadows the London Symphonies: a dancing, high-spirited piece in not-quite regular rondo form. Certain of the London Symphonies have playful woodwind flourishes towards their final bars and so it is here, until the full orchestra launches forth with the ultimate affirmative chords.

What was it that prompted a living British composer to quote from the first movement of SYMPHONY NO. 76 in E flat? The composer in question—Robert Simpson—took this simple idea (a passage not even derived from the main theme) because of its innocence.* It appears in the Trio section of Simpson's Fourth Symphony (1972) and from the composer's point-of-view is an important *motif*; the contrast of this innocent idea with what had gone before is instrumental in altering the nature of the reprise of the Scherzo.

---

* Robert Simpson, to whom I am indebted for the above reduction from his own full score, comments: "The innocence of Haydn is confronted by us with a problem; Haydn is not disturbed, but we are."

It is tempting to think of this as a tribute to Haydn, but this was not in fact the intention, being no more than the use of a fragment found to be ideal in the context. The compliment to Haydn lies in the composer's decision to identify this snatch, for it is so germane to the argument of the later work that, without one's attention having being drawn to it, it could have escaped notice. Since, however, the essence of good symphonic composition depends on the assimilation of, and respect for, the masters of the past, any such quotation, whether direct or indirect, is a straightforward sign of continuing good health in the symphony as an art form. Nevertheless, the motivation could well have lain deeper, for No. 76 is a rather "different" composition. The symphony was composed in 1782 and, had events turned out otherwise, would have been one of the group of three written in that year (Nos. 76, 77, 78) which Haydn was to have taken to England in 1783. Nothing came of these plans, however, and it is arguable if they were in Haydn's mind during the actual composition of the music. In Symphony No. 76, Haydn's intention seems to be simply to divert and entertain. The pace of the opening movement is mainly sustained through the conventional method of halving note values. The usual wind ensemble of the period, comprising flute, two oboes, two bassoons and two horns, is used, but rarely hitherto has Haydn kept them so firmly embedded in the string textures. Another clear indication of his uncharacteristic leaning towards moderation lies in the tempo markings of the second and fourth movements: *adagio ma non troppo* and *allegro ma non troppo* respectively, with even the Minuet a respectable *allegretto*. In performance there are clearly problems in achieving contrast and one is forced to the conclusion that Haydn did not really require this element. There is much beauty in the slow movement but when, three-quarters of the way through, the winds have forceful chords, the full, busy churning of the string body leaves the ear bewildered as to which line Haydn expects it to follow. The Menuetto is comfortable, falling sadly in its long *legato* lines. The broken chords which finish each section are a well-tried technique but, where in earlier times the wood-wind would be given these alone, the strings insist on muting the colouring. It is only in the swinging Trio that the off-beat oboes sharpen the texture. The Finale differs from some written at this time, being more like a first-movement in style; the solo flute is an ideal protagonist of the theme, and if at first it seems that this is to be a rondo, the repetition of the initial subject and its subsidiary makes it clear that the Finale is in sonata form after all. The moderate aspect, tempo marking apart, lies in the modest dynamics—under no circumstances could there possibly be a timpani part to this music lying undiscovered.

SYMPHONY NO. 77 in B flat is a highly individual work, bearing little resemblance to its neighbours. Its commencement has an almost comical insouciance, the lilting melodies—marked simply *vivace* but with no actual tempo—ambling happily along for all the world like a large woolly dog taking a cheerful morning promenade. Familiar Haydn effects return once more: the B flat alto horns ring loudly and boldly, and when their bright tones, together with those of the oboes, have wrung every ounce of good humour from the first theme, the composer writes another, so radiantly happy it almost bursts with pleasure. The glorious Andante Sostenuto is devotional in character. The atmosphere is like that of the famous Adagio of No. 98 but less hymn-like, for there is a new sadness. Not self-pity, but the fifty-year-old Haydn was now old enough to look back as well as forward. The Menuetto is fast—*allegro*—and would splendidly wrong-foot any dancer who attempted it, not least at the heavy interrupting chord in its second half. This leaves a full-scale sonata-form Finale, horns whooping for joy, high strings sailing up and down the scales out of happiness, and the remainder aiding the bouncing rhythms as if deciding to add to the festivities for the sheer pleasure of doing so.* Though some tricky passages need playing with accuracy, the untroubled effect given by the resultant sounds conceal the technical difficulties.

SYMPHONY NO. 78 in C minor is not a gloomy symphony by any means, but it does have its grey moments. The most interesting feature of the opening Vivace is the dark reflection of the mysteries of No. 64, because amidst the sombre exposition of the minor-keyed beginning, which in turn is none too far removed from the world of the "Trauer" Symphony, there is a curiously hopeful ray of light which fades into the mists as unexpectedly as it had appeared. It will be clear that this trilogy of Nos. 76, 77 and 78 is as unlikely a group as can be imagined, with only the orchestration and the date in common. The textures of No. 78 are fairly solid, with low horn-writing, and even in the Adagio, where these instruments have soli, the mood remains solid and stern. This time Haydn is being serious—a seriousness tempered neither by nostalgia nor sorrow: sombreness beautifully conveyed gives the audience time to reflect, and the composer himself has no personal problem to put before his listeners. The Menuetto is brighter, the gentle rocking rhythm in the bass a nicely-judged relief after the autumnal Adagio. How will Haydn offset such semi-optimism in the Trio? The answer comes in the timely injection of humour: sudden contrasts of *forte* and *piano*, with a hurdy-gurdy tune (all that is needed is a drone-bass; perhaps the harpsichordist—if any—should divert the listener by accompanying the section with only a single repeated chord throughout). As sound, however, the movement is not remarkable. The same applies, in terms of coloration, to the Finale, but the vivid Haydn

---

* Perhaps the quality of the music itself has something to do with four quite outstanding recordings of virtually equal merit being available.

dynamic changes are there and these, together with the minor key of the main theme at each return, keep balance with the earlier movements whilst still allowing a smile at the subsidiary episodes. It is curious how the flute seems to stand clear of the frequent blocks of full-orchestra tone. Haydn's masterly ear knew how to make new ideas take on an individual colouring and so ensured that they became the more memorable.

SYMPHONY NO. 79 in F is also one symphony of a group of three and as with Nos. 76 to 78 the scoring of Nos. 79 to 81 is for the basic Eighties' orchestra of flute, two oboes, two bassoons, two horns and strings. They were written between 1783 and 1784 and are full of originality, though more in the nature of formal revolution, thematic surprises and unexpected key changes. No longer, as in the mid-period works, is there "the symphony with the very low horns" or "the symphony with the violin and cello solos" or "the one with the military fanfares," for now Haydn colours his music subtly; he is sometimes content to entertain rather than shock (perhaps the reason why the symphonies between Nos. 70 and 80 are only in recent years becoming fully accepted, despite a quarter of a century of sustained Haydn enthusiasm). One may note with a wry smile one writer who gives an "appreciation" of No. 79 on a record sleeve and informs the listener that the first movement is "a little forced" and "betrays a lack of enthusiasm" and that in the slow movement "Haydn seems to have some reservations. . . ." The Minuet and Trio are said to be "somewhat short on inspiration" and finally "the last movement too is lacking in inventiveness."* It is certainly true with Haydn, as with any composer, that one cannot expect an identical high pitch of genius in every work; the early Eighties did not provide his most outstanding compositions but one can better establish a sense of proportion by comparing Haydn's symphonies of this period with those of, say, Pleyel, Dittersdorf or Wanhal. What epithets do the unsympathetic store up for *them*?

The most unusual feature of the first movement is a single downward phrase of pure Mozart; this apart, glowing melody is underpinned by a firm *staccato* bass. The Adagio Cantabile which follows is simple, touching and quietly optimistic. At length the gentle forward motion rests, and suddenly a delightful, quietly hastening section marked *un poco allegro* bustles in. Isolated from this movement it would be difficult to guess where else it might be used in a symphony—a Finale would perhaps be the place but even that would not be quite suited to such tension. One of those fine Menuetti follows, of the style in which the double bars leave a question mark in the air. The Trio is a country

---

* The disc concerned is excellent, so readers must forgive the lack of further identification for fear that the literary material might prejudice a rewarding musical performance.

dance plain and simple, with inverted use of the main material and solo flute and oboe adding delicate touches of pastel colour. The Finale, in Haydn's "homecoming" style (it could never be mistaken for anything else), spins happily along to conclude a work typical of its composer, brightly entertaining in concept yet without a single shallow moment.

SYMPHONY NO. 80 in D minor is, as the key may hint, a tragic work. Its proportions are a little unusual and complete generosity with repeats makes the slow movement unconscionably long by proportion, although the carefully measured pause at the end of the work makes the repetition of both halves of the Finale absolutely essential. The fiery first movement is the first of four quite remarkable pieces in which the thoughts of the "Sturm und Drang" period are transmuted in terms of the newer and perhaps weightier style. The second subject appears so late in the exposition that it seems almost as if it had slipped Haydn's memory, for the double bar and the repeat arrive before it has run its course. On the second time round, the long pause at this point makes the onset of the development all the more remarkable and there are other strange gaps later. The odd thing is that this second subject, which takes up virtually the whole of the development, is basically a humorous idea in broken rhythm yet the stern context almost forbids a smile. The Adagio begins in tragic sweetness, a movement of considerable stature and which somehow loses its impact if the tempo is too slow—probably on account of the pauses which, if overlong through a relaxed tempo, hinder the flow. Early on a *forte* entry comes as a great shock, for suddenly here is a yearning phrase straight out of Mozart's *Masonic Funeral Music*. Behind it there must be a deep connection which one is unlikely ever to know, but it cannot be mere coincidence that in the Trio of the grim Menuetto the plaintive tones of the *Lamentations of Jeremiah* can be heard just below the surface. another being Mozart's own use of this chant in his *Masonic Funeral Music*. Sad, repeated, syncopated notes usher in the Presto. The syncopations continue until the alteration to a regular metre occurs, inevitably sounding like syncopation in itself. As a suitable conclusion to a stark minor-keyed work, this D major Finale leaves several unanswered questions.

SYMPHONY NO. 81 in G starts with a crash,

something which has scarcely been heard since the beginning of Symphony No. 41

or Symphony No. 61.

The lyrical afterthought in No. 81 is also deceptive, for the fury of the full orchestra soon sweeps it away—a momentary stretch of peacefulness acting more as an introduction to weightier matters. It is noticeable that Haydn has something of a renewed taste for isolating concertante solos, and even bassoon accompaniments are now freed, from time to time, of the encumbrance of lower-string support. Sweeping string unisons attract the ear just before the unconventional reprise but the contrasts come now from plangent wind chords—the old concertante habits have certainly returned, although here whole sections have concertante parts as well as individual instruments and the horns take on a new brazenness towards the close of the movement. Something familiar underlies the slow movement, appearing veiled in the transitional passages and with strong oboe lines to remind one of Haydn's power to add a bitter edge to major keys—the hidden element is indefinably Hungarian. Led by flute, the strings intone a simple melody in Siciliano rhythm. It is a peaceful movement, full of pastoral serenity, yet no scenes are specifically conjured up, rather a general feeling of great space and unlimited landscapes. Such vistas were so close to Eszterháza that it is hardly surprising. The Menuetto suddenly clarifies what was previously no more than hinted at in the previous movements: those Hungarian gypsies have arrived. The bounding rhythms of the Menuetto are a barely suppressed Slavonic dance with a few stamping Germanic accents to hold the influence in central Europe, but the Trio is purely Hungarian. And in an extraordinary way, for this dance, a remarkable combination of the gentle and the wild, reaches the double bar of the Trio and repeats in conventional form. After eight more bars of quasi-development, the eight-bar recapitulation of the main Trio tune leaves the conductor simply to repeat these last sixteen bars to satisfy the formal design of this movement. Yet Haydn does something very strange: no second repeat bar appears and the composer goes to all the trouble of writing out the eight developmental bars in full for a second time. Why such extravagance? The last eight bars reveal the shock, for they are written in the minor key, the music thus becoming doubly Hungarian. A shiver of excitement must have run through the first audiences at such a great stroke of originality. Diagramatically one can map out a conventional trio as: AABABA. Since an explanation of form cannot diagnose key changes this also describes the *shape* of the Trio of No. 81. The Universal Edition score marks the last thirty-two bars for repeat *yet again*, giving the diagrammatic form AABABABABA. There is no possible reason why any conductor should observe this final instruction save to declare that the letter of the printed score had been strictly adhered to. To do so would mean that the same trio tune is stated six times (four times major, twice minor); the wonderful effect of the surprise is killed stone dead through its re-statement.

After such "revolution" Haydn's high level of inspiration is retained in one of his very finest finales. A dashing movement with a gentle falling beginning—again a parallel with No. 41—soon breaks into nervous insistent rhythms over which long-breathed melodies of great beauty are expounded. The development, though both adventurous and long, is finely calculated in that it gives a wholly major-keyed impression. Largely there is humour, elegance and lyricism throughout this work, so an aggressive Finale would not have been appropriate. The very restraint with which Haydn uses the malleable elements of which the exposition is comprised, is in itself a demonstration of his disciplined inspiration. This symphony would surely have achieved unparalleled popularity for its period given some quaint (even if irrelevant) advantage such as a colourful nickname.*

---

* One conductor who does not neglect this work is Antal Dorati. His recording as shown in the Appendix is an interpretation *par excellence*, with Haydn's joke correctly told only once. A later recording as part of the complete Haydn Symphonies by the same conductor (not recommended) actually makes the unwanted repeat, so the listener is given a choice.

7: The Paris Symphonies

The six Paris Symphonies were written in 1785 and 1786 for the Loge Olympique in Paris. It is interesting to note that in a letter to Artaria, brought to light by Jens Peter Larsen, Haydn clarified the order in which he wanted the symphonies printed, viz. 87, 85, 83, 84, 86, 82. However, he suggested to Forster at a later date the order 82, 87, 85, 84, 83, 86. The actual dates of composition clearly do not correspond, for Nos. 83 and 87 date from 1785, Nos. 82, 84 and 86 from 1786, and No. 85 from somewhere between the two.

It is interesting to note that the large Paris orchestra consisted of up to seventy strings, with doubled woodwind, but it would be unwise to conclude that Haydn had this in mind when he wrote the works, delighted though he no doubt was to find the music making such a splendidly full sound at its first performances. We know for sure that at the very least the two most fully-scored works (Nos. 82 and 86) were played at Eszterháza by the Prince's band, which at that time numbered around twenty-four players plus trumpets and drums when required—something less than one-third the size of the Paris orchestra. There is, naturally enough, no observable difference in orchestral style between the symphonies other than the expected continuous development that each succeeding year brought.

SYMPHONY NO. 82 in C, "L'ours," brings a treat withheld for twelve years: a C major Festive Symphony incorporating the spine-tingling sound of horns crooked in C alto. (Those who aver that the "Laudon" should incorporate such instruments may read "eight" rather than "twelve".) The scoring has a flute, two oboes, two bassoons, timpani and strings, in addition to the brass line which requires, in the Allegretto, two horns in F, and in the first, third and fourth movements, two horns in C alto *or* two trumpets. Once again there seems every reason not to use trumpets, although it is fairly common to employ them

In a great fury the strings fly up the scale at the rate of an octave in one-and-a-half bars. Thereafter Haydn combines fury and peasant casualness in equal measure. The ringing brilliance of this orchestra in *tutti* passages has to be heard to be believed, yet the growling held bassoon pedal-bass in the second subject (one of several theories as to why this is called the "Bear" Symphony, though this one is not especially convincing) immediately lightens to broad humour. Dissonances also creep in, especially through the insistence of the horns before the recapitulation. The final screaming fanfares of the Vivace Assai having been flung at the listener, a bouncing Allegretto variation movement enters. The element of aggression in the first movement is largely confined to a fierce joy in the second, but the Menuet takes one back to the glories of the "Maria Theresia": wind soli here and there remind one that the whole work is couched in a vein of optimism calculated to make the listener smile at these magnificent sounds as well as glory in them. A better theory concerning the name of the symphony arises at the start of the Finale. Over a drone bass a jolly flute theme plays to the accompaniment of a single repeated stroke on the drum. The theory is that in the Eighteenth century travelling entertainers had dancing bears: since it is common knowledge that such persons would play on pipe and tabor or on bagpipes so that the bear might dance, clearly anyone would recognise this when they heard all these instruments together at the beginning of the Finale—pipe (flute), tabor (drum), bagpipes (drone bass on celli and basses). At least, that is assumed to be one's immediate reaction! The Finale no longer wends its way as in the "entertainment" symphonies, rather it drives on in an uncompromising manner. The colours are vivid and varied and there is a typical Haydn effect near the close: at bar 264 the timpani enter *fortissimo*—a shattering effect since nominally the drums are twice as loud as any other instrument playing at the time (timpani *ff*, everyone else *f*.).*

SYMPHONY NO. 83 in G minor, "La poule," is so entitled because

---

* Unaccountably, only the recording under Ernest Maerzendorfer takes note of this.

of the "clucking" *motif* used as the second subject in the first movement

yet it could apply equally well to the strutting precision of the *staccato* Andante.

Whatever the reason, this minor-keyed work, scored as for "L'ours" but without timpani (or alternative trumpets), is full of high spirits, the dash of the opening movement having a wonderfully sweeping effect. The *staccato* features of the Andante, with its rows of repeated notes, is extraordinarily original. Is not the repetition of short notes followed by a long one typically hen-like? What, too, of the mad flurry up and down the scales by the strings? Haydn is not posing questions, however, and the Menuet is in finest country style; no particular country, but a homage to universal peasantry. The Finale goes in quasi-hunting style. But that it is in an inappropriate key for the period, it would seem proper for the many hammered affirmations of tonic and dominant to be supported by timpani. The orchestration, however, is turned with a steely edge to render this unnecessary, and the high-lying winds make the forward-looking development a matter of high drama.

It is not entirely clear why SYMPHONY NO. 84 in E flat should fail to be amongst Haydn's more popular works. It could be part of a general tendency to shy away from Haydn's E flat symphonies: E flat is his "comfortable" key, and the orchestra lies in such a way that the typical Haydn tricks of bold interjectory colours from the wind instruments —notably the horns—are less easily brought off. Certainly E flat always has a mellifluous influence. No. 84 is also not easy to interpret, for after a brief introduction the Allegro requires great poise. It simply will not make its proper effect if, on the one hand, it is rushed or if, on the other, the dynamics are played down. When both faults are present the work can appear superficial, which is hardly fair on the composer of such a beautiful piece of craftsmanship. The Andante is tonally colourful but needs exactitude of rhythm and careful placement of the *sforzandi* which must disturb the mood but not the rhythmic flow. The form is that of theme and variations but the whole movement moves under way with the steady tread of the fourth variation which, especially in the brilliance of the brass, has a wonderfully open-air feeling. Just before the close there is a touching farewell from the woodwinds in concertante style to a *pizzicato* accompaniment. A remarkably smooth Menuet now glides gently upon the scene—hitherto many ornaments have meant many accents but here, helped by good use of bassoons, the mood is predominantly dark and the Trio, though lighter in texture, is sad. The Finale does not bowl one over but has plenty of dash and vivacity—again, gentle beginnings and the weight of block chords to support the whirling strings. A long, quiet passage replaces the usual climactic end of the development and even the recapitulation has damped-down dynamics.

SYMPHONY NO. 85 in B flat, "La Reine de France," was reputedly a favourite of Marie Antoinette. Its scoring is the same as for Nos. 83 and 84. The slow introduction is extremely imposing, with French rhythms and rising scales giving a foretaste of the opening of Beethoven's Seventh Symphony. The theme of the Vivace is a long, smooth falling line, treated almost immediately to powerful string accompaniments in a driving rhythm. Is the descending figure in the second subject (found also in the first movement of Symphony No. 60) really a deliberate quotation from the "Farewell" symphony or merely a subconscious echo?

see examples on next page

The Romance, marked *allegretto*, is a set of variations on a popular French folk-theme: Haydn rarely writes to please his intended audience but when he does, it is only because he has something original to say with the chosen material. The Menuetto has a theme of basic simplicity, its colouring pure B flat Haydn—golden horns high up, elegant oboes setting off cross-rhythmic string ideas, horns descending to aid bassoons in moments of force, and bassoon-tone superimposed over violins for the Trio. There is nothing complicated about the Finale either: except to decide whether the form is near enough that of a rondo to be called one, since it breaks the rules by developing the material instead of just presenting alternative tunes. No matter, the Parisian audiences thrilled to it and since La Reine herself liked it success was assured.

SYMPHONY NO. 86 in D was the first symphony in this key where

85

60

45

Haydn incorporated trumpet and drum parts during composition. Only ten more years of symphonic composition remained, yet the total of fully scored D major symphonies reached five in that time (Nos. 86, 93, 96, 101 and 104). Trumpets and timpani are the only additions to the basic Paris scoring, but the orchestra is certainly used in an effective and original way. After a slow introduction, which is impressive in direct proportion to the slowness of its pulse, the Allegro Spiritoso dashes breathlessly in. Nowhere is the effect of repeated notes used so extensively as here. The effect when performed by the small orchestra at Eszterháza must have been electrifying, with the hammered repetitions reinforced at cardinal points by the harsh, military clatter of the shallow timpani of the period, beaten with hard-ended sticks, cutting viciously through the crystal-clear textures. The lacerating punctuation of the trumpets across the small string body would have had extreme brilliance. Here is one symphony where the weight and splendour of the big Paris orchestra might have been a hindrance rather than a help. Entitled Capriccio, the Largo is beautiful indeed and its cautious, detached opening notes lead to something extraordinarily moving as the music progresses. Amidst the peace there are frequent full-orchestra attacks which stir the mind. The Menuet does not change the mood entirely, although its confidence and noble structuring are in themselves enough to dispel the more serious thoughts engendered by the Capriccio. It is not until the Trio that true light-heartedness returns. The tune has an Austrian turn of phrase, the rhythm influenced by that country's dances, and all in all it only requires the words of a Christmas carol to be added to this bassoon-and-strings serenade for it to become even more popular. The Finale returns to playing upon the device of repeated notes. Again the timpani writing is very advanced but the most brilliant stroke of all lies between two exciting episodes: on the second of two first-time bars before the repeat of the exposition, there is a fermata upon a minim, at which every instrument in the orchestra crashes in with the timpani thundering out bottom A.

SYMPHONY NO. 87 in A is scored in the same way, apart from the absence of trumpets and timpani, and opens with the utmost brightness; the beautifully lucid woodwind scoring, with each colour individually audible, is once again evident (the late Seventies and early Eighties had led Haydn to neglect slightly the individuality of his inner parts in favour of overall sonority). Fresh as spring water is the innocent rise and fall of single violin notes at the end of the exposition, and even the smattering of minor keys in the development contrives to sound happy. The brightest moment of all is when, shortly before the recapitulation, Haydn simply stops composing, only to take up where he left off after a calculated indeterminate pause. Over the warmth of held horn notes the comforting (though not always comfortable) Adagio begins, cooled by flute flourishes which mould an extension of the theme with a further subject on oboes. The thought is perhaps too serious for the bassoon to be allowed to contribute its good-humoured voice to the proceedings. This is the test-case slow movement mentioned earlier in which, because of the absence of any *da capo* markings, the length in proportion to the rest of the work may be considered representative. The Menuet is another of those in which ornamental swirls give spice to the strong beats. The instrumental individuality is retained with strings dropping away to allow the wind band full play. The Trio is exceptional in that it allows the first oboe to climb extremely high —Haydn's unconventional treatment of instruments becomes more subtle and varied as time goes on. Only one basic melody is used in the Finale but it is a very flexible idea: used in canon with itself, in fragments, and fugally—responding to almost any compositional device. Although harmonically Haydn's bass lines have for long been self-sufficient, there is something ear-catching about a harpsichord in this symphony—especially in the Finale.* Something is needed to push the bass along in the style of the Finale of Symphony No. 49 and it is difficult to think of anything more appropriate than a harpsichord.

---

* Two recordings employ it: Jones and Vaughan, although the latter just misses recommendation in the Appendix.

8: The Post-Paris Symphonies

Why "Post-Paris" rather than "pre-London"? For two reasons. Symphonies Nos. 88 and 89 were to have joined the remaining six Paris Symphonies but for Haydn's decision to hand them to Johann Tost (of Tost Quartets fame) who was journeying to Paris not long after their composition (probably in 1787). Secondly, Nos. 90 and 91 were owned in autograph by the Comte d'Ogny (1757–1790)—No. 91 was actually dedicated to him—whose support of the Paris concerts, and by implication the Paris Symphonies, was critical to Haydn's symphonic success at this time. The tie with Paris is therefore still fairly strong.

As a group, Nos. 82 to 87 have many elements of consistency; those which follow are more diverse in style. SYMPHONY NO. 88 in G has some highly unusual contents, mostly concerned with orchestration and sound. The construction is straightforward enough. The first movement has a short, slow introduction, followed by a bright, lively Allegro with dancing imitative violin figures and frequent solo spots being afforded a much-favoured flute. Scoring remains one flute, two oboes, two bassoons, two horns and strings, but the first audiences would perhaps have been a little puzzled by observing trumpets and timpani sitting silent throughout the movement. Still more unnerving must have been the slow movement—a beautiful hymn-like Adagio which, after the first quiet statements of the theme, suddenly erupts as both trumpets and drums crash in for the first time ever in a Haydn slow movement.

Did Haydn consciously delay the first full entry in the symphony for so long in order to underline its effect? Possibly, and certainly it provides a heightened moment of drama. The entirely lovable Menuetto lilts upon its swinging way with a quiet drum solo at each double bar, which itself has the effect of making the music surge forward. The Trio is the culmination of Haydn's predilection for syncopation: over a bagpipe-drone the theme wends its highly irregular way, with scarcely a stress (and there are many) in the expected place. It need hardly be said that a tempo in strict relation to that of the Menuetto is essential, otherwise the syncopations have no basic rhythm to upset and the humour goes for nothing. With immense friendliness the Finale begins at a rapid trot—the theme, though turned to fugal fury before the end, is also given the trappings of horn, flute, oboe and bassoon colour with ultra-*staccato* pointing until, after a pause, a timpani-led chord heralds a brief coda. Whirling strings sweep down and up again to heighten the impact of the onslaught of wind and drums—a fitting conclusion to this highly original and, for many years now, extremely popular symphony. How comforting, too, that none of the textual problems of the mid-period symphonies are present, apart from one unauthentic soft drum-roll which some scores put into the Trio. To be correct it should not be there, but its presence does no harm to the music.

SYMPHONY NO. 89 in F begins with five abrupt chords before a mellow theme enters:

A peremptory call to attention, but the mood immediately lightens and a sheer happiness of spirit carries the music forward. Typically, as when such happiness is in evidence, a flute dances with delight. Nor are there any tragedies in the development, merely a long false reprise. It is not hard to see that Haydn is deliberately leading his audience nowhere, but he does it with such grace: even the sweeping descent of first volins against seconds is no more than mock warfare, especially since, when the strings take an angry three-note figure, all the wood-winds do is mock them by imitation. The Andante con Moto (which, like the Finale, represents a re-use of music from one of the concerti for two lyre organizzate which Haydn wrote about 1786) is indeed a worthy melody, suited to infinite variation. Serenade-like yet sad enough to offset the gladness of the first movement without altering the overall mood entirely. The wind instruments are used in a very free manner and unusual colouring is achieved through the combination of oboes with low horns, playing the melody an octave apart. The main theme is long enough to provide a full-scale movement through mere double statement followed by a minor-keyed second theme plus a return to the original. The Menuet is marvellous: the winds intone a theme which includes a sforzato at the start of the second bar—an idea which the full orchestra takes up with insistence. Another country-dance Trio follows, led by the flute, with the lower strings playing a waltz until the solo bassoon joins in the melody to set the seal on the rustic proceedings. In the Rondo-Finale, *vivace assai*, Haydn uses a very unconventional marking (*strascinando*—"dragging") at the end of the main theme. Its meaning is not entirely clear,* but either way this point can be regarded as typical of the dashing high spirits of a most original movement.

There remains just one more Festive Symphony incorporating out--and-out exploitation of high horns, trumpets and timpani—the tower-ing SYMPHONY NO. 90 in C of 1788, which promises drama from the first moments. It seems that in the few works between the Paris and London sets, Haydn was determined to flex all his compositional muscles; in so doing he proves that every style observable in past compositions has now been polished to the utmost. No. 88 stands as an excellent paradigm of all Haydn's characteristic sides—delicacy, fire, fugal writing, bucolic humour. No. 89 is more lightheartedly humorous, and even goes beyond the delightful No. 87 in that direction. No. 90 is the very summit of the C major style. Here the full-orchestra onslaughts which were so thrilling in No. 56 are woven into a pattern which includes solos for woodwind instruments, fierce, modulating string passages, and melodies held so firmly on individual instruments that even the slightest change of mood invites a change of orchestral coloura-tion also. All this is to be found in the first movement which, after a conventional full chord to begin a slow introduction, continues

---

* Antal Dorati has an exceptionally stylish interpretation of this, electing to take the high, supporting note on the violins at this point and allow it to "drag" to the lower octave with exaggerated *portamento*. This creates a delightful effect. There is, however, another view (one taken by Denis Vaughan among several others) and that is to hold the tempo back pointedly at this moment. The *portamento* is also applied but with less exaggeration. Given a firm basic rhythm (and Vaughan in particular achieves just that), the impression is every bit as effective.

hesitantly. A great shout from full orchestra indicates, however, that there is to be decisiveness in this music—and indeed there is from that moment on. The trumpet part is here reasonably independent of the horns although, since Haydn had C alto horns easily to hand but trumpets had always to be sought separately, it is quite possible that even this symphony might have been played at Eszterháza without the latter. The intensity of the first movement is gripping, the same flautist who was so high-spirited in No. 89 now expounding grander ideas. The brazen close to the movement is late Haydn *par excellence*—the unity is all the more impressive since the repeated notes in the introduction are taken up joyously in the Allegro Assai. If a conductor is careful he can relate the tempo in the ratio $1:2$ and thereby make the point more clearly.

The easy-going melody of the Andante is announced with a bassoon leading the strings in the new richly-coloured style. This is a set of variations on another of Haydn's eminently variable themes—in fact, double variations with an alternative minor-keyed section brought in after each statement of the main melody. Typically Haydn often writes "fully written-out" repeats so that even the restatements within variations are themselves varied. The striding majesty of the Menuet, with its brilliant brass writing and angular woodwind comments, is a rare gem of the C major *genre*. It is interesting to note that the trumpets leave the horn-line for the fanfarish moments. Their omission would make this a more lyrical work, yet any echo effects find the oboes adding their tone to each reflection of a horn statement: although the withdrawal of trumpet support might leave the oboes sounding a little bare, the thematic continuity would not be impaired. This seems to suggest that Haydn always had in mind the possibility of trumpets being unavailable. The Finale takes two standard basic elements of symphonic writing—drama and humour—and welds them together. Even in the Menuet, despite its regular pulse, there was never any square symmetry: a fourteen-bar length to be dealt with rather than eight-, twelve- or sixteen-. Similarly the merry theme of the Finale fails to come to the expected conclusion before the full orchestra strikes home across the rhythm; a splendidly irritable whirl of violins ends the exposition as if in desperation to say something different amidst such varied colouring, with its quasi-military overlay of brass. The development is very advanced, and despite many attempts at restating the main theme it is clear that Haydn has no intention of going more than one or two bars until the theme proper is reached. A full close plus long pause (long enough to bewilder any listeners who had let their mind wander) is the extraordinary introduction to the final onslaught of minor keys, which very shortly turns to the brilliance of C major in a triumphant conclusion.

What is there left for Haydn to do before the London series? To see how his lyrical E flat style is progressing one turns to SYMPHONY NO. 91 which also dates from 1788. The critic Bernard Jacobson has referred to Haydn's C major and E flat major traditions as reflecting two contrasting aspects of his character—"Eusebius and Florestan." This is more than a theory, for its truth is affirmed at every turn in Haydn's career. No. 91 could scarcely be further removed from No. 90, yet no one but Haydn could have written either. The slow introduction of the E flat is no more than a simple announcement of a work of tunefulness rather than tension. The curving, beauteous contours of the Allegro Assai are touched in elegantly by a firmly-moving bass line, written in such a way as not to impose unduly since the upper lines, with their casual woodwind decorations floating graciously in and out of the texture, are all-important. There is one anomaly, however: this Allegro Assai loses a great deal of its potency if it is taken quickly.* The variation movement which follows, marked *andante*, is a different matter—no harm is done if this goes at almost *allegretto*, for its bouncy accompaniments do not encourage soul-searching. The most delightful variation is the early one for bassoon; the most extraordinary, the late one for full orchestra with its massive trills beneath horns in high B flat—a sound unlike anything else in Haydn, pre-dating similar examples in the first movement of Gustav Mahler's Third Symphony (1896).

---

* There are conductors who feel a need to give it considerable breadth, among them Karl Böhm, Denis Vaughan, Eugen Jochum, Heinrich Swoboda, and Mogens Wöldike, and they bring a conviction which seems to pass by those more faithful to the score.

The Menuet is a fully-scored piece with a most tuneful Trio led by bassoon. The Universal Edition omits bassoon from the very first chord—effectively causing its melody to start on the second note (see Appendix for recordings of this movement). The Finale is based on a sweetly beautiful melody—again, it does not benefit from being rushed, although in a suitably elegant performance it may be taken at a reasonable pace given careful articulation.

The falling woodwind harmonies in the rapidly modulating section three-quarters of the way through is a new touch in Haydn to date.

The scene seems more or less set for a final stroke of symphonic originality before setting off for London. It occurs, however, in an unexpected way. In SYMPHONY NO. 92 in G of 1789—later used when Haydn received his Doctorate of Music at Oxford—one finds the experienced composer tying up a loose end of style, G major having been used in conjunction with full-scale orchestra only in Nos. 54 and 88. In view of the devastating success of No. 88 it is hardly surprising that Haydn wished to exploit the medium further. The effect of No. 92 is a continuation of the lucidity of layout of No. 88. Trumpets and drums do not shout and thunder; rather, they are given chords of short note-length which add point to certain climactic features of the music whilst avoiding the fault of overlaying the inner parts which feature light but clear woodwinds—often solo rather than in pairs. The first movement, after a dark, silky introduction, is the epitome of clarity. Woodwind solos abound, while the horns are largely reserved for *tutti* passages. The suave Adagio follows, its opening pages as noble as those of the Largo in No. 88, with a strongly staccato *minore* section. This is actually marked "staccato" at the beginning and has the staccato dots painstakingly inscribed throughout, not merely at the beginning with its implied continuance as in earlier symphonies. The smoothness of the first theme

contrasts with the sudden hammering chords by all except violins at bar 40

effectively doubling the tempo, since now there are eight accents to the bar instead of four. At bar 48 the rhythm is broken down still further

the subjective effect being of a still faster tempo.

Unfortunately there is a very bad tradition in this symphony whereby performers, not content with Haydn doubling the speed through change of note-values, actually step-up the basic tempo at bar 40 *in addition* to the written-in increase of pace. The result is often an unmusical gabble, with the inevitable weary winding down of tempo to accommodate the return of the main theme: all too often this returns at an uncomfortable halfway-speed making nonsense of the structure. Only the *Funeral March* of Beethoven's "Eroica" Symphony has suffered comparable damage through misinterpretation, where often the appearance of a *tutti* section seems to prompt a mad onsurge of tempo.

If bad performing traditions are to be exploded, then another occurs all too frequently in the third movement: an extensive and subtle Menuet in grand style with the Haydn fingerprint of notes phrased in twos:

The ultimate subtlety lies at the beginning of the Trio where the melody, if isolated, sounds as if it starts heavily on a downbeat. When following the Menuet in context, however, that seeming "downbeat" is in fact the third beat of the bar, the whole section going across the rhythm throughout. Taking the horn part, since this gives the lead, the music sounds like this:

Unfortunately, however, there is a bad tradition whereby some conductors delay the Trio by one beat, and what reaches the ear, regardless of Haydn's quite contrary instructions, is:

Gone is all the originality, the trick of syncopation killed for the whole Trio. Needless to say, the other habit of breaking the Trio from the Minuet by an indeterminate pause also has the effect of putting the accent incorrectly on the beat, since the ear still assumes the delayed first note to be the downbeat.*

The Finale brings to mind just one problem. The racing opening theme for first violins is in bare octaves over a solo cello—a wonderfully bleak effect—yet some sources have a harmonic second violin part. Perhaps later editors could not face such stark clarity in the parts, but the autograph makes it quite clear that no other harmonies were intended. It is interesting to note the insistent military trumpet and drum rhythm which becomes almost obsessive by the end of the Finale:

Yet so crisp are the textures that, for all its force, it does not overpower. Once again it does well to recall that the harsh, shallow sound of the timpani of the period would never mask the tones.

---

* In Denis Vaughan's recording it is interesting to note that the one-beat delay is to be heard in the American pressing but not in the British equivalent.

9: The London Symphonies

Some of the symphonies mentioned previously may be unknown to listeners, but there can be few music-lovers professing anything more than a passing interest in Haydn who will not have heard at least the majority of the London Symphonies. There are some earlier works which it is only possible to encounter upon records but the last twelve are played with reasonable regularity in the concert hall. Recordings themselves show very different facets of these works of genius—the final harvest of a lifetime's experience of a great composer—but how did Haydn expect them to *sound* and, indeed, how *did* they sound at their early performances in London where he directed them himself?

The short answer is "very loud and very exciting". The first group of Salomon concerts took place at the Hanover Square Rooms. The concert room held 800* and a contemporary account (in the diary of Charlotte Papendiek) describes the layout of the orchestra: an important feature of this was the steep raking, with Haydn directing from the keyboard at the front, Salomon and his group above and behind, and "at the back raised high up were the drums." On either side were

---

* By special arrangements 1500 could be accommodated.

the various wind instruments. The orchestra for the first series was about forty strong: imagine the impact in the relatively small concert room of this phalanx of wind and drums hammering out a *forte* passage. On Haydn's second visit to London the later concerts took place at the King's Theatre in the Haymarket. A greater number of instruments were used and, most important of all, although in the last concerts the orchestra was not far short of sixty strong, including some forty strings, it is clear that the woodwinds were doubled—at least in the *tutti* sections. A far cry from the upholstered Nineteenth- and Twentieth-century performances, now mercifully dying out of fashion, where some sixty strings are allowed to win an unequal battle against Haydn's original wind parts, to give a pleasant, characterless wash of beautiful sound with opaque textures. It is also interesting to recall that the Hanover Square Rooms had a vaulted ceiling: the ambience produced by the reflection of winds and percussion must have made for surprising sonority in a relatively modest-sized hall.

The proportions of the King's Theatre at that time were not much more generous: the illustrations (see plates 19) give some idea of the space provided.

Although the outlines of the London Symphonies are widely known, some of the problems of authentic style have often been overlooked. With one or two exceptions, the errors perpetrated are no longer gross, although the welcome trend towards obtaining a true "Haydn sound" has flourished very slowly. Even before the Second World War the London Symphonies had benefited from being put into better shape by Dr. Helmut Schultz and Dr. Ernst Praetorius, the latter musicologist redeeming his continuation of the misconception of the "Maria Theresia" symphony by publishing, nearly forty years ago, some refreshingly accurate revisions of these later works. Yet even this did not shake performers from their bad old ways: for example, although in 1938 Praetorius reinstated the clarinet parts, for long erroneously omitted, from the Trio of No. 103, there are still recordings dating from the stereo era in which a faulty score is used. At the same period Schultz brought to light the trumpet and timpani parts for the slow movement of No. 96, for long omitted by a Nineteenth-century editor, yet there are still recordings* which do not recognise this development.

Let us consider the London Symphonies, therefore, on the assumption that their best-known features are already familiar, and that the modern listener has, on the one hand, heard the story of the "Surprise" in Symphony No. 94 often enough to prefer an account of the rarely-heard trumpet part of the first movement of the same work, and is on the other, less interested in why the "Drum Roll" got its name than

---

* By Haitink and Walter.

in the substantial amount of music cut from the Finale which is only heard today on two select gramophone records (see Appendix).

Their dates of composition are as follows, the autograph score providing the factual basis: Nos. 93 to 96—1791; Nos. 97–98—1792 (No. 98 probably written over a period between 1791 and 1792); No. 99—1793; Nos. 100–102—1794; Nos. 103–104—1795. The exact order of the 1791 symphonies is not readily ascertainable. They seem to have been performed in the order 96, 95, 93, 94 during 1791 and 1792—this may also represent their order of composition, although the precise order of Nos. 96 and 95 cannot be verified. Very likely Haydn was working on both symphonies at the same time. These slight differences are not serious enough to prevent an examination in numerical order.

*

SYMPHONY NO. 93 in D, scored for two each of flutes, oboes, bassoons, horns, trumpets and drums with strings, has many intriguing features, including a very powerful introduction with great drum onslaughts and a majestic Allegro Assai which is problematic as to the most suitable tempo. With few problems of text to trouble one here, one is faced instead with a debate as to the very nature of the music: is it broad, noble and measured or a swift, fast waltz?* It is quite amazing how different tempi can give such contrasted effects. The one argument against a really fast tempo lies in the very subtle dynamic markings: even as early as the fourth, fifth, sixth and seventh bars of the Allegro Assai, Haydn marks second violins, originally *p*, down to *pp* in bar 5, whilst first violins, in the same short space of four bars, go from *p* to *poco f* followed by a *fz* and a return to *p*. Such detail is hard to achieve at speed,† but at what pace do these subtleties impinge most effectively upon the consciousness?

The Largo Cantabile begins with a pastoral theme (a *Ranz des Vaches* which brings to mind the Finale of Beethoven's "Pastoral"

---

* The first is best typified in an old recording of a magnificently perceptive performance by Hermann Scherchen, whose merits as a Haydn conductor have never been properly recognised; more recently Jones, Szell and Bernstein have taken a similar view. The latter concept is embodied in performances by Almeida and Maerzendorfer. The dilemma is which tempo to adopt for what is, at any speed, as near the nature of a waltz as one hears in Haydn. The *allegro assai* marking, as so often with Haydn, is not helpful. The recording by Almeida is the outcome of sessions wherein the conductor thought over the problem at length, working it out in practical terms and finally opting for the faster tempo. If this is the nearest to the truth, the analyst may not describe the music as "broad," "majestic" and so on, but rather with "rhythmic liveliness," "sudden dynamic contrast," "swift interjection of woodwind colouring," and so on.

† Although Almeida and Maerzendorfer succeed.

Symphony), expounded only by the leaders of the four string sections. Not until bar 9 does this music become anything other than a string quartet (faulty editions have for years spoilt the effect by giving the quartet passage to all the strings). One of the subtleties of the movement is the extensive inclusion of repeated timpani notes—particularly when asked to alternate between *p* and *f*. The crisp sound of these instruments, striking clearly from above the body of the orchestra, must have made a wonderful effect in the Hanover Square Rooms. At the end of the movement there is a passage of humour which is far from subtle, though none the less enjoyable, where one instrument after another (bassoon, violin, flute) loses its way tonally until the two bassoons together hammer out *fortissimo* the long sought-for bottom C.*

The Menuetto roars into its stride at once: *allegro* says Haydn, and the rumbustious dance whirls the listener along in a welter of excitement, high trumpets adding a steely descant to the proceedings. At bar 31 there begins a *pianissimo* drum roll which has become *forte* six bars later. Several conductors make this into a long timpani crescendo: the effect is thrilling and musically has total conviction—the Minuet of Symphony No. 104 may be quoted as a parallel. The Trio batters away furiously, with massive brass and drum chords which are military in feeling and tone but with a lacerating power that rings out over a heavy peasant dance.

The Finale is marked *presto ma non troppo*, presumably implying a speed faster than *allegro*; since the metre is 2/4 this means a quick pace, despite the cautionary words. Haydn intended to revise this finale but almost certainly never did; unless this is in fact the revision itself, it is difficult to see how this dashing piece could have been improved. There are many moments which link it to the rest of the symphony —including another long *pianissimo* drum roll, (the performance of which requires no more than clarity in execution, since this time a crescendo would lead to nothing in particular). After this, however, there are militaristic brass and drum fanfares which show that the aggression of the Trio is not yet forgotten.

No-one can be unfamiliar with the similarly-scored SYMPHONY NO. 94 in G, the "Surprise," (known rather differently in German as "Mit dem Paukenschlag"—"With the Timpani Stroke"). It has four vivid movements, with a slow introduction more cautious than the bold opening to No. 93. It awakes gradually with a gentle luminosity from the horns filling the harmonies. The Vivace Assai goes with a will but again there is the problem of the ultra-explicit directions, "hairpin" markings against first violin, and a wealth of phrase-marks

---

* Sometimes performers seem afraid of overdoing the vulgarity of this joke (though not Georg Szell); the criterion should perhaps be that if, in concert, none of the audience laughs, then the episode must have been underplayed.

12: Drawing by Nathaniel Dance showing three musicians of Haydn's time, identified by Edward Croft-Murray as Karl Friedrich Abel (cello), the younger Pieltain (horn), and John Christian Fischer, Gainsborough's son-in-law (oboe) (photography by Douglas Smith).

13: Performance of L'incontro improvviso (?) at Eszterháza,
with Haydn at the cembalo (Munich Theatermuseum)

14: Baryton of 1732

15: B flat alto crook (left) and A crook

16: C basso crook (left) and B flat basso coupler

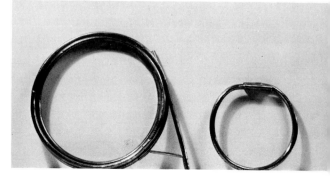

17: Horn crooked in B flat alto, attributed to Jahn of Paris (c. 1800) (Horniman Museum)

18: Same horn crooked in B flat basso, showing a C basso crook plus a B flat basso coupler (Horniman Museum)

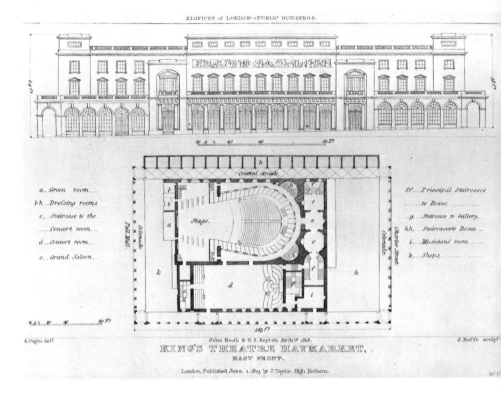

a....Green room....
bb...Dressing rooms....
c....Staircase to the
....Concert room....
d...Concert room....
e...Grand Saloon....

ff....Principal Staircases....
....to Boxes....
g....Staircase to Gallery....
hh....Staircase to Boxes....
i....Musicians' room......
k....Shops....

A.Pugin delt

John Nash & G.S. Repton Archts 1818.

J. Roffe sculpt

KING'S THEATRE HAYMARKET,
EAST FRONT.

London, Published June. 1, 1825 by J.Taylor. High Holborn.

19: The King's Theatre, Haymarket, where most of Haydn's later London Symphonies were first heard (see p. 126) (British Museum)

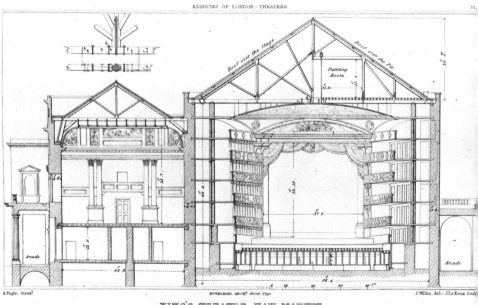

A.Pugin dirext

NOVOSIELSKI, ARCHt about 1790

J.Willis. del.—J.Le Keux sculpt

KING'S THEATRE, HAY MARKET.
TRANSVERSE SECTION, SHEWING THE CONCERT ROOM.

London, Published Augt 1,1825, by J.Taylor, High Holborn.

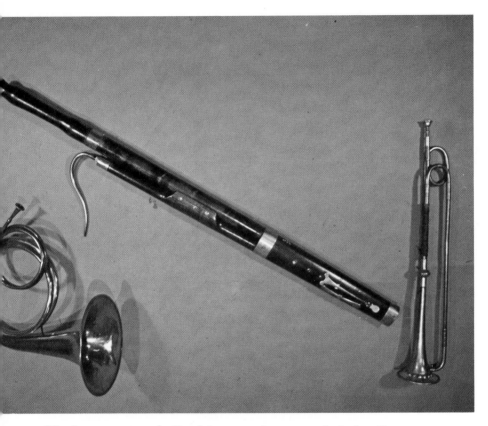

20: Instruments of Haydn's era: horn crooked in G (anonymous, Eighteenth century), bassoon (by Proser, 1777), and F trumpet crooked in D (by Kerner, 1806) (Horniman Museum)

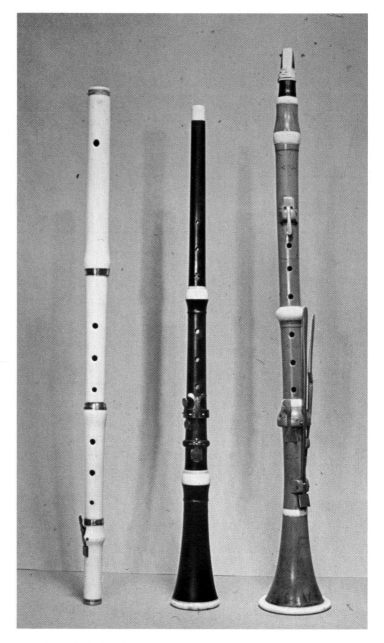

21: *Woodwind of Haydn's era: flute in ivory with silver mounts (by Cahusac, 1755–98), oboe in dark stained wood with ivory mounts (by Kusder, c. 1790), B flat clarinet in boxwood with ivory mounts (by G. Astor & Co., c. 1810) (Horniman Museum)*

on certain parts in order to bring them out and contrast them with *staccati* elsewhere. This movement cannot be taken at too rapid a pace if it is to be properly realised. The expressive violin line, surprisingly important for Haydn who so often allows other colours to break in with force, is set off by some interesting features in the brass and occasionally the timpani which, at their first entry in the development section, have retuned the G drum to A to support the massive power of the trumpets. This moment was even more thrilling as originally written by Haydn, for instead of C trumpets attacking D, as in the final version of the score, the whole movement used trumpets in G which would have screamed a sustained high A *in altissimo*. Haydn wrote this part on the assumption that such instruments would be available to him in England but after composing the first movement realised that this was not so and replaced them with the more conventional C trumpets.*

The famous Andante has is "surprise" crash at bar 16 (a chord which, in the autograph, omits trumpets). Much discussion has surrounded the movement, not so much for this one moment† but more in matters of tempo and the ability to sustain momentum. A fast pace is not the whole story, for there comes a time when the tempo is too fast to sustain Haydn's important *tenuto* markings.‡ Other careful markings occur in the massive *tutti* sections—that which commences at bar 107, for example, has only brass and first violins marked *fortissimo*, the remainder *forte*. The rumbustious Menuet has its tempo stepped up to *allegro molto*, although it is not without elegance.§ The important point about the performance of this movement is to retain a degree of rhythmic swing and an important factor in this is the correct use of the appoggiaturas. To play these as crushed notes (i.e. acciacaturas) is a serious but very widespread misconception which spoils the melody line and brings in an angularity foreign to the movement.‖ The Finale is as light-hearted as anyone could wish and

---

* Only one recording allows us to hear Haydn's original—that by Leslie Jones and the Little Orchestra of London. In the interests of consistency of tone the "G trumpet" (actually a modern valved trumpet in D), being of a brighter *timbre* than today's average orchestral instrument, was also used by the first trumpeter of the orchestra (Denis Clift) for the remainder of the recording.

† All too many performances play this down. Szell and Maerzendorfer respectively are the best protagonists of this moment.

‡ Furtwängler was notably successful in doing this and further took a courageously slow tempo—a speed which in other hands might well sound a great deal too measured.

§ Except perhaps in the alarming performance by Arturo Toscanini, who appears to regard *allegro molto* as meaning *prestissimo possibile*.

‖ Again Hermann Scherchen was the first to record a performance where these matters were properly attended to, the sour reaction of critics of the Fifties being a depressing reminder to Haydn scholars that even in that more enlightened age far too many people were prepared to accept what they were used to hearing in preference to what Haydn meant.

includes a *Paukenschlag* at bar 233 (lasting in fact for sixteen *Schlagen*) which Eugen Jochum, for instance, regards as being as important a shock as the more famous one in the Andante. How the *forte* marking came to be omitted in numerous editions, a meaningless *piano* being substituted, it is difficult to imagine, but at least the more intelligent conductors of the past (again including Hermann Scherchen) saw the dramatic intention and provided a drum *crescendo*: second best, maybe, but an intelligent emendation in the right direction in the absence of the truth.

In SYMPHONY NO. 95 in C minor, scored as for Nos. 93 and 94 but with only a single flute, one musician takes a view which opposes that of the Universal Edition in general and H. C. Robbins Landon in particular, believing that the horns, where crooked in C for the last thirty-one bars of the first movement and throughout the whole of the finale, should be played an octave below the printed notes. This is Leslie Jones, who in his recording demonstrates the brilliance of the horns when played as written at these places. If the logic of this theory is to be deduced it seems that the brightening in the first movement from C minor to C major, in conjunction with which Haydn requires the horns to change their E flat crooks to C, should be supported by horns which brighten their *timbre* from tonic E to the C above rather than descend the interval of a third to the lower C. If this is accepted, then the Finale must naturally have high horns in order to fall into line. It is very likely that no crooks for C alto were available for the first performances in England, but as so often with Haydn, the mere circumstances of early performance need not be a guide for *every* performance if one feels that the composer might have heard the music otherwise in his mind's ear. Leaving this dispute aside, it is at once obvious that this, the only London Symphony to be without a slow introduction, is a dark work of serious mood. Haydn is not concerned with vivid colours (trumpets and timpani have only two notes each in the whole of the sixty-one-bar exposition). The phrasing is also less detailed than in other works and in the major-keyed section at the end of the first movement not a slur is marked over the violins for the last twenty-nine bars. The music is hewn out with sombre fierceness and even the homely theme of the Andante (or in some authentic editions other than the autograph: Andante Cantabile) does not bring relief. Just as the first movement had some flourishes for the Konzertmeister (presumably Salomon), so the *Andante* has an extensive cello solo. Why the phrasing for this instrument differs from that of the orchestra when the main theme is repeated is rather mysterious. It is in the orchestral basses—now no longer tied unquestioningly to the apron-strings of the cellos—that there appear some of Haydn's homely comforting harmonies. This movement may be the first indication that as he grew older Haydn became prepared to look back—hitherto an uncharacteristic notion. Basses and violins in unison is another weighty expedient in this relatively short but certainly meaningful movement.

The Menuet does not change the mood at all, being full of long grace-notes which give a highly original, undulating form to the themes (here, more than anywhere else, the playing of appoggiaturas as crushed notes is ruinously unacceptable).

One may look in vain, however, for sounds other than those which are close-knit and euphonious, unless it be the timpani in the latter part, beating out a doom-laden tattoo on low C which marks the rhythm of an otherwise ultra-smooth dance. The Trio is a miniature cello concerto—again there are anomalies, for in the second part the violins are echoed by the soloist with differently marked bowing. The Finale is swift and vivacious. If the C alto theory is not accepted, then the innate sonority of the scoring gives a majesty which is more than a little unbending. At bars 44 and 45 an anomaly occurs with trumpet chords but no horns. In a footnote to the Universal Edition score there is the interesting comment that "we presume Haydn wanted horns to double trumpets"—an intriguing proposition because in order to do this they would have to have been playing in C alto! In short, the two opposing notions have a profound effect upon the basic *sound* of the symphony.

SYMPHONY NO. 96 in D has two flutes but is otherwise scored as for No. 95. This is a work which suffered more than most from unauthentic editions. Further, the gross faults have continued to be perpetrated through the use of these dubious editions and even today are still encountered. The anonymous editors did some strange things, but perhaps the addition of spurious trumpet and drum parts to the introduction, if unnecessary, was at least not greatly out of style. The downward curve of the *staccato* bassoon solo at the beginning of the Allegro gives a clue to the light-hearted nature of the early part of the movement. First violins take a subsidiary role but do insinuate a simple rhythm from the outset which bears remembering.

Indeed, it can scarcely be forgotten since the movement is rarely free
from it, particularly in the development. As usual, Haydn is preparing
the listener for a remarkable passage of highly-coloured orchestration.
At the end of the development trumpets and horns an octave apart
break the violin rhythm and hammer away at this figure:

During the recapitulation there are these massive answering fanfares,
trumpets against horns:

until eventually, twenty-five bars before the end of the movement, with
woodwinds and strings still insisting on the main theme, the following
rhythms are hammered out with immense force again and again:

with the trumpets supported by timpani over fiery violin semiquavers,
the violins becoming silent to allow the horns at the lower octave to
make their attack clear. The end of the whole movement is a triumphant
fortissimo with the trumpet rhythm now on timpani alone and the
melody high in the brass. At the Hanover Square Rooms this must
have been a thrilling sound—one, moreover, which the audience would
have heard twice, for alone among the London Symphonies Haydn asks
for the second part of the movement to be repeated as well as the first.
    The reason for the fragmented nature of the melody used for
the slow movement begins to make itself clear to the listener at about

bar five, when it is shown how easy it is to split up the component parts in concertante fashion, using strings and each woodwind section in turn to expound the melody in a most ear-catching manner. At bar 9 there is a thunderous *tutti*—how the early editions could have printed the revisions without even suspecting the presence of trumpets and timpani, especially at this point, is difficult to conceive. Haydn is now in his element: full military fanfares, variations upon a theme that do not have to be in regular form, and above all a return to his beloved concertante style. The sparing use of *pizzicato* in the bass makes for a transparent sound until at the end there appears a veritable aviary of solo instruments: solo first and second violins, violas reduced to two (then divided), and finally, amid woodwind trills and flourishes, the strings bringing the movement to rest *pianissimo*.

The probable reason for the quirks of editions lies in this being one of the first two symphonies to be copied in England; clearly the English copyists would not be nearly so familiar with Haydn's style. In the Menuetto of this symphony there are even publications which misprint the notes of the main tune. Correctly done it is a sturdy, emphatic piece. After the first double bar there is an echo of the horn-against-trumpet battle in the first movement.

After unison fanfares before the close, Haydn goes straight into a lilting Trio in which the oboe has a quaint melody with wide intervals —almost a predecessor of Twentieth-century "Dixieland" style.

In some unauthentic scores there is a marvellous effect when the trumpet doubles the opening trio phrase at the octave (making it more "Dixieland" still), a disturbing moment in some ways since the effect is so witty and Haydn-like that the ear is left wishing its authenticity could be justified.

"The last movement I recommend to be played as *pianissimo* as possible and the tempo very quick," says Haydn in a letter to Marianne von Genzinger. The movement is already a whirlwind of suppressed fury and the alteration of its marking from *vivace* in the autograph to *vivace assai* in several authentic copies and prints is certainly Haydn's intention. The first *forte* is delayed until 95 bars have been played and even then it is a wild development of the rushing theme, not merely a solid affirmation. In a quiet section before the coda, several instrumental groups take the main melody down to its component parts before, punctuated by broken timpani rhythms across held brass, the symphony is hurled to a riotous conclusion which includes a lacerating eight-bar timpani roll for good measure.

The CONCERTANTE in B flat, for oboe, bassoon, violin, cello and orchestra (known usually as the Sinfonia Concertante), was written in 1792 and first appeared at the Salomon Concerts in March of that year —probably as a counter to the success being enjoyed by Pleyel, Haydn's pupil, in rival concerts at that time. Here the Concertante was an important feature and it is obvious that Salomon would wish Haydn to better his pupil. This delightful three-movement work, with its clear-cut solo-writing and colourful orchestration, was for years known only in an arranged version. Though it never deviated as disastrously from the composer's intention as authorities have tended to assume, the original is nonetheless the version to enjoy. Without doubt the layout requires B flat alto horns to be used (their possible unavailability at early performances notwithstanding) and has a transparency* which stems directly from the clarity of the lower lines. The recitative as each soloist tries a scale or two at the beginning of the Finale is hilarious, and the benign good humour, though taking the symphony no further along the paths of development, helps one to obtain a more rounded view of the London period.

SYMPHONY NO. 97 in C is the last in the long line of C major symphonies. This time, however, Haydn abandons his typical use of horns in high C: it is clear at once that the writing is for horns in C

* Demonstrated by Antal Dorati in his recording as by no other performance.

basso and the scoring (two each of flutes, oboes, bassoons, horns, trumpets and drums, with strings) is perhaps the most Beethoven-like and Nineteenth-century inclined of any Haydn symphony to date. A new grandeur has arrived, but after the powerful *adagio* introduction the theme starts with a glance back at the old Festive style. Note how the horns here are written an octave above the trumpets—that is to say, when crooked in C-basso they are once again in unison with the trumpets as of old:

Thereafter the parts are laid out more conventionally, with the horns written at a similar pitch to the trumpets but sounding at the lower octave. There is an immediate attack upon tonic and dominant, and the first signs of the aggressiveness with which the timpani are to be employed in this symphony. This section is amazingly reminiscent of a similar passage near the opening of the "Laudon" Symphony a decade and a half earlier.

The second subject has a wonderful lilt, a true forerunner of Johann Strauss.

If the development is dramatic in a predictably powerful way, the strength of full orchestra rises at the close of the movement to a massive onslaught of quavers from every instrument. How the sound of the wind band must have blazed across the Hanover Square Rooms! Perhaps aware of the finality of these chords Haydn wrote "Laus Deo" (which is always found at the end of his works) at this point, supplementing it with "Fine Laus Deo" at the close of the symphony. The Adagio ma Non Troppo is a theme-and-variations movement which takes kindly to a swift pace. The chief feature of this relatively less complicated piece is a central major-keyed section where Haydn requires the violins to play *al ponticello* and later *vicino al ponticello*: the subtle difference in terminology is difficult to recreate in terms of sound. On modern instruments the effect is interestingly harsh and nasal in the decorative lines of notes.

The Minuet is one for a great hall full of elegant people, with a sweeping splendour and the sonority of the full wind band making it sing out gloriously. Formally it is the most adventurous of all Haydn's Minuets, for the repeats are fully written-out with different orchestration each time round. The same is true of the Trio. One focal point in the Menuetto is the tremendous *forte* timpani solos on C which slam home a series of quavers, drowning out the soft tick-tock cello accompaniment before it has finished. "But no-one could hear my bottom C with all that racket going-on," complained an eminent British cellist after a recording session. "Who wants to?" was the conductor's unsympathetic rejoinder. "You string fellows were so much dross to Haydn. Why else do you think he placed the timpani and the winds high above the rest in his London performances?" In view of the many solos written for Salomon, including a really excellent opportunity for him to shine in the Trio section of this movement, that comment could be thought uncompromising but certainly it is pertinent, in that what the cello plays *piano* is irrelevant in the face of the violent *forte* eruption from the timpani. The solo appears four times: the repeats, being written in full, occur *after* the Trio as well as *before*.

The Finale is another of Haydn's whirlwinds which starts deceptively quietly. After the theme is stated the horns play the same chord *staccato* twenty-nine times followed by another chord on trumpets which runs for another seventeen. Given exact similarity in volume between the two instruments, the effect is tense as the first big outburst strikes the ear. In mid-movement there is a thrilling flying passage for violins, barely within the bounds of playability given the *presto assai* marking. At the end there is a wonderful farewell joke: with two fermatas over successive minims, an air of doubt is created; the process is repeated (note how Haydn does not ask for the tempo to become slower) and suddenly, with the brass grabbing the melody, the coda blazes out within a few bars of the end.

Never before in a single movement of any symphony had Haydn used horns in B flat basso, nor (discounting the Concertante) trumpets or drums in the key of B flat. It is, therefore, worth looking into the required pitch for horns in SYMPHONY NO. 98 in B flat which is otherwise scored for one flute and two each of oboes, bassoons, trumpets and drums, with strings and cembalo. It should first be mentioned that no recording has ever employed horns in any key other than B flat basso for Symphony No. 98—it is also clear that it is possible to play the parts at the higher octave if required. In either octave a logical sound pattern is preserved although circumstantial evidence makes it clear that at the London performances B flat basso would have been the crook used by the horn players. This is also the modern performing tradition.

The *adagio* introduction is related to the opening of the *allegro* section in terms of minor/major, and what a manipulative theme it is—three long notes and six short, a noble rhythm (employed for the Finale of Beethoven's Fifth Symphony no less).

BEETHOVEN

The music grows sturdily and wells into a racing Allegro, in which the main theme never really lets the second subject alone, the momentum sweeping right the way through this grand movement. Only in the last twenty bars does Haydn permit himself an element of syncopation, but soon the new burnished B flat sound, aided by drums, hammers home the theme for the last time. In view of such splendour it is difficult to understand why a Nineteenth-century hack set about rearranging the brass and drum parts. Such monstrous interferences even destroyed the touches of cool flexibility in the slow movement where certain of the cello parts are for one instrument only. It is known that news of Mozart's death would have reached Haydn about the time he was writing this moving Adagio. It begins in hymn-like solemnity and proceeds with a sad sweetness, the deepest of all the movements from the first six London Symphonies. Theories that Haydn might have written it *in memoriam* of Mozart, though unfounded, are not so far-fetched, for Haydn could certainly have been affected by the melancholy news whilst writing this music. As with many poignant compositions (not least the *Funeral March* from Beethoven's "Eroica" Symphony) the chief melodic protagonist is the oboe, the beauty of whose song becomes near-unbearable towards the close.

The colours remain dark in the Menuet but the contours are strikingly bold, with powerful timpani strokes beneath the winds from the fourth to sixth bars which recall Mozart's *Don Giovanni* Overture and his "Prague" Symphony. The first double bar lightens the mood and there follows an ethereal flute solo until the theme, broken to fragments, comes to a *fortissimo* summation. The Trio is simple, with the theme given first to the bassoon and then to the flute, the section ending as all the woodwind echo the rhythm of the melody.

In 6/8 time the extensive Finale gallops away. This is one of Haydn's very longest last movements. In it he exploits not only his own great good humour, with swinging themes set against delightfully delicate subsidiary ideas, but also writes several solos—notably for Salomon but also for himself. We know that Haydn directed the concerts from the keyboard,* and here he writes himself an extended cembalo solo which, following a thematically similar one by Salomon, must have brought the house down. Haydn never laid claim to great keyboard virtuosity but the writing is quite demanding and he was probably delighted to show himself as very much the all-round musician. Certainly the passage comes as an exciting surprise close to the end of the movement. There seems no reason at all to play this work without keyboard continuo—the appearance of a harpsichord for only its solo is a weird (but common) misconception since Haydn did indicate on the lowest stave in the slow movement "Bassi continui" (or "Bassi con."). It is clear that he did not expect to sit silent at the keyboard except for his eleven-bar display-piece.

---

* It is revealing to note that in his account of a performance of *The Creation* Carpani says (as translated by Stendhal not many years after Haydn's death) "Haydn himself conducted in the modern way with a baton, as was customary for choral performances."

On his return to London in 1794 Haydn brought a new innovation: clarinets were included in the scores of the symphonies. In addition, the warmth and sunlight of the key of E flat major took a very different turn in the case of SYMPHONY NO. 99, because for the first time ever a symphony in this key had timpani and trumpets in the scoring.

The effect of the very first chord is extraordinary—isolated it could be the first chord of Beethoven's great E flat Piano Concerto. Haydn's scoring is the largest yet—two each of flutes, oboes, clarinets, bassoons, horns, trumpets and drums, with strings. This is also Beethoven's orchestra for his First, Second, Seventh and Eighth Symphonies and is actually larger by one flute than that used in Beethoven's Fourth. For once Haydn lays stress on his melodies rather than their manipulation. The introduction has important oboe and flute solos but the Vivace Assai is all vigour and panache, with a jaunty second subject incorporating an elegant ticking accompaniment. Only on its last appearance does Haydn set out to clothe it differently, for this time the oboe solo is underpinned by very deep pedal notes on second horn. The coda is a riotously glowing episode where every instrument plays *fortissimo*. The idea of low pedal notes is evident in much of the symphony and Haydn often experiments by using the second of his newly-instated clarinets for the purpose.

As with the slow movement of No. 98 there is no more than conjecture to explain the beauty and seriousness of No. 99's Adagio, written at about the time of the death of Marianne von Genzinger. This is an immensely rich piece of writing. The whole wind band is employed on the second theme of the sonata-form movement, which has a focal point just after the double bar where the timpani enter for the first time. Even though it is a slow movement they are marked *fortissimo*, as are all other instruments except trumpets and horns. The careful dynamic marking of the slow movement of the "Surprise" Symphony is recalled and there is an almost ecclesiastical solemnity about the full-bodied writing, in which the penetrating nature of the brass is deliberately subdued.

The Menuet swings in at a broad *allegretto* which has its share of swift dynamic contrasts and sudden *sforzandi*. There is even a sudden display of virtuosity by first horn—at bars 44–46—a very non-E flat thing to do:

As transposed the top note here sounds G^2. Hesitating on the note G^1, first oboe emphatically states the five-note rhythm of the Minuet before relaxing into a country dance, with well-spaced heavy beats lazily pushing the music along until a specially-composed passage urges the music back, unwillingly it almost seems, to the Minuet proper. The Finale is a rondo of the period with a charmingly cheeky two-note afterthought on the horns succeeding each statement. Plenty of syncopations break up the power of the theme when full orchestra grasp it—a cue for the woodwind to play with another idea in fragments for a while. The rondo theme is soon subjected to a thorough fugal working-out, ending in some inversions on individual instruments. Later there is even a solo for second horn, and first clarinet is similarly favoured. At this heady pace Haydn's fragments never sound fragmentary in the slightest.

SYMPHONY NO. 100 in G, "Militär" ("Military"), stands very much apart from the others in instrumentation; even the philosophy does not relate so closely to that of other London Symphonies. The slow introduction has an exciting tingle of things to come. There is also a sense of suppressed elation. The first shadow comes well into the introduction—a long *crescendo* led by the timpani. An effective touch is sometimes employed by conductors who use an old military slow open roll here, the heavy separate beats adding a chilling air of menace. Although clarinets are again employed they do not appear in this movement—since the Allegro is in Haydn's most optimistic vein, it is as though he did not wish to be bothered with new problems when writing to delight. The contrasts between *piano* and *forte*, always strong with Haydn, are here almost violent and in the development the *tutti* are always weighty and fully-scored. Even for Haydn the timpani are used extensively.* The second subject—a tune of overwhelming cheerfulness—

has been likened by Geiringer to both the first movement of Mozart's Symphony No. 40 and to the *Radetzky March* of Johann Strauss Sr. Landon says it *is* the same melody as that of the *Radetzky March*. Whatever the truth, it is, to say the least, extraordinarily military in its bearing.

The clarinets appear for the Allegretto—a movement which has

---

* Anyone who wishes to hear how the biting tone of these instruments had such an individual effect on the sound should listen to Scherchen's last recording where, notably in this movement, the timpani are everything they should be in an Eighteenth-century piece.

so much inner life that it need not be "bounced" along. The melody was originally used for the third of the lyre organizzate concerti for the King of Naples. Here, however, it is changed almost beyond recognition and soon full orchestra (the new "Beethoven" orchestra) takes it up, adding bass drum, triangle and cymbals too. A hush then falls, there is a call to arms from solo trumpet (an authentic call it seems, probably Prussian rather than Hungarian) and a thrilling timpani *crescendo* leads to a great clash of percussion—a clear encouragement at the second performance of this work for the journalist of the "Morning Chronicle" of April 9, 1794, to indulge his fancy with the now familiar words: "The sounding of the charge, the thundering of the onset, the clash of arms, the groans of the wounded, and what may well be called the hellish roar of war increase to a climax of horrid sublimity!"

The Menuet is firm but sprightly, grace-notes which are really graceful, rising scales from all departments, and repeated ornaments, elegant in the wind instruments, incisive in the strings. Trumpets and drums punctuate rather than overbear and the Trio has a duet for flute and oboe. Only towards its close do the brass and drums hammer out a threatening figure.

The Finale, amazing for the variety of keys through which it travels, is in 6/8 metre, violent *forte* interjections making it clear that this is not music to relax to. (The identical folk-melody known as *Lord Cathcart* is a derivation from Haydn's symphony, not the reverse). No sooner is one in the *tutti* sections than the key pulls wildly away from its gravitational centre. At bar 122 Haydn's timpanist lashes out with a violent *forte* solo, which erupts after five bars of hesitant single *piano* notes from violins and violas. The warning is there, and soon the might of the full percussion returns, enhanced by swirling woodwind figures. The overall upsurge of energy rides high over the repeated rhythmic pattern of the bass drum and cymbals, driving the music forward with a grimness which contrasts strangely with the exuberance of the melodic line.

SYMPHONY NO. 101 in D, "Die Uhr" ("Clock"), receives its name from the obvious place—the tick-tock rhythm of its Andante. The slow and serious introduction is enigmatic, leading as it does to a 6/8 Presto. This turns out to be more fierce than high-spirited, as witness the really bitter fermata at the end of the first subject with its vicious drum roll.* The frequent upward sweeps of detached notes for violins are exciting in impact but extremely demanding in performance. An ultra-*staccato* approach to the Andante—marked *staccato e piano* on the bassoon part—can give great point to this movement.† Absolute strictness of

---

* Maerzendorfer, and Jones in his later recording, makes this a point of high drama.
† Maerzendorfer is again triumphant.

pulse is essential—the actual pace is less important than the adherence to the chosen tempo—and the massive *minore tutti* reveals itself as a magnificent work of art if the proper amount of detail is allowed to cut through. It is a long, ornate passage—baroque in its way—but not the baroque of Telemann's music; rather, the term stems from the inspiration poured into the side chapels of the great Churches and Cathedrals of Europe—an architectural rather than a compositional impression. At one point the steady progress has a silence thrown across it—a long, unexpected pause in the notes—yet the pulse ticks on, unheard yet subconscious. It turns out to be no more than a brilliant alternative to a lengthy modulation.

The jagged Menuet is soon under way. Its themes are long, its colouring heavily influenced by the woodwind except in the quiet timpani solos after each double bar on its every appearance. The Trio has always been a thorn in the flesh to those who have insisted that Haydn was a kindly, gentlemanly fellow: the sort of man who, perhaps like his own pupil Pleyel, could be relied upon to be thoroughly conventional. Unfortunately for such folk, Haydn never fits such a pigeonhole—in this Trio the first section is written out in full twice over. One knows that this means Haydn is up to something, as was the case in the Trio of No. 81, and sure enough, mischief arrives at bars six and seven where the harmony grinds along on the same note as in the rest of the bars, giving solo flute against violins in the following harmonic clash:

The purists would have been horrified; yet when they listened to hear the mistake on the repeat it had gone:

Haydn had troubled himself to write these sixteen bars twice over simply for the pleasure of correcting this harmony on its second appearance. Needless to say, for years the standard edition had the harmony "correct" on both appearances.*

The Finale is purely fugal. It is as complex as the Finale to No. 70 but permits a larger selection of homely chords to indicate that the listener is nearing the final destination. The whirling violins are summed up by brass chords which point the direction, grouping the dissonant elements together and acting as signposts. "The key so far," they seem to say. Haydn is far from becoming a cerebral composer, however, as the massive attack of winds and drums on the tonic proves. The brief powerful coda simplifies all the complexities at a stroke.

SYMPHONY NO. 102 in B flat is the only one of the final six to abandon the clarinets. Also, having horns in B flat, it merits a moment's preliminary examination as to the required pitch of these instruments. A strong argument that Haydn was thinking in terms of alto† occurs at bars 38 to 50 in the Finale where the trumpets and horns carry a melodic sequence in unison. At bar 48 the trumpets cease to play. This is not surprising because an eleventh harmonic creeps in, which means that in order to hit the note properly it must be "stopped"—something only a horn player can do. The horns therefore finish the melody right up to bar 50—a fair indication that Haydn was thinking in terms of B flat alto since if the instruments were in B flat basso the last notes of the trumpets would be the broken end of the melody, dropping down an octave in the basso horns and being lost. It is also interesting to note the high horn entry in the Trio. It would be very difficult to play the written G *piano* on an alto horn, and an examination of the score shows that the horns are the only instruments *not* marked *piano* at this point. Perhaps Haydn knew the problem more thoroughly than one supposes.

In relation to Symphonies Nos. 98 and 102 it is unlikely that Haydn used B flat alto horns in London. The music is playable using them and, judging from aural evidence in No. 102, adds an exciting *timbre*. It is a matter of taste for the conductor who will choose accordingly (unless he does not bother to specify, in which case his players will play in B flat basso, it being the simplest expedient). It is

---

* Mercifully there have always been conductors who do not bow to what tradition has accepted. Leslie Jones, for example, has championed Haydn's original "wrong" harmony since 1924 and even before recent research clarified the point, no one would have found conductors such as Harry Newstone or Karl Haas obeying the faulty edition. Also Arturo Toscanini in his two taped recordings of the Forties adheres to Haydn's original (though his 1929 acetates used a faulty edition).

† At least three British conductors currently use horns in B flat alto in this work: Christopher Fry, Leslie Jones and Harry Newstone. Of the three only Leslie Jones has recorded the work.

an interesting discussion but in practice the difference is not so marked as might be imagined; it would be wrong for music-lovers to develop partisan preferences over such matters. Other things should take the attention—for example, would the opening of No. 102 sound more impressive with the woodwind band omitted from the two semibreve chords? Haydn certainly wrote it like that at first and this is how the early performances began, but soon he altered it to a full chord. The *largo* introduction—as often in the London Symphonies—has the thematic germ of the main section buried within it. Typical of the firm resolve of the music, the notes are largely detached. Only when the Vivace begins does the pointed phrasing, with its typical alternation of pairs of slurred notes and *staccati*, become clear. This movement is so full of melody and of orchestral complexity that it simply cannot be rushed. Phrasing is pinpoint precise in a conception of the stature of Beethoven's Fourth Symphony, a work with which No. 102 shares more than a common key. Haydn throws in fierce *fortissimo* shouts which never let the second theme settle. The development finds the same sequence of events but with the key left to wander. There are intriguing long graces in this section and across the disturbed air of the theme the first tune tries to return. Some of the most exciting passages are those where first and second violins answer each other in fierce alternation: here above all is the most convincing argument for first and second violins to be divided left and right in music of this period.* The peak of excitement arrives at bar 223 where the timpani enter softly and make a thrilling *crescendo*, hurling the listener forward to the *tutti* recapitulation at bar 227 with an impetus not to be denied. Some timpanists begin the *crescendo* earlier than marked (224 instead of 225) and this adds point; it is also a necessary device in a recording, where added time is needed for a *crescendo* effect to impinge on the listeners' consciousness. Just before the close, there is a general pause. The bassoons, violas, celli and basses then attack in a fury—nothing in music is more similar to this than the almost identical furious attack of the strings in the last bars of Beethoven's Fourth Symphony.

BEETHOVEN

Allegro ma non troppo

vla. *ff* fag;
only vla;
celli;
bassi

---

* Jones and Schönzeler use such a layout to advantage in their recordings.

HAYDN

The clear-cut Adagio is relatively brief and is deeply moving. Haydn asks for the trumpets and drums to be muted. The long stretches of repeated soft notes on timpani doubtless benefit in clarity through the muting giving them a dry quality. The effect was not required in London but appears in authentic continental manuscripts. The *timbre* is strange indeed and enhances the withdrawn feeling of the whole movement, especially as the accompanimental phrases are given largely to solo cello. One should remember that the brass mutes of the day were likely to have been of wood, and the trumpets would certainly have sounded more mellow than in modern performances, especially as they had a smoother, fuller sound in the first place. When, near the close, a single trumpet is left standing clear of the *tutti*, modern muting can make it appear unstylistically metallic, which is why many trumpeters prefer to remove the mute before that brief solo.*

The Menuet is sturdy and lengthy, although there is a school of thought which effectively reduces the feeling of longevity through a briskish tempo and strong rhythm† It is interesting to note the harmonies written higher than the melody and expounded by flute on its every statement. The horns also have rich embellishments of the melody. Against all this complexity Haydn sets a simple Trio with solo oboe, bassoon and flute. The humour of the Finale is unconfined. Each episode of the rondo theme ends with a triple wind flourish—sometimes with timpani—or is it the next section that begins with it? No chance here for the ear to work out set patterns since even the string melodies are buried in an avalanche of semiquavers. Whenever the theme is affirmed the whole orchestra stops the progress for a bout of riotous enjoyment, and after a customary set of Haydn hesitations near the end, together with wild dynamic changes, the wind and brass blaze their way to the close .

Only two problems surround the familiar SYMPHONY NO 103 in E flat, "Mit dem Paukenwirbel" ("Drum Roll"). Firstly, what sort of drum roll is intended, and secondly, does one play all of the Finale or not?

---

* Note the Leslie Jones recording.
† Maerzendorfer does this very effectively in his recording.

First things first: the timpani solo which begins the work:

This is all there is to go on—no dynamic mark of any description just Haydn's word "Intrada." One can look at the contemporary arrangements for Quintet and for Trio by Birchall but they do not help very much, for the Quintet simply says *ff* and the Trio gives a *crescendo-diminuendo* "hairpin": < >.

The remainder of the introduction is shrouded in the depths of gloom. Whether a reference to the *Dies Irae* is intended is not clear: the rhythm of the old chant is there but the notes are a long way from it; perhaps one should beware of attributing too many uses of plainchant to Haydn. The delightful Allegro con Spirito takes well to broad, explicit exposition. The sudden *forte* outburst is a fine Haydn stroke and the second subject is limited to a brief, skipping downward idea at the very end of the exposition. The development is one of those cheerfully unsuccessful searches for more than a fragment of the main theme until eventually the introduction returns—"Intrada" again being inscribed with no dynamic marks. Fifteen swift, dashing bars close the proceedings.

The Andante Più Tosto Allegretto is a jolly set of variations which seems to make even the darkness of its minor key wear a smile. The concertante element is very much at work and there is an extensive difficult section for solo violin with light accompaniment. Haydn seems to have admitted clarinets to his ensemble somewhat grudgingly since here again is a movement in which he dispenses with them, He does, however, as in so many symphonies, make good use of bottom C in the bass (presumably the London instruments were able to play it). One wonders how Haydn's band managed to go so low; what was available to him? In the end, Haydn's variation movement surrenders the minor key altogether and there follows another of those minuets with awkward corners, the clarinets returning at this point. It has an ornamented melodic line with a hard twist to the decorations. By contrast the Trio

---

* One can always steer a midway course, like Jochum in his latest recording who starts the work *ff* > but when the figure re-occurs later on uses *pp* < *ff* > *pp*. Maerzendorfer does exactly the opposite, starting with a swell-and-fade and giving *fortissimo-diminuendo* the second time. The "bad old" editions had < >, so it seems only natural to assume that the more interesting *fortissimo* beginning will probably be preferable! Needless to say, Hermann Scherchen was the first to record a *fortissimo* opening.

flows smoothly and sombrely; liquid runs from the inner parts, enhancing its smooth grace.

The Finale begins with a forceful horn call

—virtually the selfsame figure heard on the horns in bars 179–182 of the first movement.

These five notes then repeat themselves within the theme for the rest of the movement as if intent on etching themselves into one's memory. The first *forte* is longer delayed than ever and the development very lengthy; although Haydn uses only one theme, even that has the listener's wits hard at work following its thoroughly-designed inner workings. Towards the expected place for the final summing up of the themes a strangeness overcomes the atmosphere: the music should be modulating towards the home key but if anything it is drifting away —at bar 369 the music peters out for three whole bars. In restarting there are hesitant explorations of the unlikely tonal regions of C flat, as if straying into the Wolf's Glen scene from Weber's *Der Freischütz*. At last the music pulls itself together and heads for home. What possessed Haydn to strike out this wonderfully evocative passage from the autograph is a mystery. The original* is longer, less predictable and far more magical.

"The 12th which I have composed in England," says Haydn in English on the title page of SYMPHONY NO. 104 in D, "London," the last symphony he was ever to write. There is something special about this magnificent work, from its imperious outset where the timpani and brass crash in to emphasise the string fanfare—perhaps one should say

---

* On records so far, only Maerzendorfer and Dorati have played the original. In the case of Dorati his fine performance of this Finale is segregated to a separate two-disc musicological jamboree—the revision closes his excellent full-scale performance. No matter, performers cannot pretend much longer that Haydn's vastly superior original does not exist.

obliterate rather than emphasise since, whilst one cannot be sure of the full layout of the increased London orchestra at the Kings Theatre, there is no reason to suppose that the massive wind band sound would be anything other than clanguorous—especially as the first performance was probably by an orchestra with doubled woodwind. The confidence with which the main Allegro sets out provides the tenor of the whole movement. There is measured strength in the first *tutti* too, a genuine afterthought of the main melody, not merely a big instrumental contrast. The trumpets add fanfares to long-phrased melodies. Even in the final idea, Haydn's colouring remains subtle: the clarinets become integrated and a darker sound informs the quiet passages. As might be expected, the development builds firmly, the subject-matter being too serious for humorous fragmentation. The music rushes through key after key until at the peak of a roaring *fortissimo* climax there is a fermata, as the panoply of orchestral sound rings round the hall. The recapitulation can lead to only one conclusion—joyful affirmative fanfares from brass and drums.

Haydn's last slow movement does not aim for sadness or nostalgia —merely a simple theme in not too jaunty a rhythm. It is varied and turned to the minor but its basic optimism remains. The concertante side of matters is attended to by the woodwind groups with a very independent (and often rather high) horn part in G. The Menuet is as self-confident as that of the "Military" Symphony. The exciting London fingerprint is there: the long timpani *crescendo* together with another fine device—a lengthy pause which heralds a threatening trill before the final affirmation of the theme. The Trio flows on in a deceptively smooth fashion which throws the stresses upon the wrong beat. This is another of those delightfully undanceable dances which Haydn is so fond of writing.

The dancing theme which begins the Finale has many Slavonic folk connections, not least in its use of a drone bass. Various authorities also declare that the melody is sung today in many Croatian villages. A quicker way for the layman to check upon Slavonic influences, however, is to take a recording of Czech Dance No. 8, *Obkročák*, by Smetana and note the incredible similarity. The typical folk-measure of stamping repeated notes is evident throughout the whole movement. Massive held chords are a cue for the main theme to spring again from the body of the music, the timpani and basses giving the "drone." There is also a thoughtful after-subject. In the lengthy exposition it is soon swept away but in the development, heightened in intensity by the ethereal tones of the flute, it takes on a strong hint of reflectiveness, the melody falling gently down and down—a butterfly in autumn. Does one for the first, and as it happens the last, time sense a real looking-back? Was Haydn perhaps debating at this very moment whether this wonderful symphonic medium had, after all, permitted him to say all there was to say? There only remains one of the most magnificent of all Haydn's perorations. The first theme steals in half-smiling and Haydn's orchestra burnishes it to a state of glittering brilliance. With powerful *sforzandi* the horns blaze out the theme in unison across the whole orchestra, culminating in a great *fortissimo* timpani roll on D, bar after bar, as the orchestra shouts the melody for the very last time.

10: Conclusion

Haydn's music, then, developed along firm lines: if he experimented it was with progressive intent. There is no doubt that his heightened sense of drama in response to the "Sturm und Drang" influence can be taken as an excellent example of subjectivity, but romanticism is another matter. Even Beethoven stood only at the very beginning of the romantic movement. That he influenced later composers there is no doubt at all—as witness the writings of his great admirers Berlioz and Wagner—but only rarely were the passions beloved of Nineteenth-century audiences evident within Beethoven's music, for he, like Haydn, was far too concise a composer to allow soul-searching outpourings to spoil the overall architecture. It is possible to see that when Haydn and Beethoven have a theme which is coincidentally similar the contrast is between utter confidence on the one hand and dark undertones on the other—the most startling example can be found by comparing the opening of the Finale of Haydn's Symphony No. 47:

with the second subject (bars 52–55) of Beethoven's *Coriolan* Overture:

Not all composers of the Nineteenth century stressed the darker significances. For example, whilst Schubert's philosophy, as we understand it through his music, may be dissimilar to Haydn's it is surprising that commentators do not remark upon the similarity of his orchestral thinking. The staggering similarity of the following two examples—bars 126–133 of Haydn's Finale to his Symphony No. 90 (1788)

and bars 126–133 of the first movement of Schubert's Second Symphony (1815)—

seems all the more interesting when one realises that the emotional moods are different: Haydn is nearing a release of tension. Schubert is creating an atmosphere of fierce uncertainty. The incredible coincidence whereby the bar numbers prove to be identical is a fascinating addition to one's store of information but one should not try to seek further implications in this phenomenon. The point about this obvious example in particular and the link between Haydn and Schubert in general is that the similarity of their orchestral techniques has been masked by the prevalent treatment of Schubert as a soft-contoured, *legato*-inclined composer. Avoid the habitual smoothness and the contours become infinitely clearer and much more like those of Haydn.

The orchestration of Haydn's last symphonies developed logically from his early works. Formally the difference between early and late Haydn is little more than a reflection of the transition from Baroque to Classical style, whereby the Scarlatti-like binary form movements had become examples of Sonata Form; yet sonically the huge contrast between the earliest and the latest symphonies results from unrivalled inside knowledge of the orchestra and its workings. The final conclusions reached in terms of instrumentation were sufficient to serve Schubert in his first five symphonies, Beethoven in his First, Second, Fourth, Seventh and Eighth, and many lesser contemporary composers. The rapidly-changing pattern of symphonic thought after Haydn had composed his last work in this form should not be confused therefore with the instrumental means of expressing it—most composers remained quite happy with his legacy of the "classical" symphony orchestra.

Certain characteristics typify Haydn's musical handwriting. Readers can perhaps be spared the repetition of the well-worn old tag about the Irish hotel-keeper and Haydn's minuets (if the phrase about O'Reilly fitted the tune of the minuet then it was supposed to prove Haydn's authorship) but as with few other composers, Johann Christian Bach apart, Haydn did tend to have favourite rhythmic patterns for particular symphonic episodes. For example, the beginning of the first-movement Allegro in many of the symphonies written after about 1770 share a remarkably similar pattern of long-short-short (see opposite page). With such consistency in outlook the "O'Reilly" theory does not seem so far-fetched after all.

Apart from the elements of Haydn's own invention, a fascinating characteristic which appears in innumerable works throughout his lifetime is the inclusion of melodies which are either Hungarian in style or (more commonly) can actually be traced to folk tunes of known Hungarian origin. This is not at all the same thing as the "Turkish Music" which Mozart and his Viennese contemporaries sometimes wrote for the delectation of a public which was prepared to accept anything reasonably bizarre as "Turkish" (few natives of Turkey would have

50

52

53

57

58

62

66

75

78

85

93

95

99

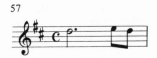

100

104

been able to relate Viennese Turkery to the music of their own country). In the case of Haydn the Hungarian melodies become part of the fabric of the music. That they are especially evident in the London Symphonies is not particularly significant, since Haydn was at that time a little more conscious of the need to catch the ears of his audience. Melodies such as that used for the second movement of Symphony No. 103:

are not so much Hungarian as generally East European. H. C. Robbins Landon has discovered that this theme has been claimed variously by the Hungarians, the Turks and the Poles, whilst a Croatian melody "Na travniku" is extremely similar. To my English ears it certainly sounds Hungarian—and that surely is as far as Haydn expected any Englishman to analyse the origins of this shadowy theme. There are innumerable dangers in ascribing hidden influences to a subjective impression—the most important being that the sheer enjoyment of the music is hampered through the introduction of a complex meaningfulness which the composer almost certainly never intended.

Where the Dance is concerned it is interesting to examine the nature of the minuets. Although Haydn did not formulate the shape of the classical symphony entirely on his own (despite what legend may say), his influence upon it by incorporating the minuet movement with considerable frequency should not be underestimated. Further, the earlier symphonies often have andantes as dance-like in nature as the minuets themselves, and even in some three-movement works a minuet forms the Finale, so there is no doubt that Haydn considered it a permanent feature of the Symphony early in his career. Half of the first thirty works are in four movements with minuet; half of the remainder are three-movement compositions which include either a minuet or a minuet-like movement. . . . This leaves only a handful of symphonic works in which no minuet is featured, since afterwards Haydn never wrote less than four movements in any symphony, nor did he fail to include a minuet.

There remain a few backwaters to be explored in looking at Haydn's minuets and one can perhaps learn something about the Hungarian influences by looking at the relevant trio sections. Some may care also to investigate the nomenclature of these movements (Menuetto, Minuetto, Menuet, etc.) in the light of national and stylistic leanings, but it does not seem that the Menuets are noticeably more French than the Menuetti or Minuetti. It would be a pity if the investigation of such sidelines were to cloud the appreciation of the mainstream of Haydn's invention.

The staggering variety of this is evidenced if one considers the nature of the earliest works: the formal exactitude, Scarlatti-like in contour, of Symphonies Nos. 1, 12, 16, 17 or 19 set against the instrumental daring of Nos. 6, 7, 8 and 13. This shows a brilliant and progressive composer already remoulding the existing forms; such early pieces have all too often been given but scant attention: in past years Haydn has, for many listeners, meant merely the "named" London Symphonies. It is the beginnings of Haydn's development which give the clue to the uniqueness of his symphonic writing no less clearly than the tuneful large-scale works of later years. The Finale of No. 8—a storm guaranteed to tax violinists' technique—is paralleled at a much later date by the grand close of No. 97—a fiery movement with detached violin notes which are required to be played at a most demanding pace. Again, as the trilogy of Symphonies Nos. 6, 7, and 8 include violin and cello soli in the slow movements, so too do Symphonies Nos. 95, 96, 98 and 102 of thirty and more years later.

The links between the earlier and the later symphonies are generally not difficult to recognise, since the key to Haydn's thought is always before us in his instrumentation. This rationalises an art which to the casual listener can at first appear to be so diverse as to be bewildering. Standard formal analysis is a useful aid to understanding compositional construction but it cannot explain important links such as those between the clean-cut lines of the first movement of Symphony No. 1 and the equivalent sections of Nos. 35 and 88. If, however, attention is paid to the instrumental layout, it can be seen at once that the forceful grouping of phrases in the bass, giving a characteristic driving force from below, links the three pieces together. Similarly, in the earlier works containing timpani Haydn immediately shows his inclination to use these instruments in martial style, their sharp tones ringing out above a deeper bass: an element equally evident in the final movement of the last London Symphony.

The sense of unity which Haydn achieves through his orchestral technique is one of the most significant characteristics of his music. There is no longer any reason why this should go unrecognised now that all of the symphonies are readily available for listening. Some of the recurring combinations of sound simply serve to place the music firmly in its Eighteenth-century setting, as in the cases when bare unison bass-writing makes keyboard continuo as essential with Haydn as with any other composer of the period. Other characteristics, however, especially the melodic use of horns high in their register, have almost no parallels in music.

Because the tonal outcome of Haydn's finely calculated complexities can now be appreciated by layman and musicologist alike, it is possible for everyone to begin to comprehend something of his character. The Eighteenth-century Hungarian countryside, where primitive rural conditions and luxurious court life were set in curious juxtaposition, is far removed from the everyday experience of most people, yet the very diversity of the masterpieces written in those surroundings helps one's understanding not only of the biographical events, but also of Haydn's need to be original in such isolated circumstances. This need he fulfilled magnificently; the symphonies, above all, bear witness to his triumph.

Appendix

Selected Writings

There are many books which can help the English-speaking reader to assimilate the biographical details of Haydn's life but not all of them are accurate and some are out of print. Works which deal more specifically with the music are very rare, and it may be that those who are able to consult memoirs of Haydn's time will find themselves brought nearer to the essence of the period than those who accept the surmises of later writers. Essential for capturing the period flavour is a book over two centuries old: Dr. Charles Burney's "The Present State of Music in Germany, the Netherlands and United Provinces," which could be read in conjunction with the same author's "General History of Music," dating from between 1776 and 1789 and reprinted in two volumes in New York in 1935. The Earl of Mount Edgecumbe's "Musical Reminiscences of an Old Amateur" depicts the nature of music in England late in Haydn's lifetime, and W. T. Parke's "Musical Memoirs" also covers the period 1784–1830, the latter year being its date of publication in London.

A modern memoir, beautifully illustrated and full of detailed information on costs and theatre production, is "The Magnificence of Eszterháza," by Mátyás Horányi. The English edition is from Barrie and Rockcliff (London, 1962). A similar, if more wide-ranging, evocation of the period is to be found in László Somfai's "Joseph Haydn: His Life in Contemporary Pictures" (produced by the Corvina Press, Budapest). The massive collection of reproductions is fascinatingly well-documented —all the well-known portraits and very many more besides are here. Faber of London published this elegant presentation in 1969; currently it is out of print but second-hand copies are to be found. A reprint of the English edition seems essential although due to the pictorial nature of its contents, most English readers would lose little by obtaining the German edition.

Of books concerned largely with the biographical aspect Karl Geiringer's "Haydn: A Creative Life in Music," issued in a revised edition by Allen and Unwin (London, 1964) is standard reading for every Haydn enthusiast. There is scarcely a well-documented detail of Haydn's life which is not to be found in this superbly researched book. It outlines the history of the composer's life in one long, chronological sweep, and to some extent the explanation of the music is subsidiary to this; the comments on the music, however, are always deeply perceptive, whilst being confined to the cooler aspects of formal description. A similar approach is taken by Rosemary Hughes in "Haydn," the revised edition by Dent being published in 1970. Although the musical descriptions are somewhat academic and the author is surprisingly unconcerned with the all-important feature of Haydn's use of instrumentation, there is real warmth in the biographical sections. Detail is by no means so far-reaching as with Geiringer but the period is conjured up with feeling and the description of the composer's last years is very moving.

H. C. Robbins Landon's monumental "The Symphonies of Joseph Haydn" (Universal Edition, Vienna, and Rockliff, London, 1955) examines the nature and sound of Haydn's music as does no other work. However much musicologists may disagree with Landon's methods or conclusions it is certain that serious popularisation of Haydn's music began with this book (and its 1961 supplement). Now out of print and in some cases, through Landon's later work, musicologically out of date, this book gives an attractive foretaste of the same author's projected five-volume complete Haydn biography.

Complete Editions of Scores

The complete editions of Haydn's scores are listed below (see also my comments on some of these on pp. 17–20). For the serious student who requires individual pocket scores for study, Universal edition provide a separately bound copy of each symphony, taken from the twelve-volume set. These miniatures are very reliable but the latest Eulenberg editions which replace some of the less authentic miniatures from that publishing house are of equal value and the names of Harry Newstone and Christa Fuhrmann (together with a few by H. C. Robbins Landon) makes it clear that the editors form a distinguished group.

H. C. Robbins Landon, "Joseph Haydn." Critical edition of the complete symphonies; twelve vols, Universal and Philharmonia, Vienna, 1963–68.

Jens Peter Larsen, and others, "Joseph Haydn: The Complete

22: *Portrait of Joseph Haydn by Johann Carl Roesler (by permission of the Faculty of Music, Oxford University)*

23: *Watercolour of the Hanover Square Rooms, London, by T. H. Shepherd, 1831 (by courtesy of the Trustees of the British Museum)*

Works," four vols, Haydn Society, Boston, and Breitkopf, Leipzig, 1950–51 (not completed).

Jens Peter Larsen, and others, "Joseph Haydn: Werke." With critical commentary; Henle, Munich, 1958 (to be completed).

Eusebius Mandyczewski, and others, "Joseph Haydn's Werke." eleven vols, Breitkopf, Leipzig, 1907–33 (not completed).

"Oeuvres complettes de Joseph Haydn," twelve vols. Breitkopf, Leipzig, 1800–1806.

Musical Instruments of Haydn's Time

In the following selection it will be seen that there is a concentration upon wind instruments. It is useful to be aware of the differences in stringed instruments but in practice the audible differences between ancient and modern is a good deal less significant. Adam Carse in "The Orchestra in the XVIIIth Century" states some heretical ideas about filling in harmonies with rewritten viola parts; similar unnecessary complications seem from the musicological point-of-view hopelessly dated, yet for all this he writes with admirable enthusiasm for the period and recreates the atmosphere of Eighteenth-century music-making with no little vividness. The remainder are admirable textbooks, with the Horniman Museum publication making an admirable supplement to Carse's writing by depicting many instruments which Carse himself owned.

Anthony Baines, "Woodwind Instruments and Their History," 1957.

Philip Bate, "The Trumpet and Trombone," second edition, 1972.

Adam Carse, "Musical Wind Instruments," 1939.

Adam Carse, "The Orchestra in the XVIIIth Century," 1950.

H. Fitzpatrick, "The Horn and Horn Playing," 1970.

Francis W. Galpin, "Old English Instruments of Music," fourth edition, 1965.

Horniman Museum, "Wind Instruments of European Art Music," 1974.

R. Morley-Pegge, "The French Horn," 1960.

Recommended Recordings

(Discographical research by Robert Dearling)

The standards upon which are based the recommendations for these recordings may be outlined as follows:

a) A reasonably high standard of performance by an orchestra of appropriate size.

b) Authenticity of text, in which are employed either the Universal Edition (of all the symphonies) or Henle publications (the London Symphonies), or similarly stylish sources.

c) Authenticity of performance: an adequate observance of Haydn's repeat schemes, including exposition sections in sonata-form movements and both halves in the early two-part movements; a consistent attitude to *da capos* in slow movements, and the observance of all repeats in minuets and trios. The use of keyboard and bassoon continuo in at least those works composed up to 1770 (the general recommendation in the Universal Edition scores). Finally, the use of correct instruments, such as alto horns and double-bass or violone where called for.

d) Clear and reasonably faithful recorded sound.

It may be assumed that the recordings listed here are satisfactory in all these respects, except where a recommendation is strong enough to override these considerations, in which case the divergencies from the standard are noted.

This list is not intended to be an exhaustive catalogue of record numbers: only U.K. and U.S.A. issue numbers are given unless the recommendation is available solely in another country, and numbers are for U.K. issues unless otherwise specified. Older record numbers have been excluded if modern pressings of the same performance exist.

Inclusion in this list is not influenced by current availability or convenience of coupling; for example, the Decca/Dorati performances are listed under individual symphony numbers even though the performances may be available only as part of a four- or six-disc set. It is, in any event, Decca's policy to reissue many of these recordings individually. The only other complete set so far released is that by Maerzendorfer. His records are available individually, and the U.K. and

U.S.A. numbers are identical, so in this case the prefix "U.S." has been omitted.

Further guidance for use:

a) Abbreviations have been kept to a minimum; the meanings of those which have been incorporated are self-evident. Names of those orchestras which appear in abbreviated form are given in full on their first appearance only.

b) Couplings of other Haydn works appear in brackets immediately before the name of the issuing company. Where only a number is given, this refers to another symphony.

c) Records are stereo, 12″ unless otherwise stated. (M)=monophonic.

d) Sets in which the discs are not available separately are indicated by "nas" after the set numbers.

Symphony "A" in B flat

Dorati—Philharmonia Hungarica.
  ("B"; 22; 63; 53 finales; 103 finale) Decca HDNK 47–48 (nas); US: London STS 15316–7 (nas).
Dorati omits the second repeat in the Andante and is crisp and idiomatic in the outer movements. It should be mentioned that Max Goberman made a recording of the work in the early Sixties but it has never been made available for sale in any form.

Symphony "B" in B flat

Dorati—Philharmonia Hungarica.
  ("A"; 22; 63; 53 finales; 103 finale) Decca HDNK 47–48 (nas); US: London STS 15316–7 (nas).
Goberman—Vienna State Opera Orchestra.
  (2; 49) US: LRM HS 11.
Both conductors observe all repeats and follow the Göttweig source in dotting the first quaver of bar 45 in the first movement. Dorati is less authentic in that he allows the wind instruments to slur some phrases in the Minuet, and he treats the repeated-note figure at the start of the Finale as a

crescendo. *His unusually rapid tempo for the slow movement stresses its Siciliana-like character.*

No. 1 in D

Böttcher—Vienna Soloists Orchestra.
  US: Mace S 9098
Dorati—Philharmonia Hungarica.
  (in set 1–19) Decca HDNA 1–6 (nas); US: London STS 15310–5 (nas).
Goberman—Vienna State Opera.
  (2; 3; *Lo speziale* Overture) CBS 61070; US: Odyssey 32–16–0006.
Goberman and Dorati observe all repeats but Böttcher is less generous, omitting the second in the first movement and both in the Andante. Slight textual deviations occur in Dorati's first movement where, for instance, bars 68–70 are played p *instead of* f. *Bars 10–11 are also played quietly, leading to a crescendo at 12 despite the dynamic for the whole section being* f *in the score. Böttcher's recording is light-toned and clean; Dorati's is smooth and comfortable but with ill-defined bass; Goberman's is more natural than either.*

No. 2 in C

Dorati—Philharmonia Hungarica.
  (in set 1–19) Decca HDNA 1–6 (nas); US: London STS 15310–5 (nas).
Goberman—Vienna State Opera.
  (1; 3; *Lo speziale* Overture) CBS 61070: Odyssey 32–16–0006.

No. 4 in D

Goberman—Vienna State Opera.
  (5; 6) CBS 61081; US: Odyssey 32–16–0034.

No. 3 in G

Dorati—Philharmonia Hungarica.
(in set 1–19) Decca HDNA 1–6 (nas;) US: London STS 15310–5 (nas).
Jones—Little Orchestra of London.
(39; 73) Pye GSGC 14021; US: Nonesuch H 71096.
Despite less polished playing and drier recording the detail and authentic style of the earlier Jones recording compares well with the more polished Dorati.

No. 5 in A

Dorati—Philharmonia Hungarica.
(in set 1–19) Decca HDNA 1–6 (nas); US: London STS 15310–5 (nas).
Goberman—Vienna State Opera.
(4; 6) CBS 61081; US: Odyssey 32–16–0034.

No. 6 in D, "Le matin"

Goberman—Vienna State Opera.
(4; 5) CBS 61081; US: Odyssey 32–16–0034.
Maerzendorfer—Vienna Chamber Orchestra.
(7) Oryx OR H 203; US: Musical Heritage OR H 203.
Goberman double-dots the slow introduction. The recording is clear and lifelike with ideal balance between bassoon and double bass in the Trio section. The string solo at this point in Maerzendorfer's performance is played on an instrument which has the sound character of a bass viol: the sleeve note describes it as merely "bass." All repeats are observed, and a harpsichord continuo appears in the second movement only.

No. 7 in C, "Le midi"

Dorati—Philharmonia Hungarica.
(in set 1–9) Decca HDNA 1–6 (nas); US: London STS 15310–5 (nas).
Maerzendorfer—Vienna Chamber.
(6) Oryx OR H 203; US: Musical Heritage OR H 203.
Maerzendorfer omits the harpsichord from all but the slow movements. In

the Finale, echo effects appear at bar 38 but are not paralleled at bar 112. Both recordings are excellently clear, the Dorati warmer but at the expense of a certain amount of impact.

No. 8 in G, "Le soir"

Dorati—Philharmonia Hungarica.
   (in set 1–19) Decca HDNA 1–6 (nas); US: London STS 15310–5 (nas).
Maerzendorfer—Vienna Chamber.
   (13) Oryx OR H 204; US: Musical Heritage OR H 204.
In Maerzendorfer's performance some grace notes in the first movement are played short, and harpsichord continuo is omitted throughout. The stereo image is biased to the right in an otherwise satisfactory recording. The Dorati version is notable for its warmth of tone but the solos are a little less accurate than with Maerzendorfer.

No. 9 in C

Goberman—Vienna State Opera.
   (10; 11) US: Odyssey 32–16–0082.

No. 10 in D

Goberman—Vienna State Opera.
   (9; 11) US: Odyssey 32–16–0082.
Goberman's recording is somewhat congested in the CBS pressing, and has traces of overloading in the first movement. It is nevertheless superior to all other versions.

No. 11 in E flat

Goberman—Vienna State Opera.
   (10; 11) US: Odyssey 32–16–0082.
Goberman, in this pressing, omits both repeats in the opening Adagio Cantabile.

No. 12 in E

Dorati—Philharmonia Hungarica.
   (in set 1–19) Decca HDNA 1–6 (nas); US: London STS 15310–5 (nas).
Goberman—Vienna State Opera.
   (13, 14) US: Odyssey 32–16–0116.
Dorati's slow and relaxed tempi result in an extremely leisurely performance,
superbly recorded. Goberman also receives a good recording but with some-
what underbalanced horns.

No. 13 in D

Goberman—Vienna State Opera.
   (12; 14) US: Odyssey 32–16–0116.
Maerzendorfer—Vienna Chamber.
   (8) Oryx OR H 204; US: Musical Heritage OR H 204.
Goberman's cello soloist in the Adagio does not always play strictly in tune,
and bars 62–82 in the finale are played sempre piano instead of the f marked.
The CBS pressing (but not the older LRM) breaks the symphony between
the two record sides. Maerzendorfer employs no continuo. Bar 59 in the first
movement is played p, and the ornaments in the slow movement are mis-
read. The very clear recording is right-biased; timpani are particularly well
caught, but horns are slightly backward.

No. 14 in A

Dorati—Philharmonia Hungarica.
   (in set 1–19) Decca HDNA 1–6 (nas); US: London STS 15310–5 (nas).
Goberman—Vienna State Opera.
   (12; 13) US: Odyssey 32–16–0116.
In Goberman's reading the second repeat in the Finale is omitted, possibly
due to editorial intervention because of the difficulty of accommodating this
work together with No. 60 on the original LRM pressing.

No. 15 in D

Böttcher—Vienna Festspiel Orchestra.
  (16; 17) Turnabout TV 34092 S.
Dorati—Philharmonia Hungarica.
  (in set 1–19) Decca HDNA 1–6 (nas); US: London STS 15310–5 (nas).
Goberman—Vienna State Opera.
  (16; 17) US: Odyssey 32–16–0166.
Böttcher's recording neglects the oboes, but otherwise this is a spacious and detailed recording. All three mentioned are of considerable merit.

No. 16 in B flat

Böttcher—Vienna Festspiel.
  (15; 17) Turnabout TV 34092 S.
Dorati—Philharmonia Hungarica.
  (in set 1–19) Decca HDNA 1–6 (nas); US: London STS 15310–5 (nas).
Goberman—Vienna State Opera.
  (15; 16) US: Odyssey 32–16–0166.
Both Böttcher and Goberman indulge in unmarked echo effects: Böttcher at bars 28–29 in the first movement, Goberman at bars 24 and 70 in the Andante. In the Turnabout recording the horns are poorly defined and there is an audible tape join in the Finale.

No. 17 in F

Böttcher—Vienna Festspiel.
  (15; 16) Turnabout TV 34092 S.
Goberman—Vienna State Opera.
  (15; 16) US: Odyssey 32–16–0166.
Unauthentic dynamics appear in Böttcher's performance, notably a crescendo at bars 44–49 in the first movement, and there are hesitations at two points in the Finale. The good recording highlights the horns. Goberman's horns are not so well balanced, but the oboe and bass lines are better defined.

No. 18 in G

Dorati—Philharmonia Hungarica.
    (in set 1–19) Decca HDNA 1–6 (nas); US: London STS 15310–5 (nas)
Mackerras—London Symphony Orchestra.
    (19; 20) US: Odyssey 32–16–0342.
An imaginatively-played harpsichord continuo in Mackerras's performance is
very forwardly balanced. Dorati's version is less impressive in this respect
but otherwise very acceptable.

No. 19 in D

Dorati—Philharmonia Hungarica.
    (in set 1–19) Decca HDNA 1–6 (nas); US: London STS 15310–5 (nas)
Goberman—Vienna State Opera.
    (18; 20) US: Odyssey 32–16–0342.

No. 20 in C

Dorati—Philharmonia Hungarica.
    (in set 20–35) Decca HDNB 7–12 (nas); US: London STS 15257–62 (nas).
Goberman—Vienna State Opera.
    (18; 19) US: Odyssey 32–16–0342.
Maerzendorfer—Vienna Chamber.
    (21) Oryx OR H 207; US: Musical Heritage OR H 207.
Only issued by CBS, Goberman's recording emerges as uncomfortably harsh
and top-heavy. In view of the generally satisfactory sound of the majority
of the Goberman series, it is to be assumed that an error has been made
in the tape-to-disc transfer process. Despite the recording, it is still possible
to recommend this performance. The other two recordings are clear and
forward, but the harpsichord continuo is lacking in Maerzendorfer's
performance.

No. 21 in A

Goberman—Vienna State Opera.
    (22) US: Odyssey 32–16–0374.

Maerzendorfer—Vienna Chamber.
   (20) Oryx OR H 207; US: Musical Heritage OR H 207.
Goberman is very stylish. Horn doubles oboe at bar 46 in the Adagio. Maerzendorfer omits the harpsichord and there is a slight lack of impetus in the second and fourth movements. Both recordings are forward and vivid.

No. 22 in E flat, "The Philosopher" (original version)

Goberman—Vienna State Opera.
   (21) US: Odyssey 32-16-0374.
Haas—London Baroque Orchestra.
   Parlophone PMA 1004 (M).
Goberman employs unauthentic phrasing at bars 66 and 67 in the first movement and at 14 and 15 in the Minuet. An alteration of tempo at bar 21 in the Minuet may be due to a tape edit. A splendid recording in which the characteristic cor anglais tone is ideally reproduced. Haas also has textual inconsistencies, the English horns adding unmarked phrasing at bars 34 and 35 in the second movement. They also join the horns in a diminuendo at bar 91 of the same movement. The recording, dating from 1951, is clear and natural, with ideal harpsichord balance. Despite these small reservations both performances are considerably superior in style to all others recorded.

No. 22 in E flat (revised version)

Dorati—Philharmonia Hungarica.
   ("A"; "B"; 53 finales; 63; 103 finale) Decca HDNK 47–48 (nas); US: London STS 15316–7 (nas).
With strong reservations about the authenticity and musical value of this version (comprising the second and fourth movements of the familiar No. 22 separated by an extremely characterless Andante Grazioso, and with flutes replacing the cors anglais), Dorati's recording is recommended only as a curiosity for the collector.

No. 23 in G

Dorati—Philharmonia Hungarica.
   (in set 20–35) Decca HDNB 7–12 (nas); US: London STS 15257–62 (nas).

Goberman—Vienna State Opera.
    (21) US: LRM HS 9.

No. 24 in D

Goberman—Vienna State Opera.
    (41) US: LRM HS 7
Maerzendorfer—Vienna Chamber.
    (26) Oryx OR H 209; US: Musical Heritage OR H 209.
In Goberman's recording a stylish cadenza in the slow movement (which is scored for solo flute and strings) was composed, just before the recording session, by H. C. Robbins Landon and the conductor, each taking alternate bars. Maerzendorfer omits the harpsichord continuo, but his clear and vivid recording favours the extremely rustic sound of the oboes and horns.

No. 25 in C

Dorati—Philharmonia Hungarica.
    (in set 20–35) Decca HDNB 7–12 (nas); US: London STS 15257–62 (nas).

No. 26 in D minor, "Lamentatione"

Heiller—Vienna Chamber.
    (36) Parlophone PMA 1016 (M); US: Haydn Society HS 9119 (M).
Maerzendorfer—Vienna Chamber.
    (24) Oryx OR H 209; US: Musical Heritage OR H 209.
Tátrai—Hungarian Chamber Orchestra.
    (27; 45) Hungaroton LPX 11458.
Heiller's recording dates from 1950 but is still clear enough to enable the performance to outclass all rivals. The first movement is taken at high speed; the horn parts appear to have been omitted from the Adagio. Maerzendorfer joins Heiller in his straight and unembellished reading of the slow movement, but he omits the harpsichord continuo.

No. 27 in G

Dorati—Philharmonia Hungarica.
(in set 20–35) HDNB 7–12 (nas); US: London STS 15257–62 (nas).
Tátrai—Hungarian Chamber.
(26; 45) Hungaroton LPX 11458.
A recording made by Max Goberman has never been made available to the public.

No. 28 in A

Dorati—Philharmonia Hungarica.
(in set 20–35) Decca HDNB 7–12 (nas); US: London STS 15257–62 (nas).

No. 29 in E

Dorati—Philharmonia Hungarica.
(in set 20–35) Decca HDNB 7–12 (nas); US: London STS 15257–62 (nas).
Jones—Little Orchestra of London.
(13; 64) US: Nonesuch H 71121.
Loibner—Vienna Academy Chamber Orchestra.
(12; 23; 30) US: Lyrichord LL 36 (M).
The Trio section of the Minuet is in the style of an accompaniment with no tune. Both Dorati and Jones leave the passage as written and omit harpsichord. In Loibner's recording, however, the harpsichordist plays the outline of a melody—a convincing example of improvisation which suits the music well.

No. 30 in C, "Alleluja"

Dorati—Philharmonia Hungarica.
(in set 20–35) Decca HDNB 7–12 (nas); US: London STS 15257–62 (nas).
Loibner—Vienna Academy Chamber Orchestra.
(12; 23; 29) US: Lyrichord LL 36 (M).
The horns, despite tradition, would sound better in C alto (together with a supporting drum part to equate the scoring with Symphony No. 48, with which No. 30 has thematic elements in common), and so it is necessary to accept two recordings which employ horns in the lower register, without

timpani. In Loibner's reading, additions to the authentic score include an sf at bar 28 of the first movement and a lightening of texture in the first of the third movement's two Trios. The second repeat in the first movement is omitted and the 1952 recording is harsh but clear. Dorati's recording is much smoother and more natural, but tends to lack the last ounce of presence.

No. 31 in D, "Hornsignal"

Dorati—Philharmonia Hungarica.
    (in set 20–35) Decca HDNB 7–12 (nas); US: London STS 15257–62 (nas).

No. 32 in C

Dorati—Philharmonia Hungarica.
    (in set 20–35) Decca HDNB 7–12 (nas); US: London STS 15257–62 (nas).
Goberman—Vienna State Opera.
    (26; *Lo speziale* Overture) US: LRM HS 14.
Maerzendorfer—Vienna Chamber.
    (33) Oryx OR H 213; US: Musical Heritage OR H 213.
Goberman slightly relaxes the tempo in the Trio of the Minuet and during the slow movement. Maerzendorfer omits the harpsichord continuo. All three recordings are bright and decisive, but Maerzendorfer's needs to be reproduced at a higher volume level than the others.

No. 33 in C

Dorati—Philharmonia Hungarica.
    (in set 20–35) Decca HDNB 7–12 (nas); US: London STS 15257–62 (nas).
Maerzendorfer—Vienna Chamber.
    (32) Oryx OR H 213; US: Musical Heritage OR H 213.
Maerzendorfer omits the second repeat of the first movement, together with harpsichord continuo; the sound of his orchestra often has more impact than Dorati's but both recordings give an excellent representation of the music.

No. 34 in D minor

Dorati—Philharmonia Hungarica.
(in set 20–35) Decca HDNB 7–12 (nas); US: London STS 15257–62 (nas).
Jones—Little Orchestra of London.
(54; 75) Pye GSGC 14047; US: Nonesuch H 71106.
A recording has been made by Max Goberman but it has never been offered for sale.

No. 35 in B flat

Dorati—Philharmonia Hungarica.
(in set 20–35) Decca HDNB 7–12 (nas); US: London STS 15257–62 (nas).
Goberman—Vienna State Opera.
(65) US: LRM HS 15.
Jones—Little Orchestra of London.
(35; 43; 80) Pye GSGC 14046; US: Nonesuch H 71131.

No. 36 in E flat

Dorati—Philharmonia Hungarica.
(in set 36–48) Decca HDNC 13–18 (nas); US: London STS 15249–54 (nas).
Heiller—Vienna Chamber.
(26) Parlophone PMA 1016 (M); US: Haydn Society HS 9119 (M).
Maerzendorfer—Vienna Chamber.
(38) Oryx OR H 215; US: Musical Heritage OR H 215.
Stadlmair—Munich Chamber.
(45) Oryx 3 C 316.
Both Stadlmair and Maerzendorfer omit the harpsichord continuo. Heiller's 1950 recording, which today sounds congested and harsh, is nevertheless of sufficient quality for recommendation to be possible. It was made before the general circulation of the authentic text, so there are many minor but unimportant divergencies.

No. 37 in C

Maerzendorfer—Vienna Chamber.
  (29; 30) Oryx OR H 211; US: Musical Heritage OR H 211.
Although Goberman recorded the work towards the end of his life, his performance has never been offered for sale. Dorati's recording should be avoided due to the unaccountable omission of trumpets and timpani from this example of Haydn's C major "festival" writing, and the use of horns in low C. The recommended performance by Maerzendorfer omits the harpsichord continuo and is none too stable rhythmically in the Minuet, but is the only version which gives some idea of the sound of the music as indicated by authentic sources. Yet even here Maerzendorfer fails to employ the high horns.

No. 38 in C

Dorati—Philharmonia Hungarica.
  (in set 36–48) Decca HDNC 13–18 (nas); US: London STS 15249–54 (nas).
Maerzendorfer—Vienna Chamber.
  (36) Oryx OR H 215; US: Musical Heritage OR H 215.
Maerzendorfer's oboe soloist adds a cadenza at bar 74 in the Finale on the repeat. Harpsichord continuo is omitted from this performance. Dorati's version does not show the highly original brass to such advantage but the tempi are held more consistently.

No. 39 in G minor

Goldberg—Netherlands Chamber Orchestra.
  Philips ABE 10168 (M) (7", 45 rpm, two sides); International Philips G 05442 R (M) (10").
Tátrai—Hungarian Chamber Orchestra.
  (47) Hungaroton LPX 11576.
Goldberg employs a harpsichord only in the Andante, and second repeats are omitted from the outer movements. The outstanding lucidity of the performance permits the listing of this mono version together with the modern stereo recording by Tátrai: a version which uses harpsichord throughout and is notably authentic in style.

No. 40 in F

Dorati—Philharmonia Hungarica.
> (in set 36–48) Decca HDNC 13–18 (nas); US: London STS 15249–54 (nas).

Goberman—Vienna State Opera.
> (13) US: LRM HS 6.

In the Trio the string parts, missing in certain sources, are added only on repeats in Goberman's recording but are employed throughout by Dorati. The latter conductor makes some dynamic emendations of questionable merit but compensates with excellent ornamentation, such as the substitution of a turn for the trill at bar 15 of the Minuet, thus bringing the passage into line with bar 37. Dorati omits the harpsichord from the Finale only, an unaccountable and unconvincing decision.

No. 41 in C

Dorati—Philharmonia Hungarica.
> (in set 36–48) Decca HDNC 13–18 (nas); US: London STS 15249–54 (nas).

Goberman—Vienna State Opera.
> (24) US: LRM HS 7.

Maerzendorfer—Vienna Chamber.
> (31) Oryx OR H 212; US: Musical Heritage OR H 212.

A reduction of tempo occurs at most appearances of the second theme in the first movement in Goberman's performance, and the Trio, perhaps due to tape editing, is faster than the surrounding Minuet. In addition, the horns in the Trio are played alto, despite the basso recommendation by Universal Edition—a most welcome and convincing emendation which is also a feature of both alternative listings. In terms of recommendation, all three are remarkable for their fidelity to both the letter and the spirit of the score.

No. 42 in D

Dorati—Philharmonia Hungarica.
> (in set 36–48) Decca HDNC 13–18 (nas); US: London STS 15249–54 (nas).

Litschauer—Vienna Chamber.
> (21) Nixa HLP 1025 (M); US: (47) Haydn Society HS 9121 (M).

Maerzendorfer—Vienna Chamber.
> (43) Oryx OR H 217; US: Musical Heritage OR H 217.

Dorati adopts an unusually slow tempo for the first movement, and his recording matches the emphatic nature of his performance. Litschauer's recording, made in 1950, also has admirable weight and impact but tends to distort at climaxes. Maerzendorfer's recording is clearer but somewhat light-toned, and he omits a short repeat in the Finale.

No. 43 in E flat, "Mercury"

Wöldike—Danish State Radio Chamber Orchestra.
   (50) Saga SPAN 6206; US: Haydn Society HS 9071 (M).
Wöldike makes an occasional slight departure from the authentic score. The stereo reprocessing of this recording, dating from 1950, is successful, and it is this PAN pressing, or the last Haydn Society issue (HS 9071), which presents the sound in the best light.

No. 44 in E minor, "Trauer"

Jones—Little Orchestra of London.
   (49; *Armida* Overture) Pye GSGC 14006; US: Nonesuch H 71032.
Pritchard—London Philharmonic Orchestra.
   (45) Classics for Pleasure CFP 40021.
Jones's tempi are overall fairly fast; his recording is clear and full. Pritchard occasionally modifies the dynamics, and the Minuet and Trio are taken at an unusually fast pace. Both repeats are observed in the outer movements.

No. 45 in F sharp minor, "Farewell"

Dorati—Philharmonia Hungarica.
   (in set 36–48) Decca HDNC 13–18 (nas); US: London STS 15249–54 (nas).
Jones—Little Orchestra of London.
   (19; 31) Pye GSGC 14001; US: Nonesuch H 71031.
Pritchard—LPO.
   (44) Classics for Pleasure CFP 40021.
Scherchen—Vienna State Opera.
   (100) US: Westminster WST 8134; Music Guild MS 160.
Tátrai—Hungarian Chamber Orchestra.
   (26; 27) Hungaroton LPX 11458.
Pritchard's is the only recording to observe both repeats in the first movement. By contrast, Scherchen omits all repeats from the symphony except

those in the third movement. In his Finale the players are heard to leave one by one, quietly bidding "auf Wiederseh'n" to one another. Tátrai's is the only version to employ harpsichord continuo.

No. 46 in B

Maerzendorfer—Vienna Chamber.
  (47) Oryx OR H 219; US: Musical Heritage OR H 219.
Newstone—Haydn Orchestra.
  (52) Oiseau Lyre OLS 135.
As in the case of No. 30, it seems necessary to pitch the horns at the higher octave, but this theory has yet to be put into practice on record. Nevertheless, both performances are highly recommendable.

No. 47 in G

Litschauer—Vienna Chamber.
  (84) Parlophone PMA 1002 (M); US: Haydn Society HS 9121 (M).
Tátrai—Hungarian Chamber Orchestra.
  (39) Hungaroton LPX 11576.
Due almost certainly to an error in editing, the second half of the Trio section in Litschauer's performance occurs three times. The recording is clear but rather dated, and the horns play sharp in the Trio. The bassoon continuo is particularly prominently balanced, as are both bassoon and harpsichord, in Tátrai's reading.

No. 48 in C, "Maria Theresia"

Goberman—Vienna State Opera.
  (4; L'infedeltà Overture) US: LRM HS 10; (56) CBS 61661.
Maerzendorfer—Vienna Chamber.
  (49) Oryx OR H 220; US: Musical Heritage OR H 220.
Wöldike—Danish State Chamber.
  (44) Decca LXT 2832 (M); US: London LL 844 (M).
The scoring of this work is as follows: two oboes, two horns in C alto, timpani, strings and continuo. (In the slow movement the horns are in F and the timpani omitted.) The recommended performances provide three different scoring solutions, all equally authentic. Goberman: two oboes, two

horns in C alto and F, timpani and strings, with harpsichord continuo in the slow movement and bassoon continuo in the remaining three movements of the symphony. A clear, fine recording. Maerzendorfer: *two oboes, two horns in C alto and F, two trumpets, timpani and strings (no continuo harpsichord). The second half of the Trio is not repeated; the recording is dry and intense, with an exceptionally clear and firm bass-line.* Wöldike: *two oboes, two F horns in the Andante, two trumpets, timpani, strings (no continuo). This recording was made before the availability of the correct text, but only occasionally does the conductor depart from Haydn's intentions, as, for instance, when he reads some of the Minuet's turns as trills. Both repeats in the first movement are omitted. The use of trumpets alone in the first, third and fourth movements was simply a matter of non-availability of C-alto hornists: a sensible and acceptable expedient which would also have been employed in Haydn's time had similar circumstances arisen.*

No. 49 in F minor, "La passione"

Goberman—Vienna State Opera.
   (2; "B") US: LRM HS 11.
Jones—Little Orchestra of London.
   (44; *Armida* Overture) Pye GSGC 14006; US: Nonesuch H 71032.
Jones indulges in some unauthentic increases of tone in the Adagio, but his harpsichordist improvises imaginatively.

No. 50 in C

Maerzendorfer—Vienna Chamber.
   (51) Oryx OR H 221; US: Musical Heritage OR H 221.
Wöldike—Danish State Chamber.
   (43) Saga SPAN 6206; US: Haydn Society HS 9071 (M).
Maerzendorfer double-dots the slow introduction and takes the Allegro di Molto at an exceptionally fast pace. The recording is clear and smooth. Wöldike makes some tiny and unimportant divergencies from the authentic text, which was not published until the year after the recording was made. The Saga PAN pressing in simulated stereo is highly satisfactory, but the Haydn Society pressing listed above is more natural and very clear.

No. 51 in B flat

Dorati—Philharmonia Hungarica.
  (in set 49–56) Decca HDND 19–22 (nas); (49) Decca SDD 359; (55)
  Decca SDD 415; (in set 49–56) US: London STS 15127–30 (nas).
Goberman—Vienna State Opera.
  (6) US: LRM HS 6.

No. 52 in C minor

Goberman—Vienna State Opera.
  (16; 19) 'US: LRM HS 16.
Heiller—Vienna State Opera.
  (56) US: Haydn Society HS 9122 (M).
Maerzendorfer—Vienna Chamber.
  (53) Oryx OR H 222; US: Musical Heritage OR H 222.
Marriner—Academy of St. Martin-in-the-Fields.
  (53) Philips 6707 013 (4 discs, nas); (53) Philips 6500 114.
Newstone—Haydn Orchestra.
  (46) Oiseau Lyre OLS 135.
Heiller's recording, the first to be issued, dates from 1950, is wiry and under-balances the horns, but is otherwise clear and satisfactory. Marriner, the most recent recording, is excellently balanced and the conductor repeats both halves of both outer movements. Goberman's LRM pressing, the last issue before that company closed down after the death of the conductor (who was also a director of the company) is rough and gritty; it is to be hoped that his performance will be issued in an up-to-date transfer.

No. 53 in D, "Imperial"

Guschlbauer—Vienna Baroque Ensemble.
  (Scherzando No. 6; *Acis* Overture; 2 bass arias); US: Musical Heritage
  MHS 768; French Erato STU 70333.
Marriner—Academy of St. Martin-in-the-Fields.
  (52) Philips 6707 013 (4 discs, nas); (52) Philips 6500 114.
Both recommendations employ Finale "B." Finale "A" is available in two recommendable performances, by Maerzendorfer as part of his complete performance (after which follows Finale "B") on Musical Heritage OR H 222, and in the Dorati "Appendices" set (Decca HDNK 47–48) which also includes Finale "C," thought to have been written by Sieber or one of

the composers associated with this Parisian publishing house. Finale "D" is the Presto movement also kown as Overture No. 4, good performances of which are to be found on US: Musical Heritage MHS 880 (issued under the same number in the UK by Oryx) by Froschauer and the Vienna Chamber Orchestra, and on German Schwann VMS 2014, Müller-Brühl conducting the Köln Chamber Orchestra.

No. 54 in G

Dorati—Philharmonia Hungarica.
  (in set 49–56) Decca HDND 19–22 (nas); US: London STS 15127–30 (nas).
Maerzendorfer—Vienna Chamber.
  (55) Oryx OR H 223; US: Musical Heritage OR H 223.
Tátrai—Hungarian Chamber.
  (56) Hungaroton LPX 11497.
Maerzendorfer's light-toned recording slightly neglects the trumpets but registers the timpani with extreme brilliance. Both repeats are played in the Finale, but the second in the first movement and both in the Adagio Assai are omitted. The resulting proportions are reflected in the respective movement timings: 5'26"; 10'10"; 3'57"; 6'57". This would seem to justify the omissions in the extensive Adagio Assai.

No. 55 in E flat, "Schoolmaster"
Goberman—Vienna State Opera.
  (15) US: LRM HS 12.
Maerzendorfer—Vienna Chamber.
  (54) Oryx OR H 223; US: Musical Heritage OR H 223.
Both recordings are vivid and clear. Goberman observes all repeats; Maerzendorfer treats the Andante Semplice to unusually sharp staccato attack; his Trio is reduced in tempo, and the bassoon is omitted from some of the repeated sections in the Finale.

No. 56 in C
Goberman—Vienna State Opera.
  (12) US: LRM HS 5; (48) CBS 61661.

Heiller—Vienna Symphony.
  (52) US: Haydn Society HS 9122 (M).
Maerzendorfer—Vienna Chamber.
  (57) Oryx OR H 224; US: Musical Heritage OR H 224.
All three recordings are dry and clear, that of Heiller, made in 1950, being thin and rather lacking in depth, but with great bite and intensity. Once again Maerzendorfer's timpani are recorded with extraordinary fidelity. Interpretatively all three performances are on an extremely high plane of excellence.

No. 57 in D

Goberman—Vienna State Opera.
  (1; 17) US: LRM HS 13.
Maerzendorfer—Vienna Chamber.
  (56) Oryx OR H 224; US: Musical Heritage OR H 224.
Both recommendations include the recently recovered and probably authentic timpani part. Goberman omits all repeats from the slow movement and the Finale. In the slow movement of Maerzendorfer's performance, untidy playing disfigures the isolated notes which separate the statements of the theme and the variations, and there is some rhythmic unsteadiness. The recording is dry and bright, with fine timpani sound.

No. 58 in F

Of the three recordings which have appeared to date, none is recommendable. Dorati's, the most recent, lacks life and rhythmic impulse; Maerzendorfer's is similarly affected and has no keyboard continuo. Lemaire is well-balanced although the sound is unsubtle and there are some wilful changes of tempo.

No. 59 in A

Blum—Esterházy Orchestra.
  (70) Philips SGL 5878; US: Vanguard VSD 71161.
Dorati—Bath Festival Chamber Orchestra.
  (81) US: Mercury SR 90436.
Blum's is a recommendable but often unauthentic reading, which omits bars

131 to the end of the Finale first time through, thus converting this section into a coda (in practice a very convincing idea). The recording is pleasantly bright. Dorati also receives excellent recording, transferred at a high level; he observes all repeats and his harpsichord continuo is forwardly balanced. His later version with the Philharmonia Hungarica is definitely less impressive and omits some repeats.

No. 60 in C, "Il distratto"

Blum—Esterházy Orchestra.
   (52) RCA Vanguard VSL 11042; US: Vanguard 2143.
Goberman—Vienna State Opera.
   (14) US: LRM HS 4.
The LRM pressing of the Goberman performance splits the work across two sides after the fourth movement. Blum's reading, accommodated complete on one side, is fractionally better recorded than even the Goberman, but he introduces a slight hesitation at the recapitulation of the first movement. Harpsichord continuo appears in the Andante.

No. 61 in D

Guschlbauer—Vienna Baroque Ensemble.
   (77) French Erato STU 70405.
Wöldike—Danish State Chamber.
   US: Haydn Society HSL 96 (M).
Wöldike's 1952 recording omits the timpani part, but is admirably clear and warm. Guschlbauer employs the drum part, and the solo oboe adds a minute cadenza in the Trio at bar 70, extending it fractionally on the repeat. The clear and otherwise faithful and well-balanced recording is marred by a fluttering effect in the central movements, particularly noticeable in the Trio section.

No. 62 in D

Almeida—Haydn Foundation Orchestra.
   (66; 67; 69) French Iramac 2–6705 (2 discs, nas); (63; 66; 67; 69–71; 73–81) Philips 6747 170 (9 discs, nas).

Dorati—Philharmonia Hungarica.
   (in set 57–64) Decca HDNE 23–26 (nas); US: London STS 15131–4 (nas).
Almeida receives a spacious and reverberant recording which is clear and well-detailed. Dorati treats the music as smaller-scale Haydn and does not attempt to give the slow movement the weight afforded it by Almeida. Therefore, two equally authentic versions give different subjective impressions.

No. 63 in C, "La Roxelane" (Conjectural original, scored for two oboes, two trumpets, two horns in C alto and basso, timpani, and strings)

Jones—Little Orchestra of London.
   (78; Overture to an English Opera) Nonesuch H 71197.
Jones employs a harpsichord continuo and amends some inconsistent phrasings in the first movement, as at bars 44–49. Horns in C alto are employed throughout although the Universal Edition specifies alto only in the last two movements. Their use in the opening movement is entirely logical, however, since the Overture which comprises the original required horns or trumpets, thereby implying the same octave for either. In the Trio section the score indicates that the oboe melody breaks off after two bars leaving the violins unsupported; Jones doubles strings with oboes throughout the section to convincing effect.

No. 63 in C, "La Roxelane" (Revised version, scored for two oboes, two horns in C basso, strings)

Dorati—Philharmonia Hungarica.
   (in set 57–64) Decca HDNE 23–26 (nas); US: London STS 15131–4 (nas).

No. 64 in A

Swoboda—Vienna Symphony.
   (91) Nixa WLP 5023 (M); US: Westminster XWN 18615 (M).
Swoboda's recording is most strongly recommended, despite its aged tonal quality and the horn mistake near the end of the slow movement. There are no significant textual problems in this work and the recommendation of only one recording which is many years old is a measure of the exceptional superiority of this version from the point-of-view of interpretation.

No. 65 in A

Dorati—Philharmonia Hungarica.
  (in set 65–72) Decca HDNF 27–30 (nas); US: London STS 15135–8 (nas).
Goberman—Vienna State Opera.
  (35) US: LRM HS 15.
Prieur—New Irish Chamber Orchestra.
  New Irish Recording Co. NIR 004.
*All three recordings provide generous repeats and are excellently recorded.
Both Dorati and Prieur indulge in (almost identical) rhythmic instability in
the third movement.*

No. 66 in B flat

Almeida—Haydn Foundation.
  (62; 67; 69) French Iramac 2–6705 (2 discs, nas); (62; 63; 67; 69–71;
  73–81) Philips 6747 170 (9 discs, nas).
Dorati—Philharmonia Hungarica.
  (in set 65–72) Decca HDNF 27–30 (nas); US: London STS 15135–8 (nas).
*Almeida takes both repeats in the first movement, and receives a superbly
balanced recording in a warm acoustic. The effect is full-blooded and impressive. Dorati is a little swifter and lighter. He is no less successful, convincing the listener of the validity of an alternative approach. There are no
problems of text.*

No 67 in F

Almeida—Haydn Foundation.
  (62; 67; 69) French Iramac 2–6705 (2 discs, nas); (62, 63; 67; 69–71;
  73–81) Philips 6747 170 (9 discs, nas).
Dorati—Philharmonia Hungarica.
  (in set 65–72) Decca HDNF 27–30 (nas); US: London STS 15135–8 (nas);
  (60) Decca SDD 358.
Tátrai—Hungarian Chamber Orchestra.
  (68) Hungaroton LPX 11571.
*The choice lies between Almeida's broad performance recorded in a "live"
but clear hall, and Dorati's more hard-driven reading in which the first*

movement is taken at an extremely fast pace. Tátrai comes between these two views. Dorati observes both repeats in the first movement, and employs a harpsichord continuo. This, however, sounds unnaturally distant and is absent from time to time.

No. 68 in B flat

Dorati—Philharmonia Hungarica.
  (in set 65–72) Decca HDNF 27–30 (nas); US: London STS 15135–8 (nas).
Maerzendorfer—Vienna Chamber.
  (69) Oryx OR H 230; US: Musical Heritage OR H 230.
Tátrai—Hungarian Chamber.
  (67) Hungaroton LPX 11571.

No. 69 in C, "Laudon"

Almeida—Haydn Foundation.
  (62; 66; 67) French Iramac 2–6705 (2 discs, nas); (62; 63; 66; 67; 70; 71; 73–81) Philips 6747 170 (9 discs, nas):
The sources appear to indicate C basso horns for this work, which makes it exceptional amongst Haydn's symphonies of the general "festive" style written before 1794. Almeida receives a well-balanced recording in which, nevertheless, the timpani would benefit from greater definition. Basso horns are used as specified; the omission of both repeats in the slow movement does nothing to mitigate the impression of excessive length.

No. 70 in D

Almeida—Haydn Foundation.
  (71; 74; 79) French Iramac 6709–10 (nas); (62; 63; 66; 67; 69; 71; 73–81) Philips 6747 170 (9 discs, nas).
Blum—Esterházy Orchestra.
  (59) Philips SGL 5878; US: Vanguard VSD 71161.
Blum gives an extremely fast opening movement in which both repeats are played. There are some anachronistic glissandi in the Trio section. A good clear recording in which the timpani have enormous impact. Almeida's recording is also natural and clear, and his steady, sane tempi represent a view of the music which greatly contrasts with Blum's reading.

No. 71 in B flat

Almeida—Haydn Foundation.
(70; 74; 79) French Iramac 6709–10 (nas); (62; 63; 66; 67; 69; 70; 73–81)
Philips 6747 170 (9 discs, nas).
Dorati—Philharmonia Hungarica..
(in set 65–72) Decca HDNF 27–30 (nas); US: London STS 15135–8 (nas).

No. 72 in D

Dorati—Philharmonia Hungarica.
(in set 65–72) Decca HDNF 27–30 (nas); US: London STS 15135–38 (nas)
Maerzendorfer—Vienna Chamber.
(73) Oryx OR H 232; US: Musical Heritage OR H 232.
Both recommended recordings are of the original version and both incorporate the questionable timpani part, Maerzendorfer generally utilising it only on repeats, although it is played during the second half of the first movement (not repeated) and in the final Presto. The possibly spurious later version of the symphony, with trumpets and amended oboe and horn parts, awaits its first recording.

No. 73 in D, "La chasse"

Dorati—Philharmonia Hungarica.
(in set 73–81) Decca HDNG 31–34 (nas); US: London STS 15182–5 (nas).
Maerzendorfer—Vienna Chamber.
(72) Oryx OR H 232; US: Musical Heritage OR H 232.
Foerster's alternative edition, most noticeable in its use of pizzicato in the slow introduction, is used only by Maerzendorfer. Both conductors employ the timpani part in the Finale (from the movement's rôle as the Overture to La fedeltà premiata); Dorati, according to the notes accompanying his issue, also uses trumpets but this is not apparent from the recording itself. Further, his bass-line is indistinct.

No. 74 in E flat

Almeida—Haydn Foundation.
(70; 71; 79) French Iramac 6709–10 (nas); (62; 63; 66; 67; 69–71; 73;

75–81) Philips 6747 170 (9 discs, nas).
Dorati—Philharmonia Hungarica.
    (in set 73–81) Decca HDNG 31–34 (nas); US: London STS 15182–5 (nas).

No. 75 in D

Almeida—Haydn Foundation.
    (in set 75–78) French Iramac 6720–21 (nas); (62; 63; 66; 67; 69–71; 73; 74; 76–81) Philips 6747 170 (9 discs, nas).
Blum—Esterházy Orchestra.
    (81) US: Vanguard VSD 71138.
Dorati—Philharmonia Hungarica.
    (in set 73–81) Decca HDNG 31–34 (nas); US: London STS 15182–5 (nas).
Dorati's trumpets are backwardly balanced in the first movement. Blum omits these instruments entirely, along with the drums, and indulges in some textual deviations and da capo inconsistencies. Almeida is very impressive, with outstandingly confident orchestral playing which gives a grand sense of scale to this work. Although musicologically Blum's omission of trumpets and drums is hard to justify, the playing is miraculously brilliant and accurate—the other versions recommended are both very satisfying and historically accurate but Blum's is nonetheless revelatory and at least as enjoyable in the long term.

No. 76 in E flat

Almeida—Haydn Foundation.
    (in set 75–78) French Iramac 6720–21 (nas); (62; 63; 66; 67; 69–71; 73–75; 77–81) Philips 6747 170 (9 discs, nas)
Dorati—Philharmonia Hungarica.
    (in set 73–81 Decca HDNG 31–34 (nas); US: London STS 15182–5 (nas).

No. 77 in B flat

Almeida—Haydn Foundation.
    (in set 75–78) French Iramac 6720–21 (nas); (62; 63; 66; 67; 69–71; 73–76; 78–81) Philips 6747 170 (9 discs, nas)
Dorati—Philharmonia Hungarica.
    (in set 73–81) Decca HDNG 31–34 (nas); US: London STS 15182–5 (nas)

Guschlbauer—Vienna Baroque Ensemble.
    (61) French Erato STU 70405.
Jones—Little Orchestra of London.
    (61) Nonesuch H 71168.
*Dorati's version is divided across two sides. Jones is the only conductor to
employ harpsichord. The satisfaction obtainable from each recommendation
is virtually identical—four really fine recorded performances.*

No. 78 in C minor

Almeida—Haydn Foundation.
    (in set 75–78) French Iramac 6720–21 (nas); (62; 63; 66; 67; 69–71;
    73–77; 79–81) Philips 6747 170 (9 discs, nas).
Dorati—Philharmonia Hungarica
    (in set 73–81) Decca HDNG 31–34 (nas); US: London STS 15182–5 (nas)
Maerzendorfer—Vienna Chamber.
    (79) Oryx OR H 235; US: Musical Heritage OR H 235.
Somogyi—Vienna Radio Orchestra.
    (22) US: Westminster WST 17095.

No. 79 in F

Almeida—Haydn Foundation.
    (70; 71; 74) French Iramac 6709–10 (nas); (62; 63; 66; 67; 69–71;
    73–78; 80; 81) Philips 6747 170 (9 discs, nas).
Dorati—Philharmonia Hungarica
    (in set 73–81) Decca HDNG 31–34 (nas); US: London STS 15182–5 (nas).
Maerzendorfer—Vienna Chamber.
    (78) Oryx OR H 235; US: Musical Heritage OR H 235.

No. 80 in D minor

Almeida—Haydn Foundation.
    (62; 63; 66; 67; 69–71; 73–79; 81) Philips 6747 170 (9 discs, nas).
Jones—Little Orchestra of London.
    (35; 43) Pye GSGC 14046; US: Nonesuch H 71131.
*It would appear from the careful rest lengths at the end of the Finale that
Haydn expected the second repeat to be played. Jones omits it but Almeida
observes it along with all the other repeats in the work.*

No. 81 in G

Almeida—Haydn Foundation.
(62; 63; 66; 67; 69–71; 73–80) Philips 6747 170 (9 discs, nas).
Blum—Esterházy Orchestra.
(75) US: Vanguard VSD 71138.
Dorati—Bath Festival Chamber Orchestra.
(59) US: Mercury SR 90436.
It has been suggested that the second half of the Trio section, while marked for repeat by Haydn as a matter of convention, should be omitted (see pp. 108–9). Both Blum and Dorati (in his Mercury edition) are generous with repeats but follow the same reasoning: that to make that particular da capo is to repeat an unrepeatable joke. Both these conductors commit definite but minor textual sins which are not to be found in Almeida's absolutely authentic recording. Dorati's later recording for Decca is not as recommendable as his first reading. It is less generous with repeats but does observe the "offending" da capo in the Trio, as does Almeida.

No. 82 in C, "Bear"

Dorati—Philharmonia Hungarica.
(in set 82–92 + Concertante) Decca HDNH 35–40 (nas); US: London STS 15229–34 (nas); (83) Decca SDD 482.
Jones—Little Orchestra of London.
(in set 82–87) Nonesuch HC 73011 (3 discs, nas).
Maerzendorfer—Vienna Chamber.
(83) Oryx OR H 237; US: Musical Heritage OR H 237.
Jones employs harpsichord continuo throughout the work. In the third movement the timpani, clearly audible elsewhere, cannot be heard.

No. 83 in G minor, "Hen"

Dorati—Philharmonia Hungarica.
(in set 82–92 + Concertante) Decca HDNH 35–40 (nas); US: London STS 15229–34 (nas); (82) Decca SDD 482.
Jones—Little Orchestra of London.
(in set 82–87) Nonesuch HC 73011 (3 discs, nas).
Maerzendorfer—Vienna Chamber.
(82) Oryx OR H 237; US: Musical Heritage OR H 237.
Of his three versions Jones's most recommendable is on the Nonesuch issue listed above, in which he uses a harpsichord continuo. Maerzendorfer's performance is also unusual in that both repeats are observed in the Finale.

No. 84 in E flat

Jones—Little Orchestra of London.
(in set 82–87) Nonesuch HC 73011 (3 discs, nas).
Vaughan—Orchestra of Naples.
(in set 82–87) RCA SRS 3004 (3 discs, nas); (in set 82–92 + Concertante)
US: RCA LSC 6805 (6 discs, nas).
Vaughan is inconsistent in his repeat scheme in the Andante, in which some grace notes are played short. Both Vaughan and Jones employ harpsichord continuo.

No. 85 in B flat, "La Reine de France"

Collegium Aureum.
(87) BASF 20 20340–9; BAC 3006.
Dorati—Philharmonia Hungarica.
(in set 82–92 + Concertante) Decca HDNH 35–40 (nas); US: London STS 15229–34 (nas); (84) Decca SDD 483.
Jones—Little Orchestra of London.
(in set 82–87) Nonesuch HC 73011 (3 discs, nas).
The Collegium Aureum, which plays unconducted, uses original or recon-structed instruments, leading to authentic timbres. The small group of strings comprises four first violins, four seconds, two violas, two cellos and one double-bass. Jones obeys an alternative source in the Finale which replaces the turns by trills from bar 142. He also uses a harpsichord continuo throughout. Although Jones uses twice the string strength employed by the Collegium Aureum, the London winds stand out more clearly.

No. 86 in D

Jones—Little Orchestra of London.
(in set 82–87) Nonesuch HC 73011 (3 discs, nas).
There are several bars in the Minuet of this performance during which the timpanist does not play. As in most of the rest of Jones's Haydn symphony readings, a harpsichord continuo is used. This relatively popular symphony has rarely been successful on records, and Jones's fine version is a welcome exception. A soft-focus recording detracts from a good Dorati performance and precludes its recommendation.

No. 87 in A

Collegium Aureum.
  (85) BASF 20 20340–9; BAC 3006.
Dorati—Philharmonia Hungarica.
  (in set 82–92+Concertante) Decca HDNH 35–40 (nas); US: London STS
  15229–34 (nas); (86) Decca SDD 484.
Jones—Little Orchestra of London.
  (in set 82–87) Nonesuch HC 73011 (3 discs, nas).
The same remarks apply for the Collegium Aureum performance as for their No. 85 (q.v.). Jones occasionally departs from the authentic score: in the first movement, for instance, bars 146–150 are taken p instead of f; and in the second movement the flute at bar 42 omits the grace-note, thus bringing the phrasing into line with that of the oboe. The Finale in this performance is outstanding and notably captures the attention more pointedly than even the excellent Decca and BASF versions. Dorati's excellent sense of shape and line throughout the work should be noted, however.

No. 88 in G

Böhm—Vienna Philharmonic Orchestra.
  (89) DGG 2530343.
Busch—Danish State Radio Orchestra.
  US: Victor LHMV 1019 (M).
Furtwängler—Berlin Philharmonic Orchestra.
  Heliodor Historical 88007 (M).
Jochum—BPO.
  (98) DGG 138823.
Amongst excellent versions of this popular work are two old recordings (Busch and Furtwängler) which remain recommendable despite their use of texts which are not ideally authentic. Karl Böhm's performance utilises a larger orchestra than is usual today in such music, but it is outstandingly well-balanced and recorded.

No. 89 in F

Böhm—VPO.
  (88) DGG 2530343.
Dorati—Philharmonia Hungarica.

(in set 82–92+Concertante) Decca HDNH 35–40 (nas); US: London STS 15229–34 (nas); (88) Decca SDD 431.

Vaughan—Orchestra of Naples.
  (in set 88–92+Concertante) RCA SRS 3002 (3 discs, nas); (in set 82–92+Concertante) US: RCA LSC 6805 (6 discs, nas).

Böhm's orchestra is larger than either of the two rival recommendations but is ideally balanced. Dorati applies the Finale's strascinando markings to the phrasing of the violins, which produce marked portamenti, rather than to the basic tempo of the music. Some grace-notes are shortened in Vaughan's reading, the tempo is unsteady in the third movement, and repeats are inconsistent. A most imaginative harpsichord continuo provides frequent stylish embellishments.

No. 90 in C

Böhm—VPO.
  (Concertante) DGG 2530398.

Dorati—Philharmonia Hungarica.
  (in set 82–92+Concertante) Decca HDNH 35–40 (nas); US: London STS 15229–34 (nas); (92) Decca SDD 412.

Maerzendorfer—Vienna Chamber.
  (91) Oryx OR H 241; US: Musical Heritage OR H 241.

Vaughan—Orchestra of Naples.
  (in set 88–92+Concertante) RCA SRS 3002 (3 discs, nas); (in set 82–92+Concertante) US: RCA LSC 6805 (6 discs, nas).

A slight low-frequency interference affects the first few minutes of the pressings of Dorati's performance, both in the HDNH set and the separate SDD issue, but this need not detract from one of the very finest of Dorati's whole series. Vaughan alone amongst these recommendations employs harpsichord and is exciting if lightweight. Böhm is bold and grand and Maerzendorfer forceful and fiery. Jones gives a comparable performance but is roughly recorded and therefore not listed.

No. 91 in E flat

Böhm—VPO.
  (92) DGG 2530524.

Jochum—Bavarian Radio Symphony Orchestra.
  (103) Heliodor 2548 147.

Vaughan—Orchestra of Naples.
  (in set 88–92+Concertante) RCA SRS 3002 (3 discs, nas); (in set 82–92+Concertante) US: RCA LSC 6805 (6 discs, nas).

The B flat horns in the slow movement are played in the lower octave in Jochum's performance. Universal Edition omits the bassoon part from the very first chord of the Trio section of the Minuet, effectively causing the bassoon melody to start on the second note; wisely Jochum rectifies this omission. The Finale in this performance is judged to perfection. Vaughan uses harpsichord and his shaping of the first movement is notably eloquent.

No. 92 in G, "Oxford"

Dorati—Philharmonia Hungarica.
    (in set 82–92+Concertante) Decca HDNH 35–40 (nas); US: London STS 15229–34 (nas).
    (90) Decca SDD 412.
Goberman—Vienna New Symphony.*
    (Overtures: *Infedeltà; Lo speziale*; songs) US: LRM 502.
Koussevitsky—Boston Symphony Orchestra.
    US: RCA LM 1102 (M).
Maerzendorfer—Vienna Chamber.
    (Concertante) Oryx OR H 242; US: Musical Heritage OR H 242.
Vaughan—Orchestra of Naples.
    (in set 88–92+Concertante) RCA SRS 3002 (3 discs, nas); (in set 82–92+Concertante) US: RCA LSC 6805 (6 discs, nas).
Böhm—VPO.
    (91) DGG 2530524.
Dixon—Prague Chamber Orchestra.
    (48) Supraphon 1 10 1202.

The Koussevitzky recording was made before the availability of authentic texts but is nevertheless recommendable: the speed and accuracy of the playing is an object-lesson. Both Dorati and Maerzendorfer suffer from slight rhythmic unsteadiness in the slow movement. Vaughan alone uses harpsichord; Maerzendorfer obtains an authentically hard, shallow timpani sound which, together with the extreme clarity of the woodwind, makes the Finale a tour-de-force. Goberman's fine version is marred in the above listed disc by the omission of the repeats in the outer movements. H. C. Robbins Landon has made it clear, however, that all repeats were observed at the recording and the special issue shown above had sections removed from the tape before pressing (presumably by the licensees). It is to be hoped that the complete performance will be presented when the inevitable reissue occurs. Böhm's majestic interpretation makes his unusually slow tempi extremely convincing. Dixon is the only conductor to keep the music strictly in tempo throughout the minore section of the Adagio. His version is also notable for crisp staccato use of brass and timpani.

---

* Actually the Vienna State Opera Orchestra, but renamed for this issue for contractual reasons.

Concertante in B flat, for oboe, bassoon, violin, cello and orchestra

Böhm—VPO.
(90) DGG 2530398.
Dorati—Philharmonia Hungarica.
(in set 82–92+Concertante) Decca HDNH 35–40 (nas); Decca SDD 445;
US: London STS 15229–34 (nas).
Vaughan—Orchestra of Naples.
(in set 88–92+Concertante) RCA SRS 3002 (3 discs, nas); (in set
82–92+Concertante) US: RCA LSC 6805 (6 discs, nas).
Guschlbauer—Bamberg Symphony Orchestra.
(Trumpet Conc.; *Incontro* Overture) French Erato STU 70652.
*Dorati's is the only performance in which the horns play in the upper
octave and the improvement in clarity of these parts is immense. In
Vaughan's recording a harpsichord is used reticently throughout; the main
theme of the first movement is "double-dotted" at bars 2, 50, 53, etc. The
recording is warm and natural, but a slight hum affects part of the first
movement. Guschlbauer's solo violinist adds embellishments at suitable points,
such as bar 162 in the first movement: his is a good, clean recording which,
however, occasionally obscures the timpani.*

No. 93 in D

Almeida—Haydn Foundation.
(in set 93–98) Philips 6747 122 (nas).
Dorati—Philharmonia Hungarica.
(in set 93–104) Decca HDNJ 41–46 (nas); US: London STS 15319–24 (nas).
Jones—Little Orchestra of London.
(in set 93–104) Nonesuch HF 73019 (nas).
Maerzendorfer—Vienna Chamber.
(94) Oryx OR H 243; US: Musical Heritage OR H 243.
Scherchen—Vienna State Opera
(94) World Record Club ST 407; (in set 93–98) US: Westminster WMS
1002.
Szell—Cleveland Orchestra.
(94) CBS 61052; US: Columbia MS 7006.
*This is one of the most successful of Dorati's recordings of the London
Symphonies, with brightly recorded brass and ideal prominence given the
percussion. A harpsichord continuo and a timpani crescendo at bar 35 of
the Minuet are "over-authentic" details which enhance the appeal of Jones's
brightly-recorded performance. Maerzendorfer gives an unusually brisk per-*

formance of the first movement, in which an unmarked crescendo occurs at bar 181. There is also a crescendo for timpani at bar 36 in the third movement, one bar later than in Jones's version. Szell receives an outstandingly well-recorded and balanced sound, presenting the brass in a particularly favourable light. Grace notes at bar 72 in the first movement are taken long, and the bassoon joke near the end of the slow movement is superbly exaggerated. Again the ear is delighted by the unmarked (but surely indispensable) timpani crescendo at bar 35 of the Minuet.

No. 94 in G, "Surprise"

Almeida—Haydn Foundation.
    (in set 93–98) Philips 6747 122 (nas).
Jones—Little Orchestra of London.
    (in set 93–104) Nonesuch HF 73019 (nas).
Maerzendorfer—Vienna Chamber.
    (93) Oryx OR H 243; US: Musical Heritage OR H 243.
Scherchen—Vienna State Opera
    (92) Nixa WLP 5137; (93) World Record Club ST 407; (in set 93–98) US: Westminster WMS 1002.

With Jones, Maerzendorfer and Scherchen the grace-notes in the Minuet are played long. The original trumpet part is employed in the first movement in Jones's reading. This conductor is the only one to have the horns playing the notes to sound as written in the Andante, and to use harpsichord throughout.

No. 95 in C minor

Almeida—Haydn Foundation.
    (in set 93–98) Philips 6747 122 (nas).
Jochum—Dresden State Orchestra.
    98) Philips 6500 216.
Jones—Little Orchestra of London.
    (in set 93–104) Nonesuch HF 73019 (nas).

Jones's is the only recommended version to amend the phrasing of the cello solo in the slow movement to bring it into line with the rest of the orchestra. His other efforts towards total authenticity include the employment of a harpsichord continuo, which adds important embellishments, and the use of the higher octave of the C horns towards the end of the first movement and in the Finale. His recording is clear but a little cold. Predominantly slow tempi and a recording of ample breadth and ambience combine to make the total effect of Jochum's Philips performance one of power and weight. This is notably preferable to Jochum's later version with *the London Philharmonic Orchestra. Almeida is strictly faithful to the score and the excellence of his version grows with hearing. The sluggish, unstylishly romantic Trio section in Klemperer's recording precludes recommendation of his clear-textured, well-detailed version.*

No. 96 in D

Almeida—Haydn Foundation.
    (in set 93–98) Philips 6747 122 (nas).
Goberman—Vienna State Opera.
    (3) US: LRM HS 8.
Jones—Little Orchestra of London.
    (in set 93–104) Nonesuch HF 73019 (6 discs, nas).
Almeida's is the only performance to observe the da capo of the second half of the first movement. The recorded balance slightly neglects the horns. The LRM pressing of the Goberman version places the Finale at the start of the second side. The recording again slightly underbalances the horns, but the orchestral playing is outstanding. Jones uses a harpsichord continuo, and his excellent brass balance, both within itself and in relation to the rest of the orchestra, is unrivalled on disc.

No. 97 in C

Almeida—Haydn Foundation.
    (in set 93–98) Philips 6747 122 (nas).
Maerzendorfer—Vienna Chamber.
    (98) Oryx OR H 245; US: Musical Heritage OR H 245.
Scherchen—Vienna Symphony.
    (in set 93–98) US: Westminster WMS 1002 (3 discs, nas); (in set 93–104) US: Westminster WN 6601 (6 discs, nas) (M).
Szell—Cleveland Orchestra.
    (98) CBS 61291; US: Columbia M-30646.
In Maerzendorfer's well-recorded reading the slurred triplets at bars 85–93 and 231–233 in the first movement are played staccato, and the pp marking at bar 38 in the slow movement is ignored. The usual uncalled-for tempo reduction is made in the Finale at bars 306–313. All repeats are omitted in the first two movements of Scherchen's recording. There are also many divergencies from the authentic text, but since the recording was made many years before the results of recent researches were publishd, textual matters may be overlooked in the light of an otherwise totally recommendable performance. The timpani interruption in the Minuet is unequalled

elsewhere. Szell's second recording tends to underbalance these instruments elsewhere, and the horns, even at crucial points such as bars 16 and 211 in the Finale, lack impact. The performance is nevertheless rewarding.

No. 98 in B flat

Goberman—Vienna State Opera.
    (22) US: LRM HS 1.
Jochum—BPO.
    (88) DGG 138823.
Maerzendorfer—Vienna Chamber.
    (97) Oryx OR H 245; US: Musical Heritage OR H 245.

Horns in all recordings are pitched in B flat basso. Jochum is the only conductor here to employ the harpsichord as a continuo throughout the symphony*; in both the other recordings the player sits silently through the whole work until his solo just before the end. Maerzendorfer's recording is clear but somewhat light in the bass. Goberman's first movement is marred by ensemble difficulties at bar 35, and the Finale—at the start of side two on the LRM pressing—is given without repeat.

No. 99 in E flat

Jones—Little Orchestra of London.
    (in set 93–104) Nonesuch HF 73019 (6 discs, nas).
Maerzendorfer—Vienna Chamber.
    (100) Oryx OR H 246; US: Musical Heritage OR H 246.
Wöldike—Vienna State Opera.
    (102) RCA Vanguard SRV 211; US: Vanguard SRV 211.

Wöldike's recording is recommendable despite a recorded sound inferior to the rest of his series of the last six symphonies. In the Finale he allows the adagio to take place at bar 185 instead of the marked point two bars later, a fault he shares with Maerzendorfer and many other artists. Only Jones avoids this pitfall on disc. Despite occasional sections of rhythmic indecision, Maerzendorfer is valuable for stylish details such as the long grace-note at bar 91 in the Trio and the timpani crescendo at bars 55 and 155 in the first movement. Again Jones is alone in using harpsichord continuo and the only real blemishes on his convincing reading are technical: a slightly hollow sound at the start of the Adagio and some noticeable tape splices.

---

* Jochum includes harpsichord throughout his other two recordings also (with the Dresden State and London Philharmonic Orchestras). The recommended version, although the oldest of the three, is interpretatively preferable and its recording is just as good and occasionally superior.

No. 100 in G, "Military"

Maerzendorfer—Vienna Chamber.
   (99) Oryx OR H 246; US: Musical Heritage OR H 246.
Scherchen—Vienna State Opera.
   (45) US: Music Guild MS 160; Westminster 8134.
Wöldike—Vienna State Opera.
   (101) RCA Vanguard SRV 187; US: Vanguard SRV 187; (45; Trumpet Concerto; Quartet Op. 74/3; *L'isola* Overture) US: Vanguard 703–4 (2 discs, nas).
In the Finale, at bar 70, Maerzendorfer uses the alternative Birchall dynamic, p replacing f, and the triangle in the final bars trills continuously in accordance with the Esterházy Archiv source. The recording is extremely vivid but slightly bass-light. The trumpet calls in the Allegretto in Scherchen's most recent performance alternate between the channels. The Finale is played much faster than in any other version. A bright and clean recording admirably balances the timpani. Wöldike has occasional unimportant departures from the authentic text, but he is recorded with immediacy and impact. The British-made RCA Vanguard pressing is the issue to seek since most of the previous issues excise some of the repeats.

No. 101 in D, "Clock"

Delogu—LPO.
   (83) Classics for Pleasure CFP 40222.
Jones—Little Orchestra of London.
   (104) Oryx BRL 18.
Maerzendorfer—Vienna Chamber.
   (102) Oryx OR H 247; US: Musical Heritage OR H 247.
Toscanini—New York Philharmonic Symphony Orchestra.
   US: Arturo Toscanini Society ATS 1034–5 (M) (nas).
All four recordings follow the latest researches in the Trio and leave uncorrected the accompanying figure on its first appearance. Maerzendorfer has a trace of instability in the Minuet, and the repeat of the second half of the Trio is omitted. Further, there are several minor textual deviations, and the Finale begins at a slightly low pitch, but the slow movement is given an ultra-staccato performance which enhances the clarity of Haydn's scoring and the point of his wit. Preserved from a radio broadcast of 1945, Toscanini's performance has perfectly adequate sound quality, and his performance is remarkably "modern" in its approximation to the much more recently published correct text. Delogu's texts are immaculate and his fast

tempi convincing; the wind passages have less period openness than in Jones's recording (his second of two), notable for its force and immediacy. The timpani playing is so accurate and stylish in this Oryx version as to merit especial mention.

No. 102 in B flat

Jones—Little Orchestra of London.
(in set 93–104) Nonesuch HF 73019 (6 discs, nas).
Maerzendorfer—Vienna Chamber.
(101) Oryx OR H 247; US: Musical Heritage OR H 247.
All the recommended recordings make a feature of the important timpani
Schönzeler—Royal Philharmonic Orchestra.
(96) Classics for Pleasure CFP 40073.
Wöldike—Vienna State Opera.
(99) RCA Vanguard SRV 211; US: Vanguard SRV 211.
crescendo which occurs at the recapitulation of the first movement. Wöldike's recording is clear but benefits from bass-cut, and his performance is presented at its most complete on the British RCA Vanguard pressing listed above. Maerzendorfer employs long grace-notes in the second subject of the first movement and in the Trio, but the left grouping of all the violins reduces some of Haydn's humorous effects. His recording is vivid and forward. Schönzeler brings out the lateral interplay of first and second violins and receives a well-balanced recording of excellent tonal quality, but there is an occasional slight blemish in playing and ensemble. Jones is the only conductor on disc to use horns in B flat alto; this factor, when combined with his division left and right of the violin groups, contributes towards an admirably clear-textured performance, recorded with weight and power.

No. 103 in E flat, "Drum Roll"

Dorati—Philharmonia Hungarica.
(in set 93–104) Decca HDNJ 41–46 (nas); US: London STS 15319–24 (nas).
Wöldike—Vienna State Opera.
(104) RCA Vanguard SRV 166; US: Vanguard SRV 166.
Dorati's Decca performance is outstandingly well-balanced and recorded and is among the best of his London readings. No less clear, but inevitably less faithful, is the 1957 stereo recording of Wöldike (which, incidentally, omits the clarinet line in the Trio). There have been available at different times a mixture of performances of this work by Wöldike, all with the same orchestra. Apparently, different "takes" from the recording sessions

have been used for different issues, the two most successful overall being the old Wing release (mono only) and the latest RCA Vanguard release for the British market. This latter is the performance to seek since it is the most recent transfer and is in genuine stereo.

No. 103 in E flat—original version of the Finale

The original ending to the Finale has been recorded twice to date. Maer-zendorfer includes it in his performance of the complete work on Oryx/ Musical Heritage OR H 248 in a light-toned recording without much impact. Dorati's version of the Finale is included in the set of two discs containing the appendices to his complete recording of the symphonies: HDNK 47–48. His recording of the whole symphony in HDNJ 41–46 includes the tra-ditional, revised Finale.

No. 104 in D, "London"
Dorati—Philharmonia Hungarica.
 (in set 93–104) Decca HDNJ 41–46 (nas); US: London STS 15319–24
 (nas).
Jones—Little Orchestra of London.
 (101) Oryx BRL 18.
Rosbaud—BPO.
 (92) Heliodor 89623; (92) Heliodor 478 425 (M).
Wöldike—Vienna State Opera.
 (103) RCA Vanguard SRV 166; US: Vanguard SRV 166.
A highly successful conclusion to Dorati's complete recording of the Haydn symphonies, and one in which the excellent balance of Symphonies Nos. 93 and 103 is maintained. Jones's second reading (the first, in the six-disc Nonesuch set of "London" Symphonies, lacked impact) is recorded with ideal balance: in particular, the horns have a thrilling "bite" in the Finale and the general attack is often more powerful than with the purposeful Dorati per-formance. Rosbaud's recording is natural and pleasing; the mono reissue is minimally purer in tone but the transcription is also excellent in the "stereo-enhanced" Heliodor. The conductor relaxes his tempo in the Finale, just before the recapitulation—an unauthentic touch but, on this occasion, brought off with subtle musical conviction. Rosbaud did not have the advantage of recent corrections, but his text does not harm the music to any great extent. Wöldike's performance also reveals the occasional moment of unauthenticity: it, too, was made before the general availability of scores bearing the fruits of recent researches. However, this is a highly recom-mendable performance in which, in the British RCA Vanguard pressings at least, the repeat schemes are satisfactory. The recorded sound is vivid and immediate.

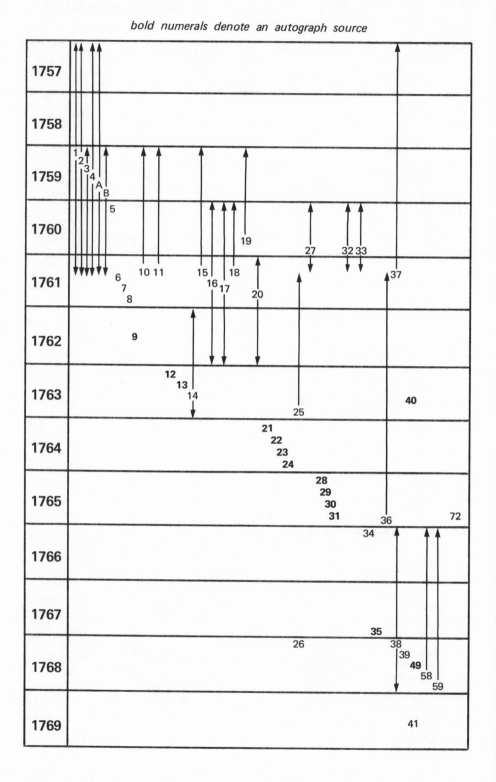

bold numerals denote an autograph source

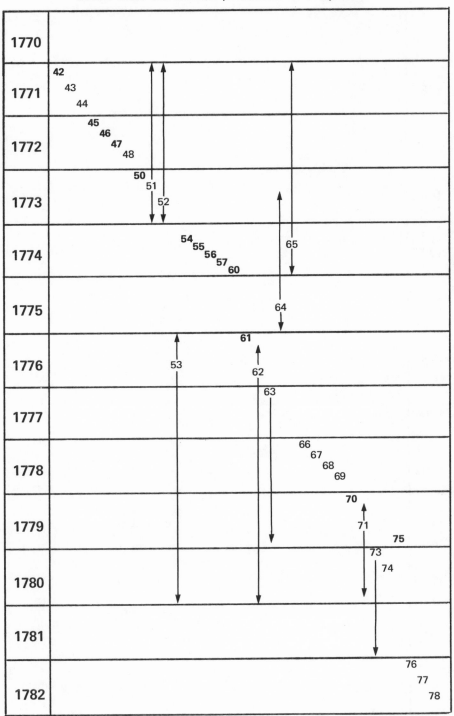

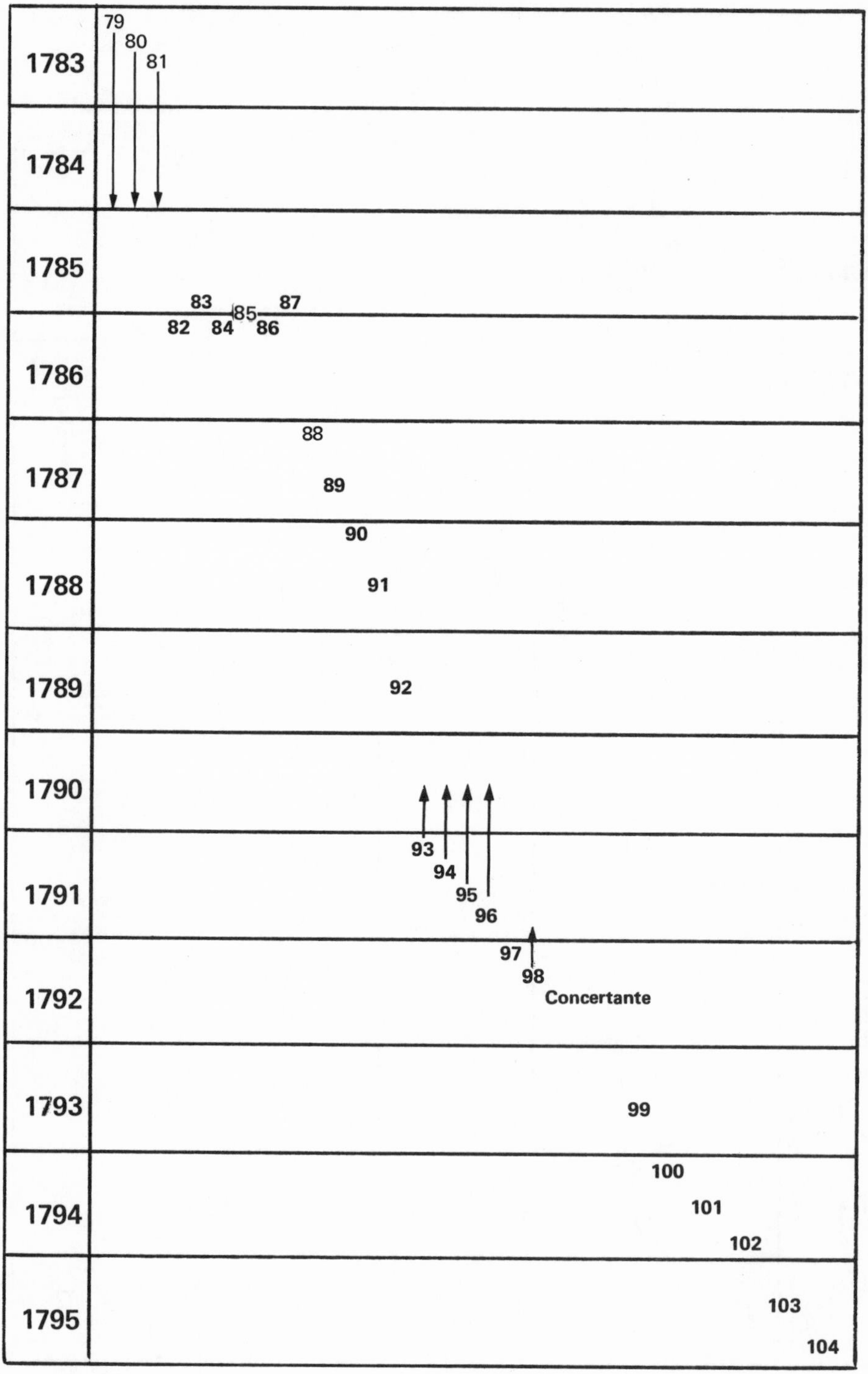
1783
1784
1785
1786
1787
1788
1789
1790
1791
1792
1793
1794
1795
79
80
81
83
85
87
82
84
86
88
89
90
91
92
93
94
95
96
97
98
Concertante
99
100
101
102
103
104

Index of Haydn's Works

Symphonies

Italics denotes a main reference

Instrumental

Choral

Operas

Singspiel

String Quartets

General Index